CHESTY PULLER

ALSO BY JOHN WUKOVITS

Pacific Alamo
Eisenhower
One Square Mile of Hell
American Commando
Black Sheep
For Crew and Country
Hell from the Heavens
Tin Can Titans
Devotion to Duty
Dogfight over Tokyo
Soldiers of a Different Cloth
Admiral "Bull" Halsey

CHESTY PULLER

A Marine Legend in World War II

JOHN WUKOVITS

CALIBER

CALIBER

An imprint of Penguin Random House LLC
penguinrandomhouse.com

LIBRARY OF CONGRESS CATALOGING-IN-PUBLICATION DATA

Names: Wukovits, John F., author.
Title: Chesty Puller: a Marine legend in World War II / John Wukovits.
Description: New York: Dutton, [2021]
Identifiers: LCCN 2020051943 (print) | LCCN 2020051944 (ebook) |
ISBN 9780593184578 (paperback) | ISBN 9780593184585 (ebook)
Subjects: LCSH: Puller, Chesty, 1898–1971. |
Generals—United States—Biography. |
United States. Marine Corps—Officers—Biography. |
World War, 1939–1945—Campaigns—Pacific Area.
Classification: LCC E746.P8 W85 2021 (print) | LCC E746.P8 (ebook) |
DDC 359.9/6092 [B]—dc23
LC record available at https://lccn.loc.gov/2020051943
LC ebook record available at https://lccn.loc.gov/2020051944

Printed in the United States of America
1st Printing

BOOK DESIGN BY TIFFANY ESTREICHER

To three historians whose
friendship and advice
helped shape my writing career—

Tom Buell
Dr. Bernard Norling
Jim Hornfischer

You assisted me more than you realize.

★ CONTENTS ★

CHESTY PULLER

PREFACE

I n writing my previous books about the war with Japan, I have encountered fascinating individuals and epic battles. Some events occurred on land and some at sea, but all shared the common thread that victory was due to the courage and determination of a handful of key people. The human element is what most attracts me to a story, and in each book, I tried to emphasize that platoons and companies do not go into battle—people do. I thus tell my stories through the experiences of those who were involved, culled largely from personal interviews, letters written during the war, and memoirs and recollections recorded years later.

I was thus delighted to receive the invitation to write a biography of famous World War II marine commander Lewis B. "Chesty" Puller, one of the dominant characters of that conflict.

I had often come across his name in the course of writing other books about the Pacific war, and long ago Burke Davis's volume *Marine! The Life of Chesty Puller* introduced me to the man, but I now had the opportunity to research the commander more deeply and discover the keys to those battlefield successes he registered during World War II.

I was not disappointed in what I discovered, for Chesty Puller was a marine's commander, a man who preferred the presence of privates and sergeants to that of generals and admirals. He compiled an impressive list of victories in the Pacific, but he never forgot that those triumphs came because young marines under his leadership were willing to die. No private had a more vocal booster than Chesty; no corporal served under a commander who better empathized with his needs than Puller.

He was not a promotions happy officer climbing the ladders of command on the backs of the men he led. He was simply a man who wanted to fight for his country and emulate the military heroes about whom he had so voraciously read as a youth in Virginia. He deserves the lofty status he has attained in Marine Corps ranks, for reams of combat events and eyewitnesses attest to his courage and undeniable leadership qualities. Utilizing both word and deed, Chesty Puller was a man who steered his men to victory.

Various sources and individuals assisted me in my research. Anyone seeking information about Chesty Puller must begin with two biographies, *Marine!*, Burke Davis's 1962 volume about the general, and Jon Hoffman's 2001 biography, *Chesty*. Those books, combined with information provided by the Marine Corps History Division and material I gathered from histories, newspaper articles, and magazine profiles of the man, enabled me to craft this work. While footnotes do not come with this edition, any reader desiring to learn the source for any of the material I used can contact me through my website, johnwuko vits.com, and I will email the relevant information.

My editor, Brent Howard, and his skilled team improved the manuscript with their helpful suggestions. Alisa Whitley, branch head and archivist for the Marine Corps History Division at Quantico, Virginia, was kind enough in this pandemic to email abundant information about the man's family background and his career, and Janis D. Jorgensen at the U.S. Naval Institute at Annapolis, Maryland, put me in touch with other resources.

Four people continue to inspire me. My dad, Tom, my mom, Grace, and brothers Tom and Fred might no longer be present to share a laugh or convey a suggestion, but they whisper their love every day. My three daughters, Amy, Julie, and Karen, lift my spirits with the pride they exhibit over my achievements, and my four grandchildren, Matthew, Megan Grace, Emma, and Katie, keep me young and laughing with their fresh outlooks on life. Each day Terri Faitel, my companion of three decades, offers her love and support, as well as adding perceptive comments about my work.

I also want to thank the three historians to whom I dedicate this book, whose advice and inspiration through the years helped me achieve my goal of writing books about the Pacific war. Tom Buell, author of two of the finest World War II biographies, opened doors with his connections, but mainly assisted me with his insightful edits and comments on my early work, undoubtedly draining dozens of red pens in the process. Dr.

Bernard Norling, my history professor and adviser at the University of Notre Dame, mailed encouragement and advice in the many single-spaced, typed letters he sent through the years to his former student.

Readers may know Jim Hornfischer as the author of *The Last Stand of the Tin Can Sailors* and other powerful volumes, but I have been fortunate to know him as much more. As my literary agent, he has helped guide me through the process of writing books for major publishers. As a fellow historian, Jim has rejoiced with me during my successes and commiserated with me during any drawbacks. Most importantly, as a friend, Jim has exhibited kindness and reinforcement. I can never sufficiently thank him.

★ CHAPTER ONE ★

"NO BRAVER MAN EVER TOOK THE FIELD"

Origins of a Warrior, June 1898–August 1941

ieutenant Edward L. Smith, Jr., a physician in civilian life now turned surgeon attached to a marine combat unit, was accustomed to dealing with frightened boys in his hometown practice, but what he saw that first night on Guadalcanal alarmed the seasoned doctor. Throughout the long, distinguished history of the Corps, marines had boasted of sending only the best into battle, but nothing in training had prepared these marines, some as young as seventeen, for the sounds and specters haunting September 18–19, 1942, their first night in the combat zone.

Even before stepping aboard the transport in Samoa for the journey to Guadalcanal, an island in the Solomons chain northeast of Australia, the men in the camp had heard stories of slaughter, blood, severed limbs, and violent Japanese banzai charges. They learned that a foe who gave no quarter had shot corpsmen, tortured captives, and hacked to death twenty-two marines on patrol not far from marine lines. They heard that in response, marines who had fought on the island since the initial landings in early August and had seen buddies die in gruesome ways had vowed to take no prisoners. In the five short weeks since the marines landed on the island, Guadalcanal had eroded into a primeval, no-holds-barred fight, a struggle marked by hand-to-hand combat and merciless jungle warfare.

In those initial hours after arriving on Guadalcanal, these wide-eyed marines stared at the jungle looming a short distance beyond their lines. No one felt safe that first night, for the darkness hid nighttime specters, real and imagined. "We lay on our ponchos and tried to sleep," recalled Lieutenant Smith, "though the grotesque shapes silhouetted against the starlit sky warned us of danger."

Shortly after midnight a distant rumble, indicating the approach of enemy aircraft, rent the sky. Parachute flares bathed the grove in an eerie green light, an indication that a more destructive bombardment from Japanese destroyers lying off Guadalcanal's coast was about to begin. Shells lit the darkness as they arced toward the marine perimeter, ending in explosions that shook the ground and kicked dirt and debris skyward. Shells smacked into the nearby airfield, toppled mammoth trees, and ignited ammunition dumps. Wounded marines moaned in pain, while others, unharmed but petrified, added their screams to those of their bloodied comrades nearby.

Suddenly another sound, tranquil and soothing, penetrated the mayhem. "I could hear the calm steady voice," wrote Lieutenant Smith, "of our battalion commander, Lieutenant Colonel Puller, through the thunder of battle, ordering his men to remain quiet and in the ground." Amid the chaos and shell explosions stood Lewis Puller, affectionately known as Chesty by his troops, infusing courage and composure into frightened young boys facing their initial battlefield test. He walked up and down his battalion's line, whispering encouragement here and words of praise there. The sight of their commander stopping at every foxhole, reminding each occupant to remain composed and keep low until the bombardment ended, calmed his unsteady troops, who figured if Chesty Puller could remain unruffled while exposed to enemy fire, they could keep their wits about them while huddling in their foxholes.

Chesty had displayed that same courage and tenacity since his days fighting rebels in Haiti in 1919. He loved to be amid the action, where he and his men met the enemy, instead of languishing behind the lines with headquarters staff. As Samuel Stavisky, a marine combat correspondent, wrote of Puller, "He continued to insert himself into the battle lines along with, and often out in front of, the grunts. He took his command post with him, at times to the consternation of his higher command. In Puller's public opinion, there were too many officers on staff and they were too far from the action to make quick, effective responses to the changing battle conditions."

Newspaper correspondents loved the man, for he was a contradiction in terms—an officer who shunned luxuries and stood in the same chow line with his enlisted, a soldier who posed as uneducated but read endlessly, a warrior who charged into battle wearing the Crusader's Cross of the Episcopal Church around his neck, and a gruff commander who wrote tender letters to his wife practically every day. "He was a blunt, profane, cigar-chewing officer who walked with his beribboned chest thrown out like a bantam rooster and with a belligerent thrust to his jaw," summed the *New York Times* in its obituary for General Puller. "He had an intense, almost noisy, loyalty to his service and a fierce contempt for weakness in men," the obituary added. "Yet he had gentler virtues, too. He was quietly religious, a devoted family man, an officer who inspired love as well as respect from those who served under him."

In 1999, correspondent Stavisky, who had witnessed many of Puller's feats while covering the war for the Marine Corps, wrote, "Chesty Puller stands tallest among the icons of the Marine Corps, the epitome of its standards and esprit de corps." General Lewis Walt, a longtime friend who served with Puller at Guadalcanal, said, "No braver man ever took the field. He was absolutely cool under fire. His rule was to hit the enemy with all you've got at the right time and in the right place. His first concern was always the enlisted men. He loved them, and I believe they loved him. He didn't send them into battle, they followed him in."

General George Patton in Europe and Admiral William "Bull" Halsey in the Pacific might lay equal claims, but few military commanders amassed as many bellicose newspaper descriptions as Puller garnered in his time during World War II and Korea. Headlines such as "Toughest S.O.B. in the Marines," "Hard-Hitting General Puller," "He Loved a Good Fight," "Hero Puller Is Idolized by Marines," and "Tough, Uncouth, and Profane: A Perfect Leatherneck" regularly appeared in articles, capturing the essence of Chesty Puller.

It is fitting that the nation's press characterized Chesty in such manner, for he came from a Virginia town replete with Civil War veterans regaling the young Puller with their stories of martial glory and courage. Those whispers in his ear remained permanent fixtures guiding Puller throughout his life.

"He Fought On and On"

When Lewis B. Puller was born on June 26, 1898, fewer than 1,000 people resided in West Point, Virginia, a community forty miles east of Richmond, the former capital of the Confederacy. Jamestown, the first English settlement in the New World, stood thirty miles south; Yorktown, where the British commander Lord Cornwallis surrendered to General George Washington to end the American Revolution, rested thirty miles southeast; and famed Civil War battlefields such as Mechanicsville, Fredericksburg, and Petersburg lay within a pleasant morning's ride.

A love for the military coursed through the blood of both his father, Matthew M. Puller, and mother, Martha Richardson Leigh. The first man bearing the same name, Lewis B. Puller, came to Virginia from England as an officer of a military company in the mid-1600s. In 1861 John Puller, Chesty's paternal grandfather, served as a Confederate captain in a local cavalry unit and rode through the Shenandoah Valley with Major

General J. E. B. Stuart. Puller's mother could claim a colonel who served in the American Revolution and an ancestor who led the 1st Virginia Infantry Regiment at Gettysburg.

Along with two older sisters and a younger brother, Puller lived in a pleasant two-story house. The youth loved reading, with adventure novels and books about military icons his favorites. He thrilled to the exploits of Julius Caesar and Hannibal, and envied the men who fought under Alexander the Great and Napoleon Bonaparte.

Equally alluring to the young Puller were the forests and streams that dominated the landscape in the West Point area. He reveled in the freedom that came in dashing across fields and through the woods on mounted steed, and he relished those times when he could grab a fishing pole or a rifle and return with dinner for the family. He learned how to track animals, how to read the telltale signs in the underbrush that might escape the casual hiker, and how to utilize vegetation as camouflage for oneself or as cover for a foe, skills that would subsequently help him survive in the jungles of Haiti, Nicaragua, and the Pacific islands. "I learned more in the woods, hunting and stalking, about the actual art of war than I ever learned in any school of any kind. Those days in the woods as a kid saved my life many a time in combat."

Living in one of the key states in the former Confederacy, Puller rubbed elbows with Civil War veterans. He sat at their feet as these aged warriors recounted tales of bravery at Manassas and Petersburg and of bloodshed at Antietam and Gettysburg. Those people brought to life the pictures of Lee, General

Thomas J. "Stonewall" Jackson, and other heralded Confederate leaders that hung in the family home.

One question about those veterans bothered Puller, however. In the Civil War his grandfather had died in battle. Why, he wondered, had not these Confederate veterans done the same instead of surrendering? When the elderly men fumbled to explain the complexities of those last days in the bitter clash, Puller replied, "I wouldn't have given up."

His childhood took an abrupt turn in 1908 when his father succumbed to cancer. His strong-willed mother grabbed the family reins and adapted to challenging new situations, and seeing her example, the son adapted as well. Martha told Lewis that she counted on him to be a man, and gave her older son responsibilities not usually handed to ten-year-olds. His next-door neighbor, Mrs. Andrew Brookes, told a reporter after World War II that "his mother depended on him a lot." She added that even though "he was young," Lewis "was a very dependable boy."

He lacked the same enthusiasm for school, where he stood in the middle of academic rankings, that he exhibited for hunting and horseback riding. Mrs. Brookes said that "he was not what you would call a thoroughly interested student," because the energetic youth preferred *doing* something rather than listening to someone else *tell* him something.

Puller excelled on the athletic fields, where he could unleash the energy that lay dormant in the classroom. He was the catcher for the high school's baseball team, the captain of both the track and basketball squads, and the star football fullback. Joseph Pumphrey, a high school buddy of Puller's, claimed that his friend displayed a stubborn refusal to quit when the contest looked bleak. "Lewis was admired here in West Point as a star of football, baseball, basketball and track. He weighed only 135 pounds at the time, but his determination on the fields of play made our teams hard to beat."

Local resident Thomas G. Pullen watched the high school football team battle one of Virginia's top squads. Although his home team lost the lopsided contest, he noticed that the fullback, rather than quit, battled for every yard. "The amazing thing was that he fought on and on, despite the hopelessness of the contest," Pullen said. "The West Point fullback ran up and down the line patting his mates on the back, kicking them, hollering and encouraging, and on the few times that his team got the ball, he made some gains."

After graduating from high school, in September 1917 Puller enrolled at the Virginia Military Institute in Lexington, Virginia, a prestigious institution 180 miles west of his hometown. Even though the school emphasized military doctrine, Puller complained that it stressed classroom instruction over actual work in the field. With the country now at war against Germany Puller, eager to join the fight before it ended, enlisted in the Marine Corps on July 25, 1918, one month after his twentieth birthday.

His hopes of reaching Europe and experiencing combat dissipated with the November armistice that terminated the conflict, but a few months later an undeterred Puller reported to Officers' Training Camp. When the Marine Corps soon announced a postwar cutback in officers and men, Puller was placed on inactive duty.

Realizing that his chances of soon becoming an officer had

vanished, at the suggestion of Captain William H. Rupertus, Puller re-enlisted as a private in the Marine Corps. He requested duty in Haiti, where that nation's military accepted marine enlisted personnel, promoted them to officers, and put them into the field to fight rebel forces. The jungles and bandits of Haiti would provide the hands-on initiation Puller sought.

"Officers Do Not Flinch Under Fire"

Puller headed to Haiti at a time when the United States had increased its presence in underdeveloped countries in the Caribbean, Central America, Asia, and the Pacific. Marine forces occupied posts in those nations to ensure calm and to keep in power rulers who favored United States interests.

These conditions offered men like Puller the opportunity to sharpen their military craft and engage in the small wars that flared between American units and native antigovernment rebels. Haiti had experienced financial and military turmoil for years, and matters had so deteriorated that in 1915 marines under Colonel L. W. T. Waller arrived to commence a two-decade-long period of occupation designed to suppress the *cacos*, the bandit forces that wreaked havoc in the northern and central regions of Haiti. American president Woodrow Wilson agreed to finance the Haitian military, the Gendarmerie d'Haiti, with marine officers serving as superior officers in the Gendarmerie and marine enlisted, like Puller, acting as junior officers.

Puller gained his initial combat experience when he commanded twenty-five men who accompanied a forty-mile mule run bringing ammunition from the nation's capital, Port-au-Prince, to outposts in the countryside. Before leaving, Puller spent two days drilling his Gendarmerie unit in how he wanted them to react in an ambush. He instructed them to listen for the sound of a bugle—one blast meant the column should turn left, and two blasts meant veer to the right—and then both days kept them in the field until dark to perfect the maneuver.

When one hundred *cacos* ambushed his column during the patrol, Puller rode out to meet the attack head on. The bandits fled against this onrush from Puller and his twenty-five Gendarmerie, and in completing this first combat assignment, Puller displayed two distinctive traits—aggressiveness under fire, and the willingness to lead from the front.

Puller continued to hone his military craft in subsequent actions, designing simple maneuvers that could be adjusted as situations warranted. "Your small wars," Puller said years later, "where the enemy invariably ambushes you is a question of split decisions."

The new commander of the Haitian Department of the South, Major Alexander A. Vandegrift, a rising star in the Marine Corps and a man Puller would frequently encounter throughout his marine career, called Puller "a master of combat patrols" for his effectiveness in fighting the *cacos*, and marked Puller as someone to watch.

The rebellion waned in late 1919 when a patrol led by Captain Herman Hanneken, another marine who in the 1940s would command alongside Puller in the Pacific, hunted down and killed the rebel leader, Charlemagne Péralte. After a sojourn in the United States, Puller returned to Haiti in March 1922, where in fighting more than forty actions, Puller learned much about jungle warfare and the tactics of successful ambushes, and proved that he could conduct himself courageously under fire while adapting to unexpected circumstances. "I think most of us profited from our long years in Haiti," wrote Vandegrift. "Whether in the Gendarmerie or the brigade, Marines learned valuable lessons in jungle and guerrilla warfare." Vandegrift was proud that many of the men who occupied top commander posts in World War II learned and "campaigned in Haiti, among them myself, Roy Geiger, Hal Turnage, Deacon Upshur, John Marston, Jerry Thomas and Lewis Puller."

Some of Puller's most important lessons came from the lower ranks. On one patrol, Lieutenant Louis Cukela, a Medal of Honor recipient from World War I, told Puller that rather than waste men by posting them to different towns, the marines should concentrate solely in the jungles and hills populated by the enemy, and remain there until every *cacos* was dead or captured. "I learned one of the great lessons of warfare from him— concentration of force," wrote Puller of his meeting with the World War I hero.

Another lesson came from a native Haitian. Sergeant Major Napoleon Lyautey, an officer in the Haitian army, used an instance from one of Puller's first battles to emphasize a point that afterward became a Puller trademark. In the early moments of the fight, Puller instinctively ducked when a bullet zipped by his head. "Captain Puller," Lyautey calmly said, "officers do not flinch under fire. They stand. The men take note of this thing. It is of first importance."

After almost five years in Haiti, which offered Puller his

initial instructions in learning how to command on the battlefield, Puller was ready to return to the United States and receive
his commission in the Marines. He did not then know it, but his
initiation into jungle warfare and into becoming a skilled young
officer had just begun.

———

The next ten years, 1923 to 1933, offered war and romance for
the young second lieutenant. He served in a variety of posts during the first five years, including stints as a post adjutant at the
Marine Barracks, Portsmouth Navy Yard, and in Basic School in
Philadelphia.

In the spring of 1926 Puller returned to his hometown of
West Point, Virginia. At a dance in nearby Urbanna, he spotted
a pretty, sixteen-year-old brunette named Virginia Evans, home
during a break from classes at St. Mary's School in North Carolina. Puller was immediately smitten. Virginia noticed him, too.
"I remarked to one of my friends that he looked so handsome in
his uniform." Puller requested a dance, and as they waltzed the
evening away, Puller suddenly asked, "Will you marry me?" Virginia declined, but was impressed that night with his determination and that Puller danced only with her.

During the ensuing years, Puller deluged her with romantic
letters, always mentioning that one day they would marry.
When he was ordered to command the guards at the Marine
Barracks, Pearl Harbor, Hawaii, he sent Virginia three expensive
orchids as a token of his admiration and promised that if she
married him, he would buy her flowers each month of her life.

After a brief time in San Diego, Puller requested a posting to

Nicaragua where, like Haiti earlier in his career, marines helped suppress a native uprising. He arrived in early December 1928, with orders to report as a staff officer with the Nicaraguan military force, the Guardia Nacional. The training in jungle warfare begun in Haiti was about to intensify.

"He Was a Common-Sense Officer"

Violent clashes among competing political factions created a volatile situation in the Central American country, where rebel leader Augusto Cesar Sandino and his militia controlled much of northern Nicaragua. The federal government ordered marines into the nation to protect American interests, and as part of the pacification effort, Puller and other marine officers would train, advise, and command the Guardia Nacional.

The isolated outposts to which Puller was assigned offered few amenities, but being located far from civilized society had its benefits as Puller was free to rely on his judgment rather than worry about interference from headquarters. Samuel Griffith, a contemporary who later fought the Japanese on Guadalcanal along with Puller, said, "I was a young officer, I had a lot of responsibility, I had to do things on my own, I had to run my own district, I was my own boss. I think I learned more in the 14 months that I was in Nicaragua—I learned a hell of a lot, about men and animals and the country."

Over the coming months, Puller led patrols into dangerous areas, hunting down bandits led by another ruthless leader, Pedro Altamirano. Recognizing Puller's value in the field, in May

1930 headquarters gave him command of Company M, a mobile striking unit tasked with heading into the jungles and mountains on prolonged expeditions, pursuing nonstop the bandits that disrupted the region.

Good fortune smiled on Puller when he welcomed as his second in command a marine whose exploits in Nicaragua were legend, Gunnery Sergeant William A. Lee. The veteran of three years in Nicaragua and Puller became fast friends. Puller admired Lee's gruff, no-nonsense demeanor and his love of combat, and Lee appreciated serving with an officer who had already gained valuable experience in Haiti. "He was a common-sense officer," said Lee years later, "and you always knew where you stood with him." Lee liked that Puller never pointed out errors to him or to anyone else in front of others, but waited until they were alone to convey his message. "He would say, 'If I'd been doing that, I'd have done it this way,' and that would be the end of it. We got on like brothers."

Relying on mobility and speed, Puller kept his men in the jungles and on the slopes of mountains for eight days at a time, refusing to give the rebels a chance to settle for long in one place. He took advantage of his terrain, traveling along small streams to cut through thick underbrush and in jungle foliage to conceal his approaches to rebel camps.

They operated under taxing conditions. In Company M everyone walked, often in temperatures that registered 110°F. The men sweltered in the dense jungle vegetation, but even when they patrolled open areas, as Lee recalled, "there wouldn't be a breath of air stirring, and everything down there—grass, cattle, everything that there is in line down there that moves, creeps, or crawls—is panting in the shade." They wound their way through heavily wooded mountainous regions, and during the rainy season trudged through terrain soaked from drenching day-long downpours. "I've seen swollen streams that were raging torrents where you couldn't move any troops or mounted units across," said Lee. "If you threw a stick in the water it would be carried off faster than a man could run."

Puller and Company M fought the rebels in numerous minor skirmishes as well as a handful of pitched battles. He captured a key Sandino subordinate, Captain Saber Manzanares, in one encounter, and killed Sandino's second in command, Marcial Rivera, in another. His prowess at defeating rebel units gained acclaim among the Guardia, and so frustrated Sandino that he placed a bounty of 5,000 pesos on the marine officer's head. Those exploits led grateful Nicaraguans to label Puller El Tigre—The Tiger.

Puller received his first Navy Cross, after the Medal of Honor the highest award bestowed on a marine, in 1930 for conducting five successful operations between February and August. According to the citation, "By his intelligent and forceful leadership without thought of his own personal safety, by great physical exertion and by suffering many hardships, Lieutenant Puller surmounted all obstacles and dealt five successive blows against organized banditry in the Republic of Nicaragua." The government of Nicaragua contributed its thanks by awarding Puller the Presidential Order of Merit.

With his thirty-month Nicaraguan tour nearing an end, Puller requested a posting to the U.S. Army Infantry School at Fort Benning, Georgia. When the news leaked, dozens of

Nicaraguans signed a letter pleading that Puller, an officer who feared no ambush and operated so effectively in the wilds of their nation, be retained in the country, but their request fell on deaf ears.

A one-year respite in the United States awaited the rising marine officer. During that interlude, he would dramatically enhance his military education and meet others like him who sought newer, and bigger, challenges.

"I'm Not About to Surrender"

The classroom lacked the field's appeal for Puller, but his year at the army's Infantry School at Fort Benning in Georgia brought him into contact with people and theories that furthered his military education. Even though the army managed the school, marine officers considered an assignment to the institution as an indication that they were marked for possible promotion.

Puller reported to Fort Benning in September 1931, where teachers discussed the best methods in commanding companies, battalions, and regiments. Puller enjoyed studying advanced battlefield tactics and utilization of weapons, but more significant was the contact Puller had with classmates, with the instructors and experts who conducted the classes, and above all, with the assistant commandant, Lieutenant General George C. Marshall. Considered one of the brightest minds in the military, General Marshall understood that field exercises and classroom debates often bore scant similarity to battlefield conditions. He contended that in the heat of combat, with bullets flying and men shouting, officers and enlisted required simplicity in orders and actions. Since battles followed their own courses rather than unfold like textbook presentations, officers needed to quickly assess the situations they confronted, think of solutions that matched the moment, and implement them without hesitation.

While learning from Marshall, Puller also impressed others. During one training exercise, Puller commanded a machine-gun detachment providing cover for an army regiment as it attempted to elude an "enemy" cavalry regiment. With the cavalry commander closing in, the army officer agreed to surrender, at which Puller snorted, "I'm not about to surrender. Is this the way you fight the war in the goddamn army? I am getting out of here!" Puller took off across country, crossed a stream, and reported to his battalion commander without yielding to the opposing force.

Puller's year in the United States ended in June 1932 with orders for his return to Nicaragua. Those newspapers that had lamented his departure the previous year now welcomed El Tigre as the man who could corral Sandino, with one publication announcing in capital letters, "MARINES BRING THE TIGER OF SEGOVIA TO FIGHT SANDINO."

Sandino's forces still disrupted the countryside as they had before, but the United States government, now dealing with the Depression and millions of unemployed workers, no longer had the desire to remain in the country. President Herbert Hoover instituted a gradual withdrawal of the American military in Nicaragua.

The American government's role may have steadily diminished, but the dangers did not. Puller and Company M averaged up to twenty miles a day in miserable conditions, engaging rebel forces five times in one week, including a vicious five-minute clash with Altamirano and eighty rebels.

One ambush occurred in late September 1932 when a local citizen informed Puller of an ancient Incan jungle trail near the Coco River used by Sandino's men as a major supply route. Puller left with forty men and eighteen pack mules to investigate the report, and traveled for two days before spotting guerrilla scouts shadowing the patrol from the hills. Puller figured an ambush awaited, but explained in his report that "my only course was to push ahead and cover as much distance as practicable."

In midmorning on September 26, a handful of rebels fired at the column, which proved to be the prelude to the main attack one hour later. From the volume of fire, Puller concluded that he had run into a rebel group of at least 150 men, heavily armed with automatic weapons, hand grenades, rifles, and dynamite bombs. With rebel bullets splintering a path in the ground toward Puller, the marine dove for the protection of a large oak tree. He shouted for the column to deploy and bring the machine gun into use, and then braved a sheet of bullets to rush toward his men and direct their movements.

Bullets smacked into Sergeant Lee's right arm and grazed his head, knocking unconscious Puller's second in command. Guerrilla fire from high ground on both flanks pinned down Puller's point, causing him to order flanking movements to the right and left by his remaining two units. The battle ended when Lee regained consciousness, grabbed the Lewis machine gun, and opened fire. Puller took advantage of Lee's action to lead charges to the tops of two ridges and clear both of rebels.

Puller led his patrol back to the city of Jinotega, the nearest Guardia base. In his report, Puller praised Bill Lee, who had not only shielded the column with the Lewis machine gun, but also displayed inordinate courage in marching back to Jinotega despite his severe wounds. "I remember he had over a hundred miles to walk, and he walked every step of that distance out."

For his efforts in this monthlong September patrol, Puller received a gold star in lieu of a second Navy Cross. The citation mentioned that during the September 26 ambush, Puller's men drove the enemy from the high ground to the right, and then utilized a flanking movement to force them from the high ground to the left. The citation added that the victory, occurring one hundred miles from any supporting force, "was largely due to the indomitable courage and persistence of the patrol commander."

Puller's last battle in Nicaragua occurred on December 26, when he and his detachment of seventy-one officers and Guardia, including Bill Lee, boarded a train to secure the area near the town of El Sauce forty miles southwest of Jinotega. President José M. Moncada had scheduled a ceremony to mark the completion of a railroad connecting El Sauce to the larger city of Léon, closer to the Pacific coast, but information indicated that guerrilla bands intended to mount an attack to disrupt the ceremony.

During the ride to El Sauce, the train approached a partially completed bridge. When the engineer, apprehensive that the tracks might dislodge and send the train careening off the bridge, balked at crossing, Puller drew his pistol, placed it at the engineer's head, and vowed to shoot him unless he continued. At the threat of gunpoint, the engineer safely navigated the bridge and moved on to El Sauce. When, upon their arrival, one hundred guerrillas attacked both sides of the train, Puller led the Guardia off the train, deployed them to both sides, and engaged in a one-hour firefight that ended with thirty-one guerrillas dead and the rebels in retreat.

The *New York Times* printed three articles near the end of the year covering Puller and the marines at El Sauce. In a front-page story, the publication mentioned that the marine officer and his Guardia "drove off with heavy casualties an insurgent band which attacked a troop train" at El Sauce, and claimed that "the crews of two work trains, on the point of being executed by their rebel captors, were rescued." The article explained that "the Guardsmen went immediately into action, directed by their commander, 1st Lieutenant Lewis B. Puller, U.S.M.C., a Virginian and holder of the Navy Cross." The ceremony ensued without further interruption, and the railroad line connecting the coastal portion of Nicaragua with an important agricultural region commenced operations.

In the first week of January 1933, Puller and the marine contingent left Nicaragua. His battles against rebel forces, in both Haiti and Nicaragua, gave him valuable lessons in commanding small units, how to earn the respect of his men, and the importance of learning from others. The education he gained in those jungles provided experience for what would later unfold in the

Pacific and instilled confidence in Puller that he was ready for something more significant.

El Tigre sought bigger battles against tougher foes. His wish would soon be granted.

"If I Hear the Beat of the Drum, I Must Leave You"

After a brief leave in the United States, on February 10, 1933, Puller left for his next overseas station as an officer in the Marine Legation Guard in Peking, China. In addition to being assistant to the officer in charge of intelligence, operations, and training, Puller received command of the Peking Horse Marines, a unit of thirty mounted marines sent to contain angry crowds and escort American citizens in and out of the Legation, the area where foreign powers established their embassies. Once each week Puller and his Horse Marines rode out to check the homes of every American living in that sector of China.

The more leisurely pace gave Puller enough time to observe the Japanese military, who had recently seized Chinese ground in their war against that nation. He and most American navy and marine officers assumed that their next war would be fought in the Pacific against Japan, whose burgeoning desire to control natural resources and island locations in the Pacific and Far East seemed destined to put Japan on a collision course with American interests in the same area. Not long after he reached the Legation, he and a friend drove twenty miles from Peking to visit the Ming Tombs, where emperors of the Ming dynasty were entombed. Along the way he noticed a Japanese battalion marching in the freezing weather, burdened with extra ammunition belts. To Puller's astonishment, each soldier also carried firewood, and when the Japanese soldiers halted, they paired off and massaged one another for fifteen minutes to loosen and warm the legs and arms numbed by the cold. After cooking and devouring their meal of rice, the soldiers began marching back to Peking.

Puller and his friend ate their picnic lunches, visited the famed life-size statues of kings at the Ming Tombs, and drove back to Peking. When the pair reached the city, Puller found that the Japanese troops had beaten them to the city, even though they had covered the distance on foot. "When I realized that this was their daily routine, I knew that they would be terrible adversaries in war."

His year in China ended in September 1934 when Puller reported for duty to command the marine guard detachment aboard the flagship in the Asiatic Fleet, the heavy cruiser USS *Augusta* (CA-31). With George Marshall, Puller had already come into contact with one officer who would play a significant role in World War II, and now, aboard *Augusta*, he met his second. Captain Chester W. Nimitz, commander of the flagship, enjoyed a steady rise in the ranks until, in the war against Japan, he held the top naval post in the Pacific.

Puller could overlook certain lapses in his men, but failure to do their duty incurred his wrath. At the mast of one of Puller's marines being disciplined for falling asleep on watch, Captain Nimitz asked Puller if he cared to comment. Most observers expected the newly arrived officer to support his marine, but

Puller replied, "I certainly do, Captain. Get rid of the son of a bitch. He's not a Marine if he goes to sleep on watch. I never want to see him again." The issue was clear to Puller—the man had been derelict in his duty and Puller would say nothing in his behalf. Captain Nimitz, who had dismissed two prior marine commanders for unsatisfactory work, liked what he saw in his new marine commander.

During his time in the Far East, Puller continued his romantic letters to Virginia. Although she declined to answer each inquiry about marriage, she admired his dedication to his nation. After expressing his love in one letter, Puller cautioned, "Even if you do marry me and make me a happy man, if I hear the beat of the drum, I must leave you." Virginia later said that "he was telling me in a nice way that the Marine Corps and duty to his country would always come first, regardless of how much he loved me. And I respected that; I respected his honesty."

"You're *Fighting* Marines"

With three years in the Pacific behind him, in June 1936, now a captain of four months, Puller returned to the United States to serve as an instructor at the Basic School in Philadelphia, established to train newly commissioned officers in the art of commanding platoon-sized units. Puller was to teach his pupils the duties and responsibilities that awaited them, and impart how best to create the esprit de corps that was so crucial to military units of all sizes.

Puller's bellowing at 6:00 a.m. every morning as he drilled

the new arrivals became so common in the Navy Yard that Colonel Allen H. ("Hal") Turnage, commander of the Basic School, joked he no longer needed a bugler to awaken everyone. When Puller noticed one of his new officers, cold and miserable while he drilled without a coat in the sleet, glance longingly at the barracks detachment marching in heavy overcoats, Puller bellowed, "Those are *barracks* Marines. You're *fighting* Marines." Turnage later claimed that the two classes in Puller's charge were the best to pass through the school.

One of those young officers, 2nd Lieutenant Wayne M. Brown, said that from the beginning Puller, whom he called the "real 'spice' of Basic School," made it clear why they had assembled and what he intended to convey. "You will draw a rifle and a pack, and for the year's course you will live the life of an enlisted Marine." Puller was everywhere, supervising them as they drilled on the field and instructing them in the classroom, always admonishing that "if you high-paid lieutenants can't do it right, how do you expect a $21-a-month private to do it right?" Puller wanted to extinguish any thoughts they had that, because they were officers, they were any better than the enlisted they would command.

Lieutenant Raymond G. Davis, one of Puller's charges at the Basic School who later became a general in the Marine Corps, said that Puller demanded perfection in every activity. During inspections, "He would go down the ranks, and if your foot was a small angle out of line, he would stop and explain it to you. He had us try on our uniforms and then inspected us individually. If he could fit a fist inside your belt, it was too loose."

Lieutenant Lewis Walt, who crossed paths with Puller on

Guadalcanal and Cape Gloucester, gave credit to Puller, his instructor at Basic School, for the successes he amassed, including actions for which he received the Navy Cross, Silver Star, and Bronze Star. He wrote Chesty after the war, "You taught us how to train men and to fight and ignore danger as though it didn't exist."

———

Lewis's pursuit of Virginia paid off in 1937 when she agreed to his latest proposal. On November 13, 1937, in Middlesex County, Virginia, at Christ Episcopal Church, a structure built on land that had been donated by a seventeenth-century Puller ancestor, the two became husband and wife.

Shortly after they were married, Lewis and Virginia attended a dance in Washington, DC, where Lewis introduced her to Nimitz, newly promoted to rear admiral. "The admiral asked me to dance and congratulated us on our recent wedding," recalled Virginia. "'Your husband is a fine officer and a fine man. You're a lucky girl,' he told me." When Virginia answered that she knew how fortunate she was to wed Lewis, the future commander of the Pacific Fleet during World War II cautioned her to accept her husband as he was, and not try to change him. "He's the kind of man we're going to need one of these days," the admiral told her. "And I remembered that advice," said Virginia. "I never tried to change Lewis. Not at all."

A fanatical warrior on the battlefield, Puller exhibited a softer side with Virginia. She never experienced that ferocious military officer every man under Puller witnessed every day; never called him El Tigre. When he was in camp or combat, other than the near nightly letters he wrote to Virginia, Puller possessed the uncanny ability to block out Virginia, hometown friends, and eventually children, so that he could focus on what had to be done to succeed on the battlefield. Once the fighting ended and Puller returned to his wife, the softer, gentler Puller materialized, far removed from the commander who led his troops into combat. Puller, a warrior-romantic, rarely allowed one facet of his personality to encroach upon another.

China

Puller was soon off to the Pacific for another year as commander of the *Augusta*'s marine detachment. From there, freshly promoted to major, Puller joined the 4th Marine Regiment in Shanghai, China, to serve as the 2nd Battalion's executive officer, the second in command.

Those early indications of Japan's militaristic intentions during his first posting in China only three years earlier had intensified, but while events in the Far East moved inevitably toward war, the mightiest democracy in the world had withdrawn into its own borders. Weary of intervening in Europe's affairs, the United States sought isolation behind its welcome barriers—the Atlantic Ocean on the European side and the Pacific Ocean on the Japanese side. Secure behind those watery borders, Americans focused upon solving their domestic problems, particularly ending the Great Depression.

The initial moves leading to World War II in the Pacific had flared in September 1931, when Japan launched an invasion into

Manchuria as Puller attended the Company Officers Course at Fort Benning. The United States joined a handful of European nations in condemning the invasion, but since those countries were then battling economic woes stemming from the 1929 Wall Street crash, they did not consider using military force to halt the moves. This refusal to take action emboldened Japan as the decade ensued.

Life in Shanghai mirrored Puller's experiences in Peking, with sports, patrols into the countryside, and military parades dominating his time. Now the father of a daughter, named Virginia Mac, Puller chafed that the United States had over the past handful of years gone out of its way to avoid open fighting with the Japanese. He hoped to return to the United States, take command of a battalion, and prepare for war. "I do not understand why we have taken all the guff from the Japanese these past few years," he wrote his wife. "Sooner or later we will be involved with the Axis powers."

Should the Japanese spark hostilities in the Far East, the United States would be unable to hold on to its Shanghai post. Some officers claimed if that occurred, they would retreat into China's interior and mount a guerrilla-style campaign against the Japanese. Puller, though, proposed an alternate course. "I don't know what the United States Government will do, I don't know what Marine Headquarters will do, and I don't know what the regiment will do, but—no orders to the contrary—I'll take my battalion and fight my way the hell back to Frisco."

Spring of 1941 dragged into summer, and yet Puller remained cloistered in Shanghai. With Europe already enveloped in warfare, and with Japan's Pacific moves certain to bring her into open conflict with the United States, Puller bristled at the thought of being left out of the fight. Should it come to war, the marines would need experienced officers, yet he remained stuck in Shanghai. "Of course I knew the war was evident," he said, "and I was just straining to get the hell out." If he languished in Shanghai, he would "be a prisoner of war for the war."

In August 1941 Puller finally left Shanghai when orders sent him to the marine base at New River, North Carolina, to assume command of the 1st Battalion, 7th Marine Regiment. The battle Puller had wanted his whole life, and the opportunity to follow in his forebears' footsteps and emulate those great commanders about whom he had so frequently read, was now at hand.

★ CHAPTER TWO ★

"THERE'S METHOD IN THE OLD MAN'S MADNESS"

Preparing to Meet the Japanese, August 1941–September 1942

P uller returned to a military scrambling to catch up after years of neglect caused by the debilitating economic effects of the Great Depression and the spirit of isolationism that gripped the nation. With Roosevelt's requests for additional military funds now finding a more cooperative response from a Congress concerned about international events, the Armed Forces began to expand their ranks and train men.

Six months before Puller left Shanghai, the 1st Marine Division had begun operating out of New River, North Carolina, a vast stretch of water, coastal swamp, and wooded areas that would eventually grow into Camp Lejeune. The critical issue was that in early 1941, the 1st Marine Division existed mostly on paper. The roster included three regiments—the 1st, 5th, and 7th

Regiments—but each was badly understrength and lacked the men and equipment needed to fight a war.

"We were racing against time and knew it, but many people in America did not," said Brigadier General Alexander Vandegrift, in 1941 the assistant division commander of Puller's division. An expansion of the Marine Corps to almost 80,000 officers and men ushered in a collection of civilians in their late teens and early twenties who joined a cadre of veteran marines.

At New River, Puller stamped his imprint on his 1st Battalion by putting into practice those military theories and tactics he had formulated from years of reading military histories and biographies, and from his own experiences in Haiti and Nicaragua. He stressed that officers should demand more of themselves than they required from their men and, above all, in combat their station was at the front, where the men could see them and where they could lead by example. He made it clear that no one, from high-ranking officers to the least experienced private, was more important than anyone else, and that no officer should feel entitled to benefits that were not also available to the enlisted. He stipulated that at chow time, the battalion would eat in reverse order—privates, corporals, and sergeants would be fed before the officers. When one marine complained about the unusual system, a veteran gunnery sergeant who had served under Puller in Nicaragua said, "You're lucky. When I was with the Old Man down in Nicaragua, the order was mules even before privates, and brother, them mules could eat! You'll find out there's method in the Old Man's madness."

One afternoon Puller came upon a private standing at attention, repeatedly saluting a 2nd lieutenant. When Puller asked the young officer for an explanation, the lieutenant answered that as punishment for failing to salute him as he walked by the officer, he was making the private snap off one hundred salutes. Rather than berate the lieutenant, Puller agreed that he was correct in disciplining the man. "But you know that an officer must return every salute he receives—now let me see you get to it, and do your share." Puller stood at the lieutenant's side until he had answered each salute.

Puller pushed his marines to give their best, in the classroom and in the field. He awoke them each day at 6:00 a.m. for rigorous physical training and after breakfast led them on hikes ranging from twelve to twenty miles. He required corpsmen wearing full gear to accompany the battalion on those marches and yanked cooks out of mess hall kitchens so they could learn how to prepare food in the field for their companies, platoons, and squads. Throughout the hikes, Puller roamed from one end of the column to the other, prodding them to greater effort and encouraging them with his presence.

Following one outing, Major Puller instructed his company officers that to more closely reflect battlefield conditions, he wanted every man in camouflage. When one officer replied that the battalion had not yet received the necessary material, Puller told them the field would provide everything they needed. His marines scoured the grounds for twigs, leaves, and branches to cover their helmets and uniforms, and spread mud on their faces and hands to better blend in with the foliage. Once finished, Puller led his men out of camp directly by marines from other battalions, who snickered at what they called "the walking forest," but due to their camouflage, before long Chesty's marines could operate undetected through forests and wade in knee-deep swamps.

Puller kept his hand in everything. On one hike, when his officers struggled to keep the column aligned while wading through a swamp, Chesty stepped in. Accustomed as a youth to navigating the country woods while hunting, he halted the line and ordered every marine who had been raised in the country to step forward. He divided those men among the platoons to act as guides, and the column encountered fewer problems from then on.

Not every officer agreed with Puller's methods. When his regimental commander, a man Puller had regarded as incompetent during their days in Nicaragua, watched Puller's battalion return to camp after being in the field, the commander exploded at their ragged appearance. "Who do you think you are, Puller, Daniel Boone?" he demanded. "Looks like a damned Halloween party. Get these men cleaned up and looking like Marines, or I'll relieve you." That evening the division's commanding officer, General Philip Torrey, called Puller to his office. Instead of a reprimand Torrey, who had also observed Puller and his men operating in camouflage, congratulated Chesty and asked where he picked up the idea. "In China," replied Puller. "The Japs and Chinese use it to perfection." Torrey issued an order that from then on, the entire 1st Marine Division was to use camouflage in the field.

With every order or action, Puller tried to instill pride. One morning as they marched onto the field, Puller overheard a marine from another unit taunting the battalion. Puller expected a handful of his marines to retaliate, but no one left the line to respond. "I was amazed that one of you didn't step out of ranks and knock him cold," he told them later. Puller said that if they did not have enough pride in their unit to respond to ridicule now, how could they fight effectively as a unit when in combat?

One of Puller's favorite times at New River occurred when his 1st Battalion challenged Hanneken's 2nd Battalion to a contest. Deeply competitive men, the two had been trying to outdo each other since their Haiti-Nicaragua days. For the exercise, Hanneken's men wore red armbands while Puller's donned white, but Puller surreptitiously told a small group of his men to put on Hanneken's red armband, sneak to Hanneken's rear, and cut his communications wire. At the same time, Puller executed a flanking movement through a swamp, surprised Hanneken at his command post, and vanquished his rival. Puller's performance caused the battalion surgeon, Lieutenant Edward Smith, to write in his diary, "I think we are going places now."

Developments in the Pacific moved swiftly while Puller trained his battalion at New River. In light of President Roosevelt's orders to halt the flow of oil, Japanese leaders could either reach a settlement with the United States and reopen the supply line from that nation, or they could continue their present policy of overseas expansion and risk war with the United States. Military leaders in Japan agreed that if diplomats could not convince President Roosevelt to lift the embargo on oil and other products by the first week in November, they would start military operations against the United States and European powers.

Alerted by intercepted messages that Japanese troops had

already embarked on transports for shipment to the Dutch East Indies and Southeast Asia, in late November Secretary of State Cordell Hull informed Roosevelt that military action could no longer be avoided. Although Roosevelt made a final attempt to keep talks going by sending a personal note to Japanese emperor Hirohito on December 6, the president knew that hostilities were imminent. When American codebreakers intercepted a Japanese message to diplomats in Washington ordering them to destroy sensitive documents and to present a note to the United States at 1:00 p.m. on December 7, Roosevelt told his top adviser, Harry Hopkins, that it meant war. A war warning raced out to every American military post in the Pacific.

"Everything was ready," wrote *Time* magazine in those tense days as the conflict drew near. "From Rangoon to Honolulu, every man was at battle stations." The magazine added, "A vast array of armies, of navies, of air fleets were stretched now in the position of track runners, in the tension of the moment before the starter's gun. A bare chance of peace remained—of a kind of peace very close to war but not quite war."

"He Was in There with Us, Pack and All"

On Sunday, December 7, Puller and Virginia drove to nearby Saluda to visit Virginia's mother. They engaged in small talk before turning to the radio for entertainment. The sudden announcement that the Japanese had attacked Pearl Harbor stunned everyone but Puller, who had been warning that a shooting war against

Japan would one day occur, but his thoughts also drifted to his friends in Peking, the post he had left only a few months earlier, who would soon become prisoners of war. Only the stroke of good fortune that had transferred him to New River had spared Chesty from sharing their grim predicament.

Before returning to his battalion, Puller discussed family finances and other key items with Virginia. Without her knowledge, he also sent money to his brother-in-law with the request that on the thirteenth day of each month, the day of their wedding, he would arrange for a dozen red roses to be sent to Virginia.

Pearl Harbor changed everything. Enlistments in the Marine Corps rocketed from 2,000 one month before the attack to almost 7,000 between Pearl Harbor and the end of December. That number doubled the next month, with the average age of the recruits at nineteen, meaning Puller and every veteran marine would have their hands full preparing these raw recruits for combat against a battle-tested opponent.

Puller, Vandegrift, and other marine officers faced daunting tasks, but at least the challenges involved young men who entered the military not to escape poor conditions at home, but because they wanted payback for December 7. "To us the real meaning of Pearl Harbor lay in the psychological transformation of our troops and those recruits who now joined us by the thousands," wrote Vandegrift. "From this time no one held the slightest doubt that we would ship out, fight, and win. Lethargy vanished, never returned." These teenagers barely out of high school would better heed their sergeants and lieutenants, for as Vandegrift added, "Suddenly a great many men realized that they knew not a damn thing about war, that a few of us professionals did, and that their chances of returning safely would improve if they learned what we offered them."

In the early months of 1942, as Puller's 1st Marine Division was the only land element ready to fight a war, Puller figured that he would soon leave for the Pacific and another battlefield, but Vandegrift, who assumed command of the division in the spring, needed time to train the rush of recruits pouring into the Corps. He replaced complacent officers with men who, like Puller, displayed a readiness to do whatever it took to prepare men and lead them into battle.

Puller welcomed Vandegrift's moves, as he had witnessed the value of thorough training since his days in Haiti. He hoped these new recruits, called "Pearl Harbor marines" by his veterans, would respond, and relied on his sergeants, the men he considered to be the backbone of the Corps, to mold them into the top-notch fighting force he wanted to take into action. He wrote that "the Corps was in fact operated by its senior noncoms and that too few officers knew the basics of their trade."

Puller was correct in leaning on those battle-scarred noncoms, who proved to be the ones who transformed the recruits from civilians to marines. Samuel B. Griffith II, executive officer of the 1st Raider Battalion on Guadalcanal, described them as "a motley bunch." They were "first sergeants yanked off 'planks' in navy yards, sergeants from recruiting duty, gunnery sergeants who had fought in France, perennial privates with disciplinary records a yard long. These were the professionals, the 'old breed' of United States Marines." He added that "they knew their weapons and they knew their tactics. They knew they were tough and they knew they were good. There were enough of them to leaven the division and to impart to the thousands of younger men a share both of the unique spirit which animated them and the skills they possessed."

At every stage of his career, Puller was a hands-on leader. Where other battalion commanders might let his lieutenants or sergeants carry the load, Puller became involved from the first day. One lieutenant in A Company of Puller's battalion said, "Major Puller never stood aside and said, 'Carry on, Sergeant,' and most officers did. He was in there with us, pack and all. He could walk down the best of us, even the kids. Other commanders rode cars in the woods, but not Puller."

Because Puller emphasized realistic training, he made certain that combat tactics, hand-to-hand fighting, and bayonet drills were constant features of his day. When he informed Colonel Pedro del Valle, commander of the 11th Marine Artillery Regiment, that he wanted his men to maneuver under live fire as often as possible, del Valle warned that employing live rounds could result in accidents, or even deaths. Puller replied that he was willing to take that chance. "What I won't chance," he said, "is taking a bunch of green kids to war before they know the sound of big guns." Del Valle agreed, and then informed Puller that he was the only commander who had asked him for artillery fire.

———

Puller received orders to embark for the Pacific in March 1942, but instead of a combat zone, the 7th Marine Regiment left to man the defenses of Samoa, an important base in the South

Pacific. On Easter Sunday, Puller led his men aboard the transport USS *Fuller* (AP-14) and exited Hampton Roads for the deployment to Samoa. The regiment was the initial contingent from the 1st Marine Division to embark for the Pacific, but unlike Vandegrift and the remainder of the division, which would soon depart for New Zealand and final combat training, Puller faced a passive defense of a remote island base. Being isolated on Samoa for an indeterminate time, he had no idea when he might leave for the battlefield, but for now he had to lean on one of his least prominent traits—patience during a time of world conflict.

"Stuck Out Here to Rot"

Once his battalion reached Samoa Puller, recently promoted to lieutenant colonel, instituted a harsh training regimen intended to have the men razor sharp and ready to enter battle whenever those orders came. He scheduled twenty-mile hikes despite the suppressing heat, during which he roamed the length of the column, goading them on and reminding them that once in combat, they would appreciate the labors they now exerted.

The men responded because like them, Puller, at forty-four more than double the age of his privates and corporals, perspired under the same sun and ran the same miles. "Puller must have marched twice the distance we did," Private Gerald White entered in his diary, "for all day long he kept marching up and down the column, jaunty as a bantam rooster, pipe clenched in his teeth, ever alert to see that men who were succumbing to the heat, exhaustion or blisters were taken care of by corpsmen.

Many times today I saw him take a BAR [Browning automatic rifle], machine gun or mortar off the shoulder of some Marine whose fanny was dragging and carry it to give the poor guy some respite."

Puller expected to see similar effort in his officers and men. When one of his company commanders, Captain Regan Fuller, who had just left the hospital after undergoing an appendectomy, collapsed two miles short of a twenty-two-mile hike, instead of reprimanding the ill officer, Puller congratulated him for going as far as he had. A marine knew Puller's opinion of his performance by how Puller addressed him. Private First Class Matthew Constentino said that every time Puller talked to them, he "called you Old Man. And then when he was a little unhappy with what you did, he'd call you Son and you better rectify the mistake or whatever to get back to Old Man again."

Puller demanded that his officers exert greater effort than their men and to make their own needs secondary to those of the enlisted. He continued his practice of making his officers wait for their food until every man had been fed, and scrutinized the chow line to ensure his order was followed. According to one marine, Puller was "the idol of his enlisted men and the bane of all second lieutenants."

One night Sergeant Stanley Oblachinski and a buddy obtained a few bottles of a local alcoholic beverage and took two Samoan beauties into the hills for an evening of romance. The party lasted well beyond their curfew of 10:00 p.m., but the marines figured that they could handily sneak back into camp. The revelry ended at 1:00 a.m. when out of the dark appeared Puller. "Oh, we were scared shitless!" said Oblachinski, who was sure he would be busted for violating the curfew. "But old Chesty just came over and sat by this little fire we had for a while, told us how we had some real tough times ahead, then took off. He didn't even ask for our names." Oblachinski breathed a sigh of relief, vowed to be more cautious in the future, and then asked himself, "What the hell was Puller doing wandering around those hills at night like that?"

Puller understood that his men would never truly know how they would react under fire or what emotions they might experience until they faced an enemy in the combat zone. Training and classroom instruction were helpful, but it was on the battlefield where a marine could begin to understand himself in the direst of conditions. "You learn a hell of a sight more in one fight than you learn in a year at Staff College," Puller said. "Reading and study is all right, but most officers spend too much time in schools."

Puller hated standing on the sidelines in Samoa while other officers steamed into combat. "Here I am, stuck out here to rot on this damned island while other people fight the war. They've marooned us," he complained to staff officers. His frustrations compounded in early August when Vandegrift led the rest of the 1st Marine Division in an assault of the Japanese-held Solomon Islands. One evening as he played bridge with his battalion surgeon, Edward Smith, Puller spoke enviously that marines along the Tenaru River on Guadalcanal had killed every Japanese soldier that charged their lines. "He was as excited as a schoolboy as he repeated the figures again and again," recalled Smith. Puller could not wait to join the action, and "you could sense his grim determination to slaughter more Japs than anyone else."

Near the end of August, almost three weeks after Vandegrift's forces had landed on Guadalcanal and adjoining islands, Puller's battalion finally boarded a transport bound for the combat zone. Vandegrift needed every man he could acquire to bolster his beleaguered marines defending a vital airfield on that island.

On Guadalcanal, Puller would add to his already impressive laurels.

"America Needed a Shot in the National Arm"

Puller's inexperienced battalion steamed to the island at a perilous moment. The nation had witnessed a roller-coaster ride of events since Pearl Harbor, with most of the ominous news directly resulting from years of military neglect. National columnists reflected the nation's military unpreparedness in their writings. Correspondent John Lardner described a country of immense buoyancy that suddenly had the rug pulled from beneath its feet. He wrote of "the picture of a country and an army and a navy at war but innocent of knowledge of war, full of fight but uncertain how to flex a fist, earnest, awkward, stumbling, getting up and falling down again, learning from day to day." Lardner added, "The first time I saw a machine gun fired by Americans in this war, it didn't work. The first time I saw an anti-aircraft gun leveled for loading, it had a broken train. The first time I saw a naval gun prepared for aiming, it didn't get aimed—because the gunnery officer called a range that the men in the gun crew couldn't find on the gun."

In early 1942 Hanson Baldwin of the *New York Times* wrote, "This is a war we can lose" and warned that "this war . . . is a war to the death, a war for life itself, a war the outcome of which is by no means certain." He said the United States was ill prepared for the conflict and the nation had to quickly drop the apathy of prewar days and focus on "one aim—victory."

The home front received welcome news in May and again in June when the United States Navy fought Japanese aircraft carriers to a draw in the Coral Sea, then changed the course of the Pacific war by sinking four Japanese carriers in the crucial Battle of Midway. The navy had struck back, but when, people wondered, would the army and marines begin assaulting enemy land bastions?

The Japanese already had their eyes on Guadalcanal as an important air base to protect their Pacific southern flank, to threaten the supply lines from the United States to Australia, and to use as a staging area for their eventual invasion of Australia. On May 3 Rear Admiral Aritomo Gotō took a naval force into Tulagi harbor, directly across from Guadalcanal, and two weeks later he landed troops and laborers on Guadalcanal to begin construction of an airfield. The discovery of this airfield by American intelligence alarmed the U.S. military for the reverse reasons the Japanese sought Guadalcanal—in Japanese hands it posed too great a threat to vital American interests in the region.

Once his 1st Marine Division, including Puller's battalion,

left the United States, General Vandegrift expected to have the necessary training time in New Zealand before conducting an assault against the enemy. The discovery of the airfield, however, altered those plans, and in late June he received orders to attack the Solomon Islands in less than five weeks. Stunned with the sudden change, Vandegrift, who did not even know the location of Guadalcanal, was tasked with leading an underprepared, underequipped division into battle against a tested enemy, at a location about which he knew little.

While Puller remained in distant Samoa, Vandegrift led most of the 1st Marine Division into battle in the Solomon Islands on August 7. A predawn stillness encompassed the armada of destroyers, cruisers, and transports approaching the South Pacific island, and as the transports began disgorging streams of marines toward Guadalcanal, Vandegrift figured he and his men faced steep odds in this first land assault against the Japanese. He believed, however, that the calculated risk was worth it. "We knew that America needed a shot in the national arm. Since December 7, 1941, our national heritage had yielded to a prideless humiliation. The Philippines were gone, Guam and Wake had fallen, the Japanese were approaching Australia."

When the first boats crashed ashore, officers and enlisted leaped from the craft and raced up the beach. When, surprisingly, they received no opposition, Vandegrift ordered the marines to advance inland. Moving in fifty-yard increments, marines reached a coconut grove and neared the airfield, the day's main objective. Conditions deteriorated the next day when Vandegrift learned that the navy, due to the lack of U.S. air cover, intended to withdraw the transports and cargo vessels early the next morning. Without naval support, the Japanese could move at will on the island, and their navy would control the waters around Guadalcanal. While the enemy could readily shuttle in needed reinforcements and equipment, the marines had to make do with whatever sparse ammunition and supplies they had.

Marines reacted angrily to what they saw as their navy brethren abandoning their posts. One private said, "I had it figured this way. Our necks were out and it was just a question of how far down the Japanese were gonna chop." With the Japanese navy in command of the seas around Guadalcanal, Vandegrift's marines were an abandoned, underequipped division facing the might of the Japanese surface and land units.

Vandegrift ordered his marines to pull back and hold a six-mile-long by three-mile-deep perimeter around Henderson Field, which lay along Guadalcanal's northern coast near the Lunga River. Outside the marine defensive perimeter, alternating stretches of jungle and grassy plains led to interior hills and mountains, all of which the Japanese controlled. Two rivers—the Tenaru along the eastern flank and the Matanikau beyond their lines to the west—would be the sites of decisive battles in the coming months for control of Henderson Field and for the land outside the perimeter, but until reinforcements would enable him to patrol deeper into the jungle and operate beyond the perimeter, Vandegrift had to confine his operations to the area around the airfield.

The evening of August 12 brought additional alarming news when Lieutenant Colonel Frank B. Goettge, the division intelligence officer, led a patrol of twenty-five men into the jungle to pursue reports that a group of Japanese soldiers was ready to surrender. Instead of finding a dispirited enemy, the men walked into a trap and most were slaughtered. Sergeant Frank L. Few, one of three survivors, told a reporter that the Japanese, instead of taking the men prisoners, sliced the marines to death with their swords. "It was the end of the rest on the beach. The Japs closed in and hacked up our people. I could see swords flashing in the sun."

From that moment, marines vowed that if the enemy wanted a dirty war, they would get one. The notion of "kill or be killed" took hold, and both sides adhered to an unspoken pledge that no prisoners would be taken. "For the rest of our time on Guadalcanal we met Japanese brutality with an equally brutal response," said Gunnery Sergeant Thurman Miller. "The Japanese became less than human to us, and many of us descended to their level, not just taking revenge but also taking body parts, even skulls, as souvenirs." He added that "the spiraling cycle of revenge reduced both sides to base animal instincts. We were killing machines fueled by hatred."

Shortly after midnight on August 21 Vandegrift was awakened with news that close to 1,000 Japanese were attempting to punch through 200 marines manning the defense line on the east side of the Tenaru River and retake the airfield. The fighting continued until daylight, at which time the marines received their first look at the damage they had inflicted. As one recalled, "Dead Japs were piled in rows and on top of each other from our gun positions outward. Some were only wounded and continued to fire after playing dead."

The marines on the Tenaru line killed eight hundred Japanese while losing forty-three dead in repelling the enemy. In doing so in their first major action, they gained confidence that they were the equal to a Japanese land force that had compiled an impressive list of Pacific triumphs. "We beat the Japanese at the Tenaru," wrote Vandegrift of his first major action in the Pacific. "Yesterday the Jap seemed something almost superhuman, a kind of mechanical juggernaut that swept inexorably through the Philippines, through the Dutch East Indies, over the beaches at Guam and Wake Island, through the jungles of New Guinea." He added, "But today *we* [italics his] had beaten the Jap. The Jap no longer seemed superhuman. The Jap was a physical thing, a soldier in uniform, carrying a rifle and firing machine guns and mortars and charging stupidly against barbed wire and rifles and machine guns."

Vandegrift's tenuous hold on Guadalcanal could slip away at any time, however. In September 1942, shortly before Puller arrived, 19,000 men of the 1st Marine Division maintained a fragile perimeter of a few square miles around Henderson Field, while the Japanese commanded the rest of Guadalcanal. The exhausted marines, hemmed in by the sea on one side and the Japanese on the other three, dug in, subsisted on meager rations and captured rice, and battled the Japanese while on patrols as well as dysentery and malaria.

In mid-September Vandegrift chatted with Hanson Baldwin, the respected *New York Times* military correspondent. Baldwin, who had recently arrived from the United States, told Vandegrift that top officials in Washington, DC, were pessimistic that the marines would prevail. Vandegrift admitted they were hanging on by a slender thread, but said the Japanese had miscalculated American determination and skill, and insisted that despite disease and insufficient food and ammunition, his division would hold.

Vandegrift said that on Guadalcanal he had to alter much of his prior thinking about waging war. "In order to meet them successfully in jungle fighting," he explained to Baldwin, "we shall have to throw away the rule books of war and go back to the French and Indian Wars again." Standing armies meeting on vast battlefields would be replaced by companies and battalions engaged in smaller-scale clashes and speedy firefights, actions that perfectly suited Puller's notions of combat forged in the wilds of Haiti and the jungles of Nicaragua.

———

Vandegrift and Puller faced an equally determined Japanese commander. Major General Kiyotake Kawaguchi's 35th Infantry Brigade had overrun Borneo in December 1941, and as August ended, he landed his brigade at Guadalcanal to knock Vandegrift's marines off the island and restore it to Japanese control.

Two weeks later, with Puller's transport at sea, Kawaguchi moved on Henderson Field. The gifted officer planned a three-pronged attack, striking simultaneously from the east, west, and south. Vandegrift concluded that the Japanese would hit a ridge one mile south of the airfield that, in their hands, would give Kawaguchi a commanding view of the airfield, and ordered Lieutenant Colonel Merritt Edson, Puller's equal in gaining legendary status in the Corps for his heroics in Nicaragua, to place his 400 1st Marine Raiders along the ridge to prevent Kawaguchi from seizing the vital position.

Edson, called by correspondent Richard Tregaskis "the bravest, the most effective killing machine I met in fifteen years as a war correspondent," stood with his men on the ridge, waiting for the enemy. On September 12 at 9:00 p.m., a Japanese aircraft dropped a flare over the area. Thirty minutes later Japanese cruisers bombarded the ridge for twenty minutes, after which Kawaguchi's men swarmed down the banks of the Lunga River straight at Edson. Grenades exploded and bullets smacked into the terrain along the length of the Raider line, but the marines held. Japanese bullets hit so close to Edson that he at times issued commands as he lay on his stomach, but by daylight on September 14 Kawaguchi's attacks halted. Edson lost 31 killed and 104 wounded, but half of Kawaguchi's men lay on the ridge's slopes and crest. For the moment, Henderson Field was safe, but if Vandegrift hoped to retain the airfield, he needed Puller's men.

"Well, Puller, You Finally Found the War"

Correspondent Tregaskis had witnessed much of the fighting since the August 7 landings. He obtained material from interviews with generals and colonels, but his best copy came from the casual conversations he conducted with lower ranks, where majors and lieutenants, sergeants and privates conveyed the reality of combat. He turned their words into newspaper articles, and kept a diary that would become a bestselling book the next year and then a popular home front motion picture.

On Friday, September 18, Tregaskis visited headquarters near Henderson Field for a morning chat with a colonel. Instead of summarizing the previous day's actions, the officer quietly suggested that the correspondent stroll shoreward. "I can't say anything more about it, but I'd recommend that you go for a walk on the beach." Intrigued by the mystery, Tregaskis strode toward the water. Moments later cargo ships and transports, escorted by destroyers, steamed into view to disgorge fresh men of the 7th Marine Regiment to bolster Vandegrift's defense of Henderson Field.

On one of those transports, Chesty Puller inspected his battalion before he led the men ashore to join the rest of the division in savage combat around the airfield. Puller had no doubt he would be as successful in South Pacific jungles as he had been in Haiti and Nicaragua. He commanded a larger unit than when he pursued Sandino, but he could still operate in much the same manner as he had in those earlier clashes. As Solomon Island jungles would be too restrictive to allow large-scale movements, the decisions and actions of a battalion commander, the highest-ranking officer remaining in close contact with the men on the front, would be crucial to success, for he was the officer most seen by the marine infantrymen and he was the man from whom they would take their cue.

The tenets of that success centered around the thought that every unit, from platoon-size to battalion, was only as courageous as its leader, and as such, Chesty maintained that the ideal commander exhibited courage in battle and led from the front.

In a memo on leadership written for a magazine correspondent, Puller argued that a commander had to be "warlike. A savagely fighting leader of combat troops. Shows positive taste for fighting, but with good common sense. Won't order his men where he won't go himself. Swears at his officers and men, but knows their names and makes them feel they are intimate with him. A driving, furious, fighting type whose men both respect and fear him."

Puller could barely discern the island's shoreline from the transport that foggy morning. The other vessels approaching Guadalcanal provided a sense of comfort, but soon Puller and his marines, many of whom had no experience and little notion of what combat was like, would drop into the Higgins boats for the short journey toward the beach, exposed to enemy fire as they neared the island.

In the early daylight, Marines emerged from sweltering holds and climbed to the deck. Men cursed the heat as they advanced toward rails, grabbed onto the netting, and descended into the bobbing Higgins boats that would take them to land.

As his boat neared the beach, Puller waded ashore and stepped through intricately woven barbed-wire entanglements toward a coconut grove beyond the sand, where he planned to assemble his men. Telltale signs of warfare had transformed the grove into a battle-scarred landscape. Splintered, charred trees contrasted with the luscious jungle foliage beyond, and marine trenches carved paths into what had once been a well-tended grove. Camouflaged machine-gun emplacements and sandbag-reinforced dugouts dotted the grove and beaches, while a handful of twisted, burned Japanese fighter aircraft cautioned Puller that the skies harbored enemy threats every bit as dangerous as those hidden in Guadalcanal's jungle.

When Puller left his landing craft, Lieutenant Colonel Merrill B. Twining, an old friend of Puller's who knew how impatient Chesty was to join the fighting, greeted him. Unsuccessfully masking a smirk, he said, "Well, Puller, you finally found the war. Did you get lost on the way? Where have you been?"

Puller brushed aside Twining's welcome and asked where he could find the Japanese. Someone handed him one of the hastily prepared, inaccurate maps used in those early days of Solomons combat, but after one glance Puller tossed it away. "Hell, I can't make head nor tails of this," grumped Puller. "Just show me where they are!" Upon learning their location, Chesty blurted, "All right. Let's go get 'em."

Richard Tregaskis and the marines who had been on the island since August had eagerly awaited the appearance of reinforcements, and Puller's battalion, as well as the rest of the 7th Marines, breathed life into men who had suffered a string of numbing blows. "All along the beach our weary veterans stood and watched the process, passively," wrote Tregaskis in his diary. "We had been talking about reinforcements, and waiting for a long time." Unlike the marines with whom Tregaskis had endured naval shellings, aerial bombings, and jungle ambushes, Puller's unscathed marines "wore clean utility suits and new helmets, and talked tough and loud as they came ashore." One veteran quizzed a few of Puller's men and told his buddies, "Chees, these guys want to tell *us* about the war," before remembering that he had been as boastful in the hours before his August 7 landing. "And we knew then that it would take some time with these men, as it had with us, to get rid of that loud surface toughness and develop the cool, quiet fortitude that comes with battle experience."

Merritt Edson was not surprised that Puller's men exuded confidence, for they adopted the demeanor of their heralded commander. The five-foot-ten Puller infused confidence in his marines as he directed the movements of his three companies of almost 800 officers and men. A trademark wrinkled cap rested atop a face weathered by years of hard duty, and the forty-four-year-old inhaled on a pipe clenched tightly in his teeth. Resting in his pocket, as it had been every time Puller went into combat for the last twenty years, was the oft-read and much-underlined copy of Caesar's *Gallic Wars*. Edson, who would be awarded the Medal of Honor for his actions in the Solomons, said to his executive officer upon Puller's arrival, "There comes the greatest fighting man in the Marine Corps. We'll have some competition now."

For the remainder of that first day, Puller supervised his men while they unloaded ammunition and other supplies and shifted it from the beach to the sheltered areas in the coconut grove. Once finished, he led the battalion five hundred yards to the grove, where they dug in and prepared for their first night on Guadalcanal.

"Everyone Was Jittery That Night"

As daylight faded, Puller surveyed the scene facing the coconut grove. Between his men and the defensive perimeter line stood

Henderson Field and its aircraft. Looking westward, the Lunga River lay to his right, while along the eastward edge of the perimeter, the Tenaru River meandered north toward Sealark Channel, where massive naval clashes would ensue in the coming weeks. Behind lay the beaches that, along with the rivers on each flank and the jungle to their front, encased the marines in a tight defensive cocoon. Puller posted sentries and handed out passwords for the night, and then let his men settle in. He hoped they would catch a few hours of sleep, but doubted that any of the novice marines would enjoy more than a handful of minutes here and there.

A commander's impact in battle can often be affected by the moves he takes before combat, and this was never truer than on the battalion's first night on Guadalcanal. Puller assumed that his gunny sergeants and other veterans would be fine, but his Pearl Harbor recruits would need reinforcement, as they were about to face a new, terrifying moment for which they had little preparation.

He was correct. During that initial night, mental demons haunted their minds and imaginations. Shrieking birds became enemy soldiers shouting commands, each branch waving in the wind was an enemy to dread, and every sound became a peril. A jungle animal scurrying about the grove morphed into a Japanese soldier sneaking toward their foxhole, intent on slicing throats with a bayonet or blowing men to pieces with a hand grenade.

"Everyone was jittery that night," wrote Sergeant Joseph Goble, who along with the other untested marines had heard the tales of Japanese atrocities that marked combat on Guadalcanal.

Skittish sentries or marines in their foxholes fired at unfamiliar sounds, which in turn prompted others to do the same, but in the midst of chaos Puller's presence, puffing on his pipe and checking on positions, calmed his marines, especially when shortly after midnight Japanese cruiser and destroyer shells ripped into the grove, terrifying the young marines with their screeching noise and violent eruptions. Chesty Puller's booming voice reminded his marines to remain composed and stay in their positions until the shelling ended. The thirty-minute bombardment killed three marines and wounded two others, but Puller's demeanor helped steady frightened young men facing their initial battlefield test.

Lieutenant Smith treated the two wounded marines, but when he inspected the dead marines, one lay with outstretched arms as if welcoming a friend, and the other man's uniform hung in shreds, revealing a disemboweled torso. Smith tried to consume a can of cold vegetable hash and hardtack, but tossed it away after witnessing those scenes. He wrote that because of what Puller's marines had experienced that first night, "I looked at the faces of the young men who sat speechless beside me. Already they seemed older."

Compared to what lay ahead, that night was a pale foreshadowing.

The addition of the 7th Marine Regiment enabled Vandegrift to employ measures he could not implement in the early weeks of fighting. He installed younger, more aggressive leaders to replace a handful of ineffective commanders, including Puller's regimental superior, Colonel James W. Webb. The dour, unassertive Webb had failed to impress Vandegrift, and when Webb waded ashore at Guadalcanal in a neat uniform, as if he were about to participate in a parade instead of combat, Vandegrift decided to replace him with the regiment's executive officer, Lieutenant Colonel Amor L. Sims.

With 19,000 Marines now under his command, Vandegrift divided the perimeter into ten sectors. Three 1st Division battalions guarded the three beach sectors, while others, including Puller's 1st Battalion, 7th Marines, moved into positions along two of the seven sectors manning the outer line. The perimeter meandered along high ground, but in the jungle-filled low areas in between, where the dense undergrowth made it impossible to connect a solid line, Vandegrift relied on del Valle's artillery to block the enemy's path. Marines strung double rows of barbed wire in front of foxholes and logged and sandbagged machine-gun emplacements.

Vandegrift also extended his line nearer to the Matanikau River on the west and to the Tenaru to the east. He had already engaged the Japanese in the fierce August battle along the Tenaru, but Vandegrift now expected the Japanese to take advantage of the terrain bordering the Matanikau on his right for future clashes. From its origin deep in the foothills, the Matanikau coursed through a deep, narrow valley, flanked on each side by steep ridges, before reaching Sealark Channel 1,400 yards east of Point Cruz, a narrow peninsula extending 500 yards into the water. Due to the terrain, river crossings could only be made at select points, each defended by Japanese infantry emplaced on ridge tops who could exact a heavy toll on approaching units.

Even with the reinforcements, Vandegrift still lacked enough marines to completely man the perimeter, but he was stronger and in better shape compared to earlier. He could also now send patrols deeper into the jungle to determine where and how strong the Japanese were, information that would allow him to better organize his defense of Henderson Field.

Puller moved his battalion into its assigned sector, the center of Vandegrift's perimeter. His line extended to the right across Edson's Ridge (so named after the unit led by Lieutenant Colonel Merritt Edson) to the Lunga River, where his battalion connected with the 3d Battalion, 2nd Marines. A few weeks before, in bloody, hand-to-hand combat, Edson had spurned one Japanese attempt to break through this area and sweep across Henderson Field, but additional thrusts against this vital spot in the line, the exact spot where Puller inserted his unit, were certain to follow.

Puller's men dug in and scrounged for material that could strengthen their foxholes and bunkers. They broke apart wooden crates to use as slats and chopped down coconut tree trunks from Lever Brothers plantations to form makeshift roofs over their positions, which they reinforced with camouflaged sandbags, clumps of grass, and palm fronds. Beyond the barbed wire, which had been laid out in concentric rings, marines fashioned interlocking fields of fire one hundred yards deep and burned the kunai grass to their front so the Japanese would be forced to attack across open fields. Mortar crews and artillery registered the likely Japanese assembly points and trails in the jungle ravines between the ridges, and marines booby-trapped every approach.

They were as prepared as possible, but before the enemy assaulted Henderson, Vandegrift had something else in mind for his most recent addition.

"The Face of a Tenacious Bulldog"

Since landing on Guadalcanal, Vandegrift had lacked intelligence about the enemy's movements and numbers. He knew the Japanese controlled most of the island, but since their main bodies operated beyond the range of Vandegrift's patrols, he had no idea what the enemy might be planning or where they might be assembling. Aviators in marine aircraft attempted to locate concentrations of Japanese, but the thick jungle foliage concealed them from view. Vandegrift had in those early weeks tethered his patrols to brief one-mile excursions into the jungle, but the added troops now allowed him to dispatch patrols farther from the perimeter and for longer periods of time.

In an effort to discover whether the Japanese were amassing forces beyond the Matanikau River, five miles west of the perimeter, for another assault on the airfield, Vandegrift ordered Puller to take his battalion's eight hundred marines on a two-day patrol of the jungle to the south and west. He told Puller to determine if Japanese units had moved closer to Henderson Field, and to break up any concentrations he came across.

When he discussed the patrol with his battalion commander, Colonel Sims told Puller that he might have to keep patrolling after dark. "That's fine," replied Puller, eager to get started on his first combat foray of this war. "Couldn't be better. My men are prepared to spend the night right on the trail. And that's the best place to be if you want to move anywhere."

The press officer for the 1st Marine Division, Lieutenant Herbert C. Merillat, observed of the man about to disappear for two days in the jungle that Puller "had a short, sturdy body with a head that seemed mostly forehead. Beneath that impressive dome was the face of a tenacious bulldog." He added that Puller "liked to strike out on his own without much control from higher headquarters—one of those who preferred to be out of touch with Division, unless he was in trouble. He was one of the most colorful and effective troop leaders in the Corps."

With Puller at the head, the column of marines filtered from the perimeter early in the morning of September 20. Even though the sun had barely risen, men perspired in heat that quickly dried their dungarees from the nighttime dew. Puller walked the length of the line reminding his marines to conserve their water by taking only a few sips at a time. They first wound through open fields of chest-high kunai grass just beyond the perimeter. Each step coughed up hundreds of insects, but of even greater concern was that the tall grass provided perfect shelter for a Japanese sniper or a machine-gun nest.

After navigating the open fields, the battalion disappeared into the jungle. The column had wound south less than eight hundred yards and had crossed the Lunga River at Pioneer Bridge when a burst of fire from three Japanese stragglers hiding near the structure killed one marine. Walking with the column, Captain James Hayes said every marine hit the dirt and scurried for jungle growth along the trail—save one. Puller stood in the open and "walked up and down the line talking as if he were on parade. He told us it was all right and that this was nothing to worry about, just small stuff. We began to get up again." Hayes added, "The men saw what kind of a man they had and the word went down the column as fast as light. We lost our fear—or some of it."

Ignoring gunfire had become ingrained in Puller since Haiti, when Sergeant Major Napoleon Lyautey had admonished the young marine that officers should never flinch in combat. Puller remembered Lyautey's words, recognized that quality as a crucial trait of a successful leader, and employed it at Guadalcanal, for if an officer failed to exhibit courage, how could he ask his men to rise to the same challenge?

With their first minor skirmish behind them, the column continued its plunge deeper into the jungle, where they soon realized that on Guadalcanal, they battled two enemies—the Japanese and their ally, the jungle. Correspondent John Hersey, who accompanied marines on numerous patrols, pointed out that, while the American military possessed certain advantages, "the jungle was Jap."

The thick undergrowth offered obstacles few had seen. Tentacle-like webs formed by the foliage and vines ensnarled the marines, who became especially wary of the wicked, hook-festooned liana vines that lacerated their skin. To make headway, they had to hack through dense foliage, at times placing a hand on the pack of the man in front to avoid being separated. They often could see only a few feet ahead, meaning that a Japanese sniper could be lurking in the jungle unobserved until it was too late, and they became wary of banyan tree roots stretching across the trail, which tripped some of the heavily burdened marines. As a result the line, which resembled a slender green snake slowly winding through the jungle, moved in fits and starts, with the men at the end of the line having difficulty keeping pace with those ahead. Numerous streams and rivers cut the trail, and Guadalcanal's daily rains added to the misery. The extra moisture soaked their uniforms, making the men feel as if they had donned medieval suits of armor, and when the sun returned and temperatures soared above the 100°F mark, the marines wilted in the increased heat and humidity.

The island's animal life offered its own terrors. As they moved nearer to Japanese-held Mount Austen, south of Henderson, the screech of parrots and macaws and the screams of monkeys unnerved them. One bird produced a noise that sounded like a person banging two blocks of wood together, and another creature imitated a barking dog.

Land crabs and lizards scurried everywhere, warthogs munched on coconuts, and three-foot-long iguanas and four-inch-wide spiders became common sights. Spiderwebs hung loosely from tree to tree, and as one marine recalled, "These damn spiders just sat in the middle, and you'd see them swaying in the wind. Those I didn't care for, and they were all over the damn place." So, too, were the hundreds of centipedes in the fields, some as long as a finger, that crawled up their legs, or the dozens of leeches that fastened onto them whenever they crossed a stream or swampy area. Men tied the bottoms of their pants to their boots and draped handkerchiefs from their helmets down over their necks to reduce exposure to the clouds of mosquitoes that made Guadalcanal their domain, but nothing completely succeeded.

The worst part about jungle combat, though, was the suspense. Day or night, few could relax their vigilance for even a moment, as each step could mean death from Japanese soldiers waiting to kill them. At least they had Chesty, who operated as if the jungle were his backyard. Haiti and Nicaragua had offered perfect instruction in jungle combat, and he coached his men on what to spot as dangerous and what to ignore, and to remember that the Japanese could be anywhere.

The patrol wound up hills so steep that in places his marines grabbed onto the undergrowth to move forward. When they reached a grassy knoll where Puller planned to stop for the night, a handful of Japanese ambushed the group, and for the second time during this first day of his battalion's combat action, Puller walked about, exposing himself to Japanese fire while shouting orders for three men to bring up a machine gun. "It was the greatest exhibition of utter disregard for personal safety I ever saw," said Captain Robert H. Haggerty, who joined his platoon in hitting the dirt.

After chasing off the Japanese, Puller organized his battalion for the night. He reassured the wounded that they would be treated back in the perimeter the next day and reminded his men not to fire at anything unless they could clearly determine the target. The hungry, exhausted men spent a restless night, half expecting to be attacked in enemy-controlled territory. Since anything moving was considered hostile, the ironclad rule was never to leave your position. Most lay in place clutching their rifles, with a bayonet on the ground beside them, and tried to discern whether the noises they heard were animals moving in the jungle or an enemy soldier hoping to kill them. Like their first night, few enjoyed any sleep.

Once daylight arrived, Puller set out to patrol along ridges and through ravines. To his disappointment, in the day's heat many of his marines, still not masters of their fears, drained their canteens of water by noon. As he had done in Nicaragua, Puller maintained minimal contact with headquarters, which he contended was populated by officers he referred to as "paper shufflers" or "potted palms." He was the commander on the scene, and he trusted his judgment more than theirs. The day's patrolling met sporadic fire that wounded two men before Puller reentered the Henderson Field perimeter and entrenched his battalion for the evening.

Puller lost three marines during his patrol but reported the good news to Vandegrift that he had uncovered no traces of a large enemy concentration in that area. His patrol could be considered a success in that he fulfilled Vandegrift's mission, but more importantly, for two days his young marines had hacked through Guadalcanal jungles, labored up ridge slopes, and had engaged the enemy, all of which heightened their self-confidence. Puller was disappointed that too many of his marines had failed to maintain discipline and had instead fired wildly in the night, requiring him to issue stern warnings about the matter, but Chesty figured that until his men had experienced more combat on Guadalcanal, and had become accustomed to the sights and sounds around them, the shooting was likely to be an issue.

In their first week on Guadalcanal, Puller's battalion had completed its initiation into battle. With his unruffled presence, he had helped jittery marines make it through a first night that might otherwise have been overwhelming, and he had then led them in a successful patrol deep into Japanese-held jungle. The men had been embroiled in a pair of minor skirmishes, but Puller knew that their true tests lay ahead. While this first week would make them better warriors, his marines needed a full-scale battle against enemy battalions and regiments, filled with bursting mortar shells and hand-to-hand combat with screaming Japanese soldiers, to completely transform from civilians to battle-tested marines.

The Matanikau River would provide the opportunity.

★ CHAPTER THREE ★

"YOU'RE NOT GOING TO THROW THESE MEN AWAY!"

Chesty Rescues His Men, September–October 1942

F rom the end of September through October, the Matani-kau River occupied center stage in the battle for the possession of Guadalcanal, for whoever controlled the river and the land adjoining its banks gained a huge advantage in determining the eventual outcome. If Vandegrift could expand his perimeter west to the banks of the Matanikau, he would help protect Henderson Field by pushing enemy artillery beyond their effective range, but should the Japanese seize that region, they would gain a valuable launching point for a major thrust against the perimeter that could give them control of Henderson Field and force the evacuation of Vandegrift's marines from Guadalcanal. That watery barrier thus became crucial to both Americans and Japanese commanders.

Japanese concern over developments on Guadalcanal caused

the Imperial General Staff to send its top military planner, Lieutenant Colonel Masanobu Tsuji, to Rabaul, Papua New Guinea, in mid-September. Tsuji had been lauded for planning many of the earlier Japanese successes, including operations in Burma, French Indochina, and the Philippines. Superiors in Tokyo hoped that Tsuji's arrival in Rabaul, along with his strategic thinking, would energize Japanese commanders into eradicating the American presence on Guadalcanal.

"He Shouted Battle Orders in a Bellow"

The Matanikau is a light brown stream winding through a jungle valley five miles west of Henderson Field. During the rainy season, water cascaded down the sides of mountains into the river before working northward toward Ironbottom Sound, and once the rainy season ended, receding waters deposited a sandbar at the river's mouth. A handful of crossings along the river's length led to the land west of the Matanikau, where a series of parallel ridges handed the Japanese perfect terrain for checking marine expansion in that direction.

Vandegrift's chief concern was that the Japanese, by controlling the waters off Guadalcanal, would shuttle in longer-range artillery that could place the airfield and perimeter under constant bombardment. The perimeter meant far more to Chesty's marines. It was not much, land-wise at least, but it was theirs, and as small as the perimeter was compared to enemy-controlled territory, it provided a sense of security, a sanctuary in which marines could share a cup of coffee with a buddy or scribble a hurried note home. They had left safe havens in the United States to enlist in the marines, but now, thousands of miles from family and friends, they had fashioned a rudimentary replacement. Should the Japanese bring in artillery possessing the ability to hurl shells into that perimeter, or control land east of the Matanikau from which even their smaller guns could be effective, those marines would lose that refuge.

To deal with that threat, Vandegrift paired two of his best commanders, Puller and Edson. He told Puller to locate and reconnoiter a trail leading from Edson's Ridge, scout the slopes of Mount Austen, and then cross the Matanikau 2,000 yards upstream from the beaches at a Japanese-laid wooden span called One Log Bridge. After reaching the west side of the river, he was to move north and destroy any Japanese forces standing in the region. Vandegrift ordered Edson to follow in Puller's wake and continue farther west beyond the river before veering north toward the sea, from where he could threaten enemy troops from the rear. At the same time, Edson was to establish a patrol base west of the Matanikau that would provide an early warning system signaling Japanese movement toward the river and serve as a base from which to mount patrols and stage offensives. Vandegrift estimated that Puller and Edson might face 400 Japanese in the area, but because of faulty intelligence, he was unaware that the Japanese commander, Major General Kiyotake Kawaguchi, had posted 1,900 men of Colonel Akinosuke Oka's 124th Infantry Regiment along the river.

Vandegrift held high expectations for the 7th Regiment as it offered the services of two jungle war heroes in Puller as well as Hanneken. Their tenacity and leadership could help defeat the

Japanese, but Vandegrift's chief of staff, Lieutenant Colonel Gerald C. Thomas, figured Puller would be the real spark. "We thought if any person could get a battalion up the river and get it across and get above the Japanese," he later explained, "it would be Lewie Puller."

On September 23 Puller and his battalion deployed to the Matanikau and their first major action of the war. Martin Clemens, a British officer who doubled as a coastwatcher in the Solomon Islands, was accustomed to dealing with rough, hardened personalities from his time in the islands, and he concluded that Puller was perfectly suited for the task. Puller's chin reminded Clemens of a bulldozer blade, and he said that "Puller, a fellow pipe smoker, naturally appealed to me. He was a tough old soldier, and if anyone could get round the Japs he was the man."

Puller had not felt such a rush of anticipation since he fought the rebels in Nicaragua in the previous decade. Patrols, whether in Central American jungles or those on Guadalcanal, served their purpose, but Puller had long sought the chance to command troops in a major battle, just as Robert E. Lee and his other Civil War heroes had done. Now, it appeared, he would have his opportunity.

The column wound through the jungle until they reached Mount Austen, where Puller ordered his men to dig in for what he hoped would be a restful night. With rumors of enemy troops prowling on the nearer side of the river, he figured they would need the sleep for what might be a fierce encounter with the Japanese the next day.

They continued across the slopes of Mount Austen toward

the Matanikau the following morning, with Puller again at the head of the column. Toward evening the point unit killed two Japanese soldiers eating, and when Puller joined the unit, enemy fire knocked a bowl of rice from his hands and killed one man near him. Everyone hit the dirt but Puller, who alternately stood to issue orders, fell to the ground and rolled over, and rose again to encourage his marines. "He kept that up for several minutes: hit the deck, roll," said the point's platoon commander, Captain Regan Fuller. "Stand and bellow orders, then down again, spinning. He knew the Nips would zero in on him while he was yelling orders, and he kept 'em buffaloed. He came out of it without a scratch."

Puller ordered one of his three companies to follow him and assist Fuller's A Company, which was pinned down by thick, accurate gunfire. Puller's booming voice cut through the noise as he sidled from spot to spot, hollering inspiration and shuffling men about. "He shouted battle orders in a bellow that would have rattled the Halls of Montezuma," said Corporal Kerry Lane, a marine who in his career held every rank from private to lieutenant colonel. "He stalked about under enemy fire as though he was daring the enemy to hit him. Puller had an abiding love for the enlisted men who did the killing and dying and a sneering hatred for the stuffy officer who did the sitting and meddling. He thrived on combat and he became a legend to his troops."

Puller led the marines so close to the enemy that he shot three Japanese with his sidearm. However, supported by heavy weapons that Puller's men lacked, the Japanese held their ground against Chesty's inexperienced marines. With darkness rapidly approaching, Puller collected his wounded and withdrew to a ridge three hundred yards away to dig in for the night. The heated battle cost Puller twenty-five wounded and ten dead, including his runner, Private First Class Richard Wehr, and 1st Lieutenant Alvin Cockrell, the rising young commander of B Company. After listening to reports from his other company commanders, Puller concluded that in their fright, his men forgot to execute the basic battle tactics he had imparted during training.

Puller had to detach more than one hundred men—four to a stretcher—to carry the wounded through the jungles and across streams back to the perimeter. When Puller asked headquarters to send reinforcements so he could continue his mission, Vandegrift, knowing that Chesty would not cavalierly make such a request, dispatched the 2nd Battalion from the 5th Marine Regiment, along with an order giving Puller, the commander on the scene, the option of continuing to the Matanikau or returning to Henderson Field.

The fresh battalion reported to Puller in midmorning on September 25. With the additional numbers, Puller split off two of his three companies, under the command of his executive officer, Major Otho L. Rogers, to escort the wounded back to the perimeter's aid stations while he continued to the river with C Company and the newly arrived battalion from the 5th Marines. This unusual decision—to break up his battalion and march into combat with only a portion of the men he had trained, supplemented with unfamiliar men from another battalion—would come back to haunt Puller, as would his decision to place the inexperienced Major Rogers in command of A and B Companies.

After his two companies left for the perimeter, Puller buried his dead and turned westward. Upon reaching the Matanikau and finding that enemy forces had been massing in the area of One Log Bridge, instead of crossing to the west with his entire force as he and headquarters had planned, Puller detached one platoon to act as a diversionary unit while he slid northward along the east bank toward the river's mouth in hopes of locating an undefended crossing. According to Lieutenant Colonel Thomas, though, "the Japs had picked him up, and they defended all the possible crossings." Puller, "in an effort to get across, just eased down [north] the river" until he reached the mouth. When Puller attempted to cross the Matanikau River, a stream of machine-gun and mortar fire from Colonel Oka's 9th Company forced Puller to pull back, this time with six wounded.

Vandegrift altered his plans and ordered Colonel Edson and his Raiders to meet Puller at the river mouth, where Edson assumed command of the combined force. After consulting with Puller, Edson sent Lieutenant Colonel Samuel B. Griffith and his Raiders, accompanied by Puller's C Company, up the east bank of the Matanikau to One Log Bridge, with orders to fight their way across, turn northward, and attack Japanese forces west of the Matanikau. While Griffith moved into position, the 2nd Battalion, 5th Marines would mount a supporting attack for the Raiders.

Puller, without forces to lead, remained with Edson at his command post. He hated being separated from his men in the crucial moments before battle, but under orders to stay where he was, Puller could do nothing but watch as the Raiders and his C Company left from the river's mouth early in the morning of September 27. His chance to command men in a major battle seemed to be slipping away.

As this unit neared One Log Bridge in midmorning, they walked into withering crossfire from Japanese forces now posted on the east side and from others still emplaced on the west. Within the first few moments, enemy fire killed Major Kenneth D. Bailey, a Raider who was posthumously awarded a Medal of Honor for his actions in defending Henderson Field two weeks earlier, and wounded Colonel Griffith. Outgunned and losing men, Griffith began falling back, but when he tried to inform Edson of his retreat, Edson received only a badly garbled report because a Japanese bomb had disrupted their communications. While Edson and Vandegrift believed Griffith had successfully crossed to the west bank of the Matanikau and was already advancing northward for an attack, Griffith actually remained on the east side.

Hoping to launch an attack with stronger forces, Edson contacted Vandegrift and asked that the two companies under Major Rogers be rushed to his sector as soon as they had successfully escorted the wounded back to the perimeter. Under the misconception that Griffith would be attacking on the west side, Edson ordered the 5th Marines to charge from the river's mouth while boats shuttled Rogers's two companies along the coast for a landing near Point Cruz west of the Japanese. If successful, the units would mount a pincer attack from three sides—Griffith marching up from the south, Rogers attacking from the west, and the 5th Marines plunging across the Matanikau's mouth from the east.

Unfortunately, the Japanese had already turned back Griffith at One Log Bridge, and while Rogers landed to the west, the Japanese repulsed the 5th Marines' assault at the river's mouth. Two legs of the pincer attack had collapsed, leaving the two companies of Puller's marines, led by an untested officer, to carry the day.

Back at the command post, Puller paced back and forth, frustrated with the passive role he had been assigned while the men he had so meticulously trained entered the battle he so sorely sought.

"Puller Quickly Came to the Rescue of His Boys"

Inside the Henderson perimeter, Puller's executive officer, Major Rogers, was attending Sunday religious services when Vandegrift sent him a message to report to headquarters. He was also to have the two companies he had brought back from Puller's front lines assembled and ready to leave upon his return. While Captain Charles W. Kelly, Jr., withdrew the men from their defensive positions along the perimeter and prepared them for departure, Rogers, a shy officer with little combat experience, received Vandegrift's directives. Upon rejoining his men, he failed to relay to Kelly or any other officer the details of their mission other than that his 400 marines would be landing in two waves behind enemy lines one mile west of the Matanikau.

After delivering a brief pep talk, Rogers and the marines boarded Higgins boats for the short trip to Point Cruz, four miles due west of the village of Kukum.

At the same time in Ironbottom Sound, the USS *Monssen* (DD-436) steamed in to escort the landing craft carrying Rogers to Point Cruz. The destroyer took station in the van, with the Higgins boats strung behind like ducklings following their mother, and set a westward course beyond the Matanikau.

When the vessels reached their destination, the *Monssen* hovered offshore to shell the landing zone while the Higgins boats shifted into a circular pattern and organized into two waves. Once aligned, they swerved shoreward, but coral accumulations nudged the boats to the right of the planned beach. Coast Guard officers manning the boats warned Rogers that because of this alteration, he needed to swing to the left as soon as he hit the beach.

Shortly after 1:00 p.m. the marines landed in two waves and rushed to the jungle cover lining the beach. Once out of his boat, Rogers failed to make the necessary adjustment for landing at the incorrect location and instead led his men directly inland to regroup and organize for Vandegrift's plan to trap the Japanese.

A trap unfolded, but not the one Rogers had in mind. Among other omissions, Vandegrift's intelligence officers had failed to detect the presence of Colonel Oka's heavily fortified 2nd Battalion, 124th Infantry, one mile west of the landing beach, and were oblivious to the Japanese elements rushing down from One Log Bridge. Oka had, in fact, calmly watched Rogers approach the beach, and then pulled his men back to allow the marines to advance 500 yards inland before launching his surprise attack.

Rogers filtered through the coconut grove to the summit of Hill 84, where he ordered his marines to dig in and establish a defensive perimeter. He gathered his officers and noncommissioned officers to provide details about their mission, but before he could begin his explanation, marines spotted one of Oka's columns closing in from the beach. Rogers, who had expected no more than a few hundred Japanese, now feared he was greatly outnumbered and in peril of being surrounded.

Before Rogers could issue orders to his officers, a direct hit from a mortar shell killed the major, hurling pieces of his body in all directions. Captain Kelly immediately stepped in, but lacking details as to what he should do, he had to improvise. He hurriedly inspected the marine line while the Japanese column and two other enemy groups maneuvered into positions for their final assault.

Several hundred Japanese charged up the slopes, firing at Kelly's marines as they tightened a ring around the trapped men. The Japanese advanced so near to the trapped Americans that Master Gunnery Sergeant Roy Fowel, a mortarman with a legendary reputation for uncanny accuracy, pointed his mortar tubes almost straight upward to ensure that the rounds exploded directly in front of marine lines. Kelly was certain that his men would mount a stiff defense but concluded that few, if any, would survive what appeared to be boiling into a fight to the death.

The Japanese had now overcome all three parts of Vandegrift's assault. Japanese gunfire prevented the 5th Marines from crossing the Matanikau's mouth, their infantry had checked the Raiders at One Log Bridge, and Oka's battalion stood on the verge of annihilating Rogers's men at Hill 84. According to the action report, "it was obvious that this battalion was in a dangerous position."

Back at Edson's command post, Chesty Puller fumed over the lack of information about his men. He had not long before assumed that Rogers remained in the perimeter with two of his three companies, but his men had been whisked away from beneath him and sent to Point Cruz. Chesty's barely concealed irritation that Rogers and his marines would attack without their battalion commander in the lead permeated the command post.

His men on Hill 84 needed him. For all he knew, they were at that moment out of ammunition and fighting for their lives, lunging at the enemy in hand-to-hand combat. He believed that if he could reach his men, he might possibly save some, but if not, he would at least perish with those marines he called his own. Instead, he chafed and muttered at the command post and stood by while Edson made the decisions.

Unable to contact Vandegrift, Kelly told some marines to remove their white undershirts and spell out in huge letters, "HELP" on the crest of the hill. The chances were slim, but he hoped that an aircraft operating out of Henderson would spot it and relay the information to headquarters.

Good fortune smiled on Kelly. After completing his usual

scouting mission over Ironbottom Sound in his Douglas SBD Dauntless dive bomber and scout plane, 1st Lieutenant Dale Leslie, a dive-bomber pilot from Marine scout-bombing squadron VMSB-231, was on the homeward leg to Henderson with his gunner, Private First Class Reed Ramsey. While over Hill 84, however, Leslie noticed the four large white letters pleading for assistance. Figuring a group of marines needed aid, Leslie radioed the information to Vandegrift's headquarters, who in turn passed it along to Edson.

At almost the same time a radio call from Griffith at One Log Bridge informed Edson that the Raiders had been prevented from crossing the river. Listening nearby, Puller waited for Edson to send units to assist Griffith at the bridge and Kelly atop Hill 84, but to his consternation, Edson read the note and said, "All right. I guess we'd better call them off. They can't seem to cross the river."

Edson's orders for his Raiders to disengage from the fighting would leave Puller's men cut off and alone on Hill 84, a situation Puller could not accept. Puller asked Edson for permission to organize a relief force to save his surrounded men, fully assuming his request would be approved, but again to his astonishment Edson turned him down. "Most of my battalion will be out there alone, cut off without support," Puller heatedly objected. "You're not going to throw these men away!" When Edson refused to budge, Chesty stormed out of the command post and stomped toward the beach.

Edson might have known that Puller would never abandon his marines, something Chesty had made evident in Haiti and Nicaragua in the 1920s and 1930s. At Vandegrift's headquarters, press officer for the 1st Marine Division, Lieutenant Herbert C. Merillat, knew as much and wrote later, "Puller quickly came to the rescue of his boys."

Puller grabbed a signalman and rushed to the beach, where he told the man to signal a request to the *Monssen* to send a boat ashore to pick up Puller. The destroyer's captain, Commander Roland N. Smoot, worried that the man on the beach waving signal flags might be part of a Japanese trick, ordered one of his signalmen to use semaphore flags and relay the question, "WHO WON THE WORLD SERIES IN 1941?" When Smoot received the correct response, "YANKEES IN FIVE," Smoot ordered a whaleboat lowered over the side to get Puller.

The whaleboat returned with Puller, an aide, and two other marines. Puller saluted Smoot and explained, "I've got a whole group of my men up there in the hills. I've got to get them out of trouble." He explained that they had been ambushed after Smoot had earlier deposited them at Point Cruz, and said, "They are trapped up there. Let me tell you where to shoot."

Puller and Smoot devised a plan to rescue Kelly's unit on the hill. While Smoot arranged for landing craft to follow the *Monssen* shoreward to evacuate Puller's men, Chesty conferred with the *Monssen*'s gunnery officer to plan what the ship's war diary said was a "shore bombardment against Japanese and assist in recover of [a] battalion of Marines by landing boats."

Vandegrift was not optimistic about Puller's tactics. He had already seen his own three-pronged plan collapse, and now one of his best battalion commanders might be lost in what threatened to be a failed rescue attempt. The strategic situation on and around Guadalcanal was tenuous at best, and Vandegrift could not afford to have a leader like Puller removed from the roster when he most needed the hard-hitting colonel. Lieutenant Merillat mentioned "the gloom at the CP that night" as Vandegrift waited for word about the operation's outcome.

"Fight Your Way. Only Hope."

Gloom hardly described the peril Puller's two outnumbered battalions faced on Hill 84. Wounded marines mounted a gallant defense, but despite their valor, the enemy inched closer to the crest. One sword-wielding Japanese officer burst out of the foliage and beheaded a private, and in places along the line hand-to-hand combat flared, but just as all seemed lost, hope emerged from the sea. "It looked as if we were finished," said Sergeant Robert D. Raysbrook. "But around the point steamed one of our destroyers. Boy, were we glad to see her!"

Sergeant Goble glanced toward the water and saw a "destroyer belching smoke and heading towards us." The *Monssen*, with Chesty Puller rapidly issuing instructions, rushed to their rescue. A signalman on the bridge used both signal light and semaphore flags to instruct the marines on the summit that they needed to abandon their hilltop positions and rush back to the beach.

Sergeant Raysbrook grabbed the semaphore flags, stood amid the gunfire, and relayed Kelly's responses. "Mortar fire was landing all around me and the blasts kept knocking me off my feet," he said. As Smoot took the *Monssen* closer to shore, Chesty scanned the crest with his binoculars and spotted Raysbrook signaling Kelly's answer about pulling back to the beach. "Engaged. Cannot return." Puller fired back a stark, five-word response. "Fight your way. Only hope." As Kelly received those dire words, Puller added a last, desperate directive. "Give me your boundaries right and left. Will use ship's fire."

The *Monssen*'s five-inch guns ripped into the jungle to carve a path of retreat for Kelly's unit. Starting at the beach, shell explosions slowly advanced up the hill toward the crest, slicing into the Japanese while also threatening to envelop the besieged marines as well. "Then I saw fire from the destroyer's 5-inch guns and I hit the ground fast!" said Sergeant Goble. "The destroyer fired salvo after salvo, hitting the coconut grove below us. We all cheered! Trees were falling, Japs were screaming." Once the escape route had been completed and Kelly's men were ready to leave, Puller told the *Monssen*'s gunnery officer to shift fire to the right and left of the path to block the Japanese as his men hurried down the hill to the beach.

Someone removed Major Rogers's identification tag before departing, and Sergeant Goble grabbed the officer's binoculars, but when Japanese artillery zeroed in on the retreating group, the marines could no longer afford to linger. Clusters of men leapfrogged each other toward shore. A handful of marines held ground on each side of the path and mounted a covering fire while their buddies pulled back fifty yards; they then turned and did the same for the first group.

With the Japanese advancing closer and threatening to move between the marines and the beach, Platoon Sergeant Anthony Malanowski shouted to Captain Regan Fuller that he would remain behind to fend off the enemy while Fuller and others carried the wounded to the landing craft. "I'll handle the rear and be with you in a few minutes," promised the sergeant. When Malanowski took his position behind a coconut log, one of his closest friends, Platoon Sergeant Stan McLeod, asked, "You okay, Ski?" Malanowski loaded an automatic rifle and said, "Yes, Mac, you go on down. I'll just be a few minutes." Fuller and McLeod joined others at the beach, but Malanowski sacrificed his life while giving McLeod and other marines time to reach the boats, an action for which he was awarded the Navy Cross posthumously.

Puller's marines waded into the water and dropped low to the surface to present smaller targets, but the first landing craft stalled at sea, as if hesitant to risk the enemy's guns to move in for the rescue. Interlocking Japanese fire from Point Cruz to the east and Kokumbona to the west churned the offshore waters, hitting three Coast Guard coxswains aboard the landing craft, and at that sight, the following coxswains halted their boats, uncertain if they should continue or turn back toward the *Monssen*. Caught between a rapidly approaching enemy from the jungle and an indecisive group of coxswains at sea, some of Chesty's marines feared they would be hacked to pieces as had occurred to members of the Goettge Patrol the previous month.

Bold action by two men prevented a slaughter. To goad the boats in, Captain Fuller waded out as far as he could and threatened to shoot the coxswains if they did not immediately head for shore. At the same time, flying his Dauntless over Point Cruz, Lieutenant Leslie made repeated passes above the boats, circling lower each time so his gunner could fire the aircraft's machine gun into the onrushing Japanese soldiers.

When Puller noticed the confusion unfolding offshore and saw a few of the boats edging back toward the destroyer without retrieving any of his men, he issued a torrent of profanity. According to Chester Thomason, one of the sailors aboard the *Monssen*, "When Puller saw that the boats were mostly empty, he was furious, and he screamed at the boat coxswains to go back in and not leave the beach until all of the Marines alive had been picked up." To ensure his orders were followed, Puller climbed into one of the craft and ordered the coxswain to take it into what by now was a watery cauldron of bullets, shouts, and blood. Each time he passed by a lingering boat, Puller bellowed orders to those coxswains to follow him in or face charges.

With Puller at the point, the boats began filing toward shore. The sight of their forty-four-year-old commander racing to their rescue lifted the spirits of his marines, who only seconds earlier had expected to die on the sand. Once Chesty's boat landed, he stood at the edge of the beach for twenty minutes, directing the evacuation while under constant Japanese gunfire.

Bravery was common that day on the beach. Marines carrying the stretcher-laden wounded to the boats could have hopped into the landing craft with them, but instead turned back into Japanese gunfire to retrieve more of their buddies. In one boat twenty yards out to sea, coxswain Ray Evans held the tiller in one hand and fired at the enemy with the other, while his Coast Guard companion in the boat, Signalman First Class Douglas Munro, sprayed the beach with gunfire. "And there was a very narrow little sand beach, the jungle came down within five or six feet of the water," said Evans. "So there was hardly any beach [and] the boats' bows were almost up into the brush! We would lay off kind of behind them, and act as a covering for them, and as they filled up, we would just send in more boats."

Due to coral formations, some boats could close in no more than thirty yards offshore, so Captain Kelly ordered his men to carry the wounded to the waiting boats despite the hundreds of bullets that shot out from the jungle. "We were up to our necks with the wounded, trying to hold them up and get them into the boats," said one of the marines, Ed Poppendick. "When it was your turn, you went; until then you laid in the water facing the jungle. Finally, my turn came, and I waded out to get into the boat. One of the sailors in it remarked to me, 'I never saw so many beat up guys as you.'" When each boat was packed with Puller's men, many of them badly wounded, one by one the boats backed away and turned east toward the Henderson Field perimeter. Finally, with the first Japanese soldiers barely twenty yards away, the last marine left the beach.

In the last boat, Evans and Munro maintained their covering fire while the other craft ferried Puller's marines out of danger. After the last man had been retrieved, Evans and Munro pulled away, but they had not gone far when Evans spotted a line of waterspouts kicked up by Japanese bullets making a path directly toward Munro. Evans shouted to his friend, but the engine noise drowned out his warning as bullets tore into the back of Munro's head. "Did they get off?" Munro asked Evans with his last words, but before Evans could reply, Munro died. The Coast Guard signalman was later awarded the Medal of Honor posthumously for his deeds.

Faulty steering on Evans's craft momentarily slowed the boat's departure, providing time for a lone marine to rush out of his hiding spot in the jungle, screaming for Evans to wait as he splashed his way to the boat. Now carrying the last marine from the beach, Evans joined the other craft and returned to the perimeter.

Smoot and Puller developed an instant rapport during the rescue. Smoot's speedy responses to the unexpected developments impressed Chesty, and in the few calm moments sprinkled throughout the hectic day, they exchanged light banter. Smoot offered Puller a steak dinner, hot shower, and a kit containing clean clothes, cigarettes, and cookies, and when Puller thanked Smoot, he added that he would still not trade places with the commander for any amount of money, even though Smoot and his crew enjoyed items that would have been worth their weight in gold to marines mired in Guadalcanal's jungles. Smoot, surprised with that answer, said, "You mean to tell me you'd go back and go into that messy stuff over there and get yourself filthy and live on C rations? You've come to see the kind of life I lead out here and you prefer yours?"

"I sure do," answered Puller. "When you get hit, where are you? When *I* get hit, I *know* where I am."

"We Haven't Seen Anything Yet"

Once back at the perimeter, Puller waited until the next morning before gathering his exhausted officers to examine the fighting both along the Matanikau and during the evacuation, which cost twenty-four dead and thirty-two wounded. When they discussed lessons they could extract from what could only be described as a defeat, Chesty stressed that the battalion had at least now been blooded, and that they were not to blame themselves for anything that had occurred. "Concentrate on building a better combat unit," he said, "because that's the best hope of all of us surviving." He told them that if anyone was to blame, it should be him, as they lacked the combat experience that he had gained in Haiti and Nicaragua. "You'll come along fast," he reminded them, "and there'll be work for us. Let's be ready when our time comes." He again stressed that he wanted his officers to station themselves at the front, which he learned had not always been the case in this fight. "Never do I want to see that again in my command. I want to see my officers leading." He added, "There are many qualities in a man, but one that is absolutely necessary in an infantry leader is stark courage," for as he explained, an officer exhibiting bravery—or adversely, fear—infuses his unit with that same quality.

He then advised them to leave the meeting and check on every private, corporal, and sergeant in their units. The men had to know that their officer not only endured the same conditions, in and out of battle, as his men, but also that the officer cared for them. "Now take care of your men, and make yourselves ready. We haven't seen anything yet." In conducting this meeting, Puller used as a teaching moment the aftermath of a bungled action that might have adversely impacted his marines. He viewed the moment as an opportunity to steady his battalion, to boost morale, and to focus their attention on future conflicts, instead of dwelling on the past.

Puller's superiors could hardly conclude anything other than the Second Battle of the Matanikau, which Puller's men called "the Dead Man's Patrol" and "Little Dunkirk," was a defeat for the marines. Before the mission started, intelligence had erred in grossly underestimating Japanese strength in the region beyond the river, and instead of an organized outing, the battle devolved into a series of improvised actions. Vandegrift and his planners at headquarters had hoped to discover enemy strength west of the perimeter, but after Puller's initial contact along the Matanikau, according to Colonel Twining, a staff officer who helped devise the Guadalcanal operation, "Our reaction to these losses was an unconscious shift of emphasis from reconnaissance to attack. We began an utterly piecemeal series of reinforcements and attacks that descended to a sour nadir on the afternoon of the twenty-seventh. What began as a sound and sensible reconnaissance operation ended as an improvised, complex, jury-rigged attack for which we had no plan and had made no preparations."

Twining accepted blame for agreeing with Vandegrift and Edson for the "improvised, off-the-cuff landing near Point Cruz. It was I, not they, who was in a position to exercise a cooler and more detached judgment." Twining believed that his acquiescence "may well have swayed General Vandegrift's judgment when he gave final approval."

Twining called the event an "unlucky operation" that left the Japanese in position to cross the Matanikau in sufficient numbers to threaten the western flank of the perimeter, and allowed them to move artillery into place to hamstring operations at Henderson Field. In his opinion, "This was the only thoroughly unsuccessful operation of the entire Guadalcanal campaign."

Vandegrift agreed. According to his official action report, the decision to land troops behind the Japanese "represented a continuation of the same fundamental error, piecemeal commitment and sketchy arrangements for support." Colonel Thomas placed the blame on Vandegrift and his staff, later saying that "it was not a well arranged affair. It's one that we [headquarters] should have stopped, but we didn't. We were just trying to do something, and it just didn't work out."

As usual, Puller had his own opinion. He considered his sidelining to be a costly blunder and concluded that Vandegrift had erred in sending the 2nd Battalion, 5th Marines to reinforce him, which meant that he had to command a mixed unit instead of only his 1st Battalion. However, Puller ignored his mistake in sending Rogers and two of his companies back with the wounded instead of allowing the fresh reinforcements to escort those marines to the perimeter. Had Puller done so, he would have commanded only the men he had trained and led onto Guadalcanal.

Even in defeat, praise for Puller's role outweighs the criticism. By leaving Edson's command post and returning to the battlefield to save his marines, Puller snatched a small victory from an otherwise disappointing performance. His quick response in rushing to the beach and arranging for the *Monssen* to escort landing craft beyond the Matanikau—actions that some might have considered acts of insubordination—saved his trapped men from annihilation and handed Vandegrift a partial victory. This brilliant evacuation, combined with everything his marines already knew about their commander, strengthened their trust that Chesty would never let them down, and that when plans went awry, he could improvise with the best. Puller might not have commanded a decisive battle to compare with those of Robert E. Lee, but he had staved off the extermination of his marines who thought all had been lost. He remained confident that his long-desired fight awaited, if not on Guadalcanal, then somewhere else in the Pacific. In the meantime, he could take satisfaction that he had played a prominent role in a daring operation.

Vandegrift's official report stated, "The successful withdrawal of this battalion in the face of the enemy was due to its fighting qualities, brilliant improvisation on the part of those responsible for the movement and to the great good fortune which attended it. This compensated in large part for the numerous misfortunes of the day."

Despite the medals—Munro's Medal of Honor, Chesty's Bronze Star for his work aboard the *Monssen*, and Navy Crosses for Raysbrook and Malanowski—the outcome left the Japanese in firm control of the Matanikau. The fighting failed to ease the pressure on the airfield and Vandegrift's perimeter, which continued to be at risk of being dismantled first by enemy artillery and offshore shelling, and then by direct assault. Vandegrift had to find a way to improve his situation, or the entire Guadalcanal operation was in peril.

———

Similar thoughts circulated back home as readers absorbed the dismal news. Hanson Baldwin explained in a *New York Times* article published the same day, that the fighting on Guadalcanal "has re-emphasized what former Ambassador [to Japan] Joseph C. Grew has already stressed—that the Japanese will never quit until they are killed or utterly crushed." He added that "the danger to Guadalcanal and our other holdings in the southeastern Solomons is real," and that the fighting "has developed into a battle for the Southern Pacific. The battle is a sprawling, intermittent sea, air and land action in which the stakes are high—perhaps eventual victory itself." He compared the situation to that of the marines holding Jones Beach, a popular state park along the southern shores of Long Island, while the Japanese controlled the other 95 percent of Long Island. Baldwin cautioned that this enabled the Japanese to pour in reinforcements and set the stage for a climactic battle in the near future.

"Get Off Your Ass and Come Up Here Where the Fighting Is"

In August and September, Japanese assaults had consisted of piecemeal attacks in which units had been tossed into battle as they arrived. Impatient that Henderson remained in American hands, though, and outraged that Puller had removed his companies from Point Cruz from under their noses, Japanese senior officers altered their tactics and committed one of their most heralded outfits.

Called the Sendai Division after the Sendai region north of Tokyo where it was recruited, the unit boasted an honorable heritage. Founded in 1870 by Emperor Meiji, the men of the Sendai considered themselves the Emperor's division. The veteran troops had fought in China, and in the early weeks of 1942 had invaded and seized Java. With that elite force at their disposal,

Japanese commanders planned to finally shove the marines off Guadalcanal, control the Solomons and the strategic supply routes to Australia, and cement Japanese domination in the South Pacific.

Under Lieutenant General Masao Maruyama, the Sendai began landing in mid-September, with the final units arriving in the first week of October. The general emphasized to his Sendai that the world would be scrutinizing the events of the next few weeks, and that Japan expected them to give their all. "Do not expect to return," he warned, "not even one man, if the occupation is not successful."

With additional men pouring into the island, Maruyama planned an October 9 attack to achieve two objectives. His forces would move across the mouth of the Matanikau to establish forward artillery positions that could subject Henderson Field to additional destructive bombardments, and to secure a staging area east of the river from which to launch a decisive infantry attack against the airfield. Maruyama could not know, however, that Vandegrift had plans of his own for the same terrain.

Following the evacuation from Point Cruz, Puller moved his men into position along the perimeter. For the next week he sent patrols into the jungle to scout for the Japanese, while the rest of the battalion strengthened their defensive positions skirting the airfield. During the relatively quiet period, Puller told his marines to catch up on food and rest, encouraged them to write letters home, and urged them to attend religious services. Each day he visited the marines along the perimeter, asking questions to determine their morale. Chesty knew that hard fighting lay ahead, and he wanted to make sure that his battalion was ready.

His men carried the grime and dirt of the jungle on their faces and clothing. His battalion surgeon, Lieutenant Smith, wrote that these young marines had fought and died "in the hot, impenetrable, disease-ridden jungle," that they had run through interlocking fields of machine-gun fire, and had, when they needed medical attention, joked that they were fine. "It's all right, Doc," a marine would say, "it will take more than a God-damned Jap to kill me!"

Puller's men had lain in filthy swamps swarming with malaria-spreading mosquitoes and had swatted away throngs of flies that attacked their bodies and infested their rations. They had eaten cold hash and beans out of helmets still dented and dirty from combat and had gone weeks without showering. Socks and underwear had rotted away in the heat and humidity.

Seeking extra calories that their meager food supply could not provide, they added worms to their oatmeal for extra nourishment and laughed that they could consume moldy chocolate they never would have touched back home. Captured Japanese rice became a staple, until they had seen so much they could not digest more. "We got so that we hated the sight of rice as much as we did the faces of the Japs from whom we had captured it," wrote Lieutenant Smith. Men lost as much as forty pounds, and at times the marines were so weary from malaria-induced aches and chills that they could hardly walk. Smith sent the most serious malaria cases back to a field hospital near Henderson for treatment, but the main criterion there was, "If he could walk and shoulder his rifle, and if he was free of the acute symptoms of his disease, he was ready to be sent back to us."

The brief lull ended in early October, when patrols picked up indications that the Japanese were massing their forces west of the Matanikau for another assault on Henderson Field. Vandegrift intended to thwart them by springing his own offensive in which the 5th Marine Regiment and Edson's Raiders would advance along the coast for an attack at the mouth of the Matanikau, while three separate units crossed One Log Bridge to swing behind and close in on the enemy from the west. The Whaling Group, consisting of a scout-sniper unit and a battalion of the 2nd Marines organized by Lieutenant Colonel William J. Whaling, would swerve north and advance along the west bank; Hanneken's 2nd Battalion would thrust 600 yards beyond the Whaling Group before turning north to attack; and Puller would lead his battalion 500 yards farther west than Hanneken, head north toward the shore, and join the Whaling Group and Hanneken's battalion to pin the Japanese near the river's mouth. While Vandegrift's plan mirrored his previous tactics, recent reinforcements enabled him to send a stronger force into a fight that, if successful, would secure Henderson from enemy artillery and permit Vandegrift to expand his perimeter.

Puller and Hanneken began filing along the coastal road in midmorning on October 7. After turning south, they reached One Log Bridge before digging in for the night and preparing to cross the next day. At the mouth a mile north, meanwhile,

Edson engaged a Japanese battalion east of the river, forcing them back in fighting that Puller could hear at One Log Bridge.

In heavy rain, Puller started crossing the Matanikau early the next afternoon, but he spent so much time ushering his battalion along the narrow One Log Bridge that he had little daylight left in which to accomplish anything more. The tedious crossing annoyed Puller, as intelligence reported that a large Japanese force had left the Japanese base at Rabaul 660 miles to the northwest. Vandegrift urged him to quickly secure the far side of the Matanikau from Japanese control and pull his battalion back to the perimeter before those reinforcements put Vandegrift at a further disadvantage.

Shortly before 7:00 a.m. on October 9, Hanneken and Puller resumed their advances. When they came under heavy Japanese machine-gun fire, Hanneken suggested that Puller send a company northwest to outflank the enemy, but as Puller's men conducted the move, Vandegrift suddenly ordered Hanneken to break off, move to the river's mouth, and secure the western side.

Hanneken's removal left Puller to fight the inland battle alone. When the regiment's commander, Colonel Amor Sims, who had established his command post east of the Matanikau a mile back, ordered Puller to slide farther west to avoid casualties, Puller shouted into the phone that Sims stood too far from the scene to issue pertinent orders. "If you'd get off your ass and come up here where the fighting is, you could see the situation," Chesty admonished his superior. Operating without interference from Sims, Puller dispersed the enemy before continuing north to the coast.

When they reached high ground 1,500 yards inland from Point Cruz, Puller came upon a Japanese battalion bivouacked in a wooded ravine to his front and left. In optimal position to trap the enemy, he laid down a barrage with his machine guns and mortars and called in del Valle's big guns for support. Artillery and mortar rounds drenched the ravine with Japanese blood, and whenever the enemy scaled the slopes to escape the artillery, Puller's riflemen and machine guns cut them down before they reached the crest. The Japanese faced the option of dying on the slopes or being eviscerated by artillery and mortar shells in the ravine.

"Hey, Old Man, bring your guns [mortars] up here," Puller shouted to Private First Class Matthew Constentino during the battle. As Constentino recalled later, the Japanese would "run up the ridge and the riflemen would shoot them. They'd go down the valley and we'd shoot them." This continued until Puller turned to Constentino and asked, "Hey, Old Man, how many more rounds we got?"

"I think we got six rounds left, Colonel," the private replied.

"Ah, let's save those," said Puller, who had overseen the decimation of an enemy battalion of 700 men and was ready to pull out. "We might need those going back home." Although a handful of Japanese made it back to their lines, Puller had destroyed the 2nd Battalion, 4th Infantry.

With the first decisive win for his battalion in his pocket, Puller turned back toward the perimeter to be in line for the imminent attack by those Japanese reinforcements barreling down from Rabaul. His marines reached the perimeter with renewed confidence gained from defeating a fresh Japanese battalion. Vandegrift needed that self-assurance, as he expected that his marines, which included Puller's battalion, would soon be engaged in the climactic struggle for control of Henderson Field and domination of Guadalcanal. The critical battlefield encounter Puller had long sought was finally at his doorstep.

CHAPTER FOUR

"I GAVE THANKS TO GOD AND PULLER"

Battle for Henderson Field, October 15–25, 1942

Vandegrift's conclusions proved correct. The same day that Puller's marines annihilated the Japanese battalion in the ravine, General Haruyoshi Hyakutake arrived on Guadalcanal to personally direct the attack against Henderson Field. His predecessors had failed to neutralize the Americans on the island, but Hyakutake was not about to allow his name to be added to that infamous list. He planned to concentrate everything he possessed, every man and every weapon, in a massive assault against Vandegrift's perimeter. Senior army commanders in Japan had promised their navy cohorts that the forces on Guadalcanal would control Henderson Field no later than October 25. Hyakutake intended to meet that deadline.

"They Are Landin' 'Em Faster Than We Can Kill 'Em"

Since the August American landings, Japanese army commanders had blundered by committing their forces piecemeal. Hyakutake altered those tactics and mapped a comprehensive offensive involving four simultaneous assaults that would hit Vandegrift from all sides. While one column of troops crossed the mouth of the Matanikau and attacked from the west against Vandegrift's perimeter, a second column would strike from the southwest as a third hit Koli Point five miles to the east of Henderson. The fourth, and most potent, arm, consisting of the 7,000 men of Maruyama's Sendai Division, would punch through the middle of the perimeter, sweep across Henderson Field, and terminate the American presence on the island.

The Japanese commander possessed the forces to achieve his goal. Japanese destroyers continued their nightly delivery runs, which added reinforcements and supplies to the troops already fighting on Guadalcanal. By mid-October Hyakutake had increased his force to about 20,000 men, practically matching Vandegrift's numbers, with more yet to arrive.

The enemy buildup alarmed not only Vandegrift, who wired a priority dispatch about his predicament to Admiral Nimitz, but especially the marines who had been hotly contesting the Japanese in the jungles and fields. "Glum faces today," scribbled the press officer, Lieutenant Merillat, in his diary on October 15. "Six transports were brazenly unloading this morning within sight of Kukum." Merillat wrote that since the marines lacked the aviation fuel needed to keep planes in the air around the clock, "the Japs have the run of the waters around Guadalcanal. They have landed unknown thousands of troops in the past two nights. They have made determined attempts to knock out the airfield, and have come close to succeeding, what with bombings, artillery shelling, and naval gunfire." He then added a feeling shared by every marine fighting on Guadalcanal: "Where is our Navy, everyone wants to know." A show of force by their naval comrades might impede that stream of enemy forces pouring into the island.

Marines closer to shore seethed at watching those enemy destroyers deliver troops whose sole intent was to kill them. They figured that it was only a matter of time before those reinforcements, supplemented by the veteran combat units already on the island, would make their move against Henderson. Walking about the perimeter, Merillat heard some say, "They are landin' 'em faster than we can kill 'em."

Their outlook worsened in mid-October when Hyakutake increased the frequency of air attacks and brought in long-range artillery to punish Henderson Field and the marine lines. Battalion surgeon Smith said that every day at noon, Puller's marines prepared for yet another inevitable air attack, which unfortunately occurred like clockwork.

The Japanese commander utilized every resource at his disposal to wear down the marines, but without question, Puller's men and other "old breed" veterans described naval bombardments staged from Japanese ships steaming back and forth in Ironbottom Sound as their worst experiences. Throughout the long night of October 13–14, for instance, Japanese warships, including the mighty battleships *Haruna* and *Kongo*, hurled

almost 1,000 12-inch and 14-inch shells at the marines, destroying or damaging half the aircraft at Henderson and gouging immense craters in the field. The flashes of the warships' main
guns, followed a second later by the deep-throated boom of the
salvos, heralded the approach of more shells on their way toward
Henderson Field. "Then rushing through the night, straining
like an airy boxcar, came the huge projectiles," wrote one marine. When the shells hit, the ground rocked, dugout walls
shook, and curtains of dirt half-buried the helpless marines.
"Your stomach is squeezed, as though a monster hand were
kneading it into dough; you gasp for breath like the football
player who falls heavily and has the wind knocked out of him."

Helpless against the cascading shells, marines closed their
eyes and prayed or cursed as they crouched lower in their foxholes to avoid the shrapnel propelled by the exploding shells.
Lieutenant Merillat rushed to one bunker, where he "huddled
with about a dozen others, at the bottom of a quaking heap,
while we went through the worst bombardment we have yet
had. The shelter shook as if it was set in jelly. Bombs, artillery,
big naval shells made it sheer hell."

Vandegrift called the shells that ripped into his area "mon-
sters," and expressed his frustration that "I could do nothing to
disrupt the raid. We owned no night fighters; our artillery could
not reach the ships. Like everyone else in the perimeter I sat out
the bombardment, hoping against a direct hit on my dugout."
After the shelling finally ended, one officer entered Vandegrift's
command post, his face streaked with tears and his body trem-
bling, and asked to be relieved because "I cannot stand another
shelling and I do not want to crack up in front of my men."

Vandegrift granted the officer's wish and ordered him evacuated from the island.

Every marine along the perimeter knew that Japanese artillery and naval guns were only preludes to an imminent major attack. All they could do was wait and hope that enough men survived the bombardments to mount an effective defense when the storm hit.

Across the lines, Lieutenant General Maruyama, who had boasted about accepting Vandegrift's capitulation, conveyed the battle's importance to his Sendai. He told his men before the October 22 attempt to take Henderson, "This is the decisive battle between Japan and the United States in which the rise or fall of the Japanese Empire will be decided." He cautioned that "if we do not succeed in the occupation of these islands, no one should expect to return alive to Japan" and said that they must overcome any hardship "and push on unendingly by displaying invincible teamwork. Hit the proud enemy with an iron fist so he will not be able to rise again."

Maruyama moved out on October 16, but heavy rains and near-impenetrable jungle terrain slowed his progress. For three days the Japanese advanced single file through dense jungle, first moving south before turning eastward across the Matanikau. Once near Mount Austen, Maruyama swerved to the north until he pulled within one mile of the airfield, where he split his force and sent them along four separate trails for their final approach to the perimeter.

The challenging trek, however, required Japanese soldiers,

each carrying sixty pounds of equipment as well as an artillery shell, to nudge the heavy guns up and down ridges. Those rigors slowed the advance and forced Maruyama to request a post-ponement of his assault until October 24. Hyakutake approved the change but failed to relay the information to Major General Tadishi Sumiyoshi, who commanded the Sendai unit earmarked to attack across the Matanikau's mouth. Maruyama reached his jumping-off point in the jungle on October 23, where the 7,000 soldiers under his command prepared to hit the center of Van-degrift's perimeter—precisely where Puller had just inserted his battalion.

Across the open field from Maruyama, Puller inspected his line to make certain that his machine guns created interlocking fields of fire and to ensure that his marines were ready. Now one mile apart, Puller and Maruyama were about to engage in the decisive battle for control of Henderson Field, a contest in which the Japanese outnumbered Puller and his 800 marines nine to one. Over the next few days, Chesty Puller would display his talents as a gifted battlefield commander and help cement his reputation as one of the greatest marines of all times.

"I'll Have to Charge You with Desertion"

Vandegrift had been conducting moves of his own to fortify the perimeter. The arrival of the 164th Infantry Regiment allowed him to rearrange his units into five sectors, ranging from the army regiment in the east holding 6,500 yards along the Tenaru on Vandegrift's left edge, to the 5th Marine Regiment on the far right, defending the airfield's western end from an attack coming from the Matanikau. In the middle of the line, in Sector 3, Puller's 1st Battalion, with Hanneken's 2nd Battalion to his right, stood across the same route the Japanese had used to charge Henderson Field in September. Since Vandegrift expected the Japanese to mount their strongest attempt from across the Matanikau and not at Puller, he concentrated his strength on the western side of the perimeter. Puller, as events turned out, was left to bear the brunt of Maruyama's attack.

Since moving into the left half of Sector 3, alongside Hanneken's 2nd Battalion, Puller's men strung barbed wire, dug bunkers and foxholes, carried extra ammunition from the beaches, sharpened their bayonets, and established machine-gun fire lanes in the narrow slice of open ground between the marines and the jungle. On October 21 Colonel Sims ordered Puller to station an observation post under Platoon Sergeant Ralph Briggs on a grassy knoll 1,500 yards forward of the perimeter. Puller thought Sims wasted good men with this action, as a small unit operating that distance from the perimeter would most likely be cut off and slaughtered by the Japanese, but he followed orders.

The Japanese made their first move two days later. Uninformed about Maruyama's postponement, Major General Sumiyoshi, who commanded the Sendai troops designated to attack across the Matanikau, hit marine positions east of the river with an artillery and mortar barrage. Once the bombardment ended, nine tanks lumbered across the sandspit, leading Sumiyoshi's troops in a furious charge against Vandegrift's right flank. Marines along the perimeter concentrated their fire on the tanks, while del Valle's artillery decimated his infantry. Before Sumi-yoshi made any headway, his nine tanks were smoking ruins amid hundreds of dead Japanese.

Sumiyoshi's attack reinforced Vandegrift's belief that Maruyama's main thrust would originate from the west. Because marine patrols scouring the jungle south and east of the airfield had not penetrated deeply enough, they had missed evidence that the Sendai were on the move. Vandegrift thus shifted Hanneken's 2nd Battalion from its position adjoining Puller to the western flank alongside the 3rd Battalion, 1st Marines, where together they would defend what Vandegrift considered the crucial sector.

Puller's three companies now manned the southern sector alone. They guarded a 2,500-yard defense line stretching westward from the right flank of the 164th Infantry across the southern slopes of Edson's Ridge to the Lunga River. Puller requested additional marines to insert into his thin line of defense, now weakened by Hanneken's removal, but Vandegrift assured him that the Japanese would focus along the Matanikau to Puller's right.

Concerned about filling the gap left by Hanneken's departure, Puller moved into the line every spare marine. He phoned Sims for permission to pull Briggs's platoon back to the perimeter, arguing that they were being needlessly sacrificed, but Sims chose to leave them isolated at the knoll.

Puller improvised by forming a composite company. He took a platoon reinforced with machine guns from each of A, B, and C Companies and poured them into Hanneken's deserted location. While this diluted the other portions of his line, Chesty had no alternative but to spread out his men to cover with his marines an area that had been defended by two battalions.

Facing a grassy plain outside his perimeter that ended a short distance away in thick jungle, Puller stretched his marines along the one-and-a-half-mile-long line. Manning his perimeter from left to right were A Company under Captain Regan Fuller on the left flank, Captain Marshall Moore's C Company teamed with B Company under Captain Robert H. Haggerty in the center, and Captain Charles W. Kelly, Jr., commanding the composite company on the far right. Machine guns and mortars provided extra support in each company's sector, along with a handful of 37mm antitank guns interspersed along the perimeter.

All day long on October 24, Puller's marines strung double lines of barbed wire along the perimeter and attached empty metallic ration cans filled with rocks to make noise if the Japanese approached in the dark. They further cleared fields of fire for their machine guns, piled dirt atop wooden slats to protect their guns and themselves, and placed hand grenades near their side for quick use. Certain that machine guns would prove vital, Puller scrounged the back lines for more, and nearly doubled the number of those weapons on his battalion's line.

As his men prepared for battle, Puller walked back and forth along the 2,500-yard perimeter, the ever-present pipe firmly clenched in his teeth, checking that each gun position was properly placed. Private First Class Robert Leckie, a member of the 2nd Battalion, 1st Marines, caught a glimpse of Puller and later wrote how impressed he was with the bullish colonel. "He was a man of only five feet six inches in height, but with an enormous rib cage stuck on a pair of matchstick legs—the barrel chest crowned by a great commanding head with strong out-thrust jaw." He reminded his men of what they had learned in training and reassured them that if everyone did his job, victory would be theirs. With his presence, Chesty calmed his young men and infused confidence into a group that, while they had already experienced combat since their arrival on Guadalcanal, were far from the skilled warriors they eventually would be.

When Puller came upon one marine continuing to shovel deeper in his foxhole, even though it was already sufficient to protect him, he said, "Son, if you dig that hole any deeper I'll have to charge you with desertion." The machine gunner, Sergeant John Basilone from the battalion's weapons company, smiled as Chesty walked back to his command post, which was nothing more than a solitary field telephone ten yards behind the front lines. As a small-unit commander in the jungles of Nicaragua, Puller stood with his men. Now, as a battalion commander in the jungles of Guadalcanal, he intended to do the same for his riflemen and mortarmen as Maruyama's Sendai drew close.

"Nips Are Out There"

While Puller prepared his men for the crucial defense of Henderson Field, government officials and senior military commanders worried over the outcome of the Guadalcanal fighting. They sensed that the battles over the next few weeks would determine whether the United States controlled the island, which would place them on the path to changing the course of events in the South Pacific, or suffered a defeat whose repercussions would reverberate through Washington, DC, and alarm civilians at home.

At his headquarters in Pearl Harbor almost 4,000 miles from Puller, Admiral Chester W. Nimitz, commander in chief, Pacific Fleet, had concluded the week before that "it now appears that we are unable to control the sea in the Guadalcanal area. Thus our supply of the positions will only be done at great expense to us. The situation is not hopeless, but it is certainly critical." He needed to ship every available man and weapon to Guadalcanal, but many of those resources had already been earmarked for the upcoming November landings in North Africa.

When a reporter asked Secretary of the Navy Frank Knox if he thought the marines could hold on to Guadalcanal, his response was far from reassuring. "I certainly hope so and expect so. I will not make any predictions, but every man will give a good account of himself. What I am trying to say is that there is a good stiff fight going on. Everybody hopes we can hold on." On the same day that Puller teased Sergeant Basilone about the depth of his foxhole, President Franklin Roosevelt shared Nimitz's concern and penned a note to his Joint Chiefs of Staff saying, "My anxiety about the Southwest Pacific is to make sure that every possible weapon gets into that area to hold Guadalcanal."

Newspaper articles and editorials informed the public of the perilous situation on Guadalcanal. In the *New York Times*, reporter Charles Hurd wrote that "brief Navy communiqués now indicate that the island is the site of a life-and-death struggle," and wondered, "Is Guadalcanal to be the story of a desperate adventure, or is this apparent climax part of a delicately executed tactical plan by the American forces in the southwestern Pacific?" He added that if the Japanese controlled the island, "it would be the southern anchor of a battle line extending all the way from the Asiatic coast and a point of departure for a dangerous drive on our supply lines. In Allied hands it would be a base from which to begin the task of rolling back the Japanese."

Those dire statements wound their way back to Puller's men. Lieutenant Smith said that each evening he and others would gather a short distance from the front lines to listen to news broadcasts on the only radio in the regiment. He mentioned that when the broadcaster turned to the Pacific, he would "in a mournful voice tell us that we were in grave danger, that Washington was deeply concerned about the plight of the men on Guadalcanal. The little island fortress might fall at any time." Smith and the group scoffed at the pessimism, and one evening in response to those sentiments a private blurted, "Well, I'll be a sad son-of-a-bitch! Don't they know we got Marines on this island?" When the announcer talked of home front labor strikes and absenteeism hampering war production, the laughter ceased. "In shocked silence the men listened," said Lieutenant Smith. "Then in the gathering darkness they melted into the jungle to man their guns for the night watch which might be— who could know?—their last. Life here was too short to waste time with the problems back home."

A partial solution to their problems had already been put in place. Vandegrift's immediate superior in the Pacific, Vice

Admiral Robert L. Ghormley, the military commander, was the wrong man for the task at hand. He remained at his headquarters in Nouméa, 900 miles southeast of Guadalcanal, preferring to operate inside the cramped, sweltering conditions of his quarters aboard the tender *Argonne,* a vessel so tiny that Ghormley's staff officers nicknamed her the *Agony Maru.* The admiral had visited neither the marines fighting for their lives on Guadalcanal nor Vandegrift's command post. Ghormley's lack of leadership infected his staff, stifled morale among naval and marine units, and caused concern in Pearl Harbor, where Admiral Nimitz asked journalists returning from Guadalcanal for their thoughts on the matter. Hanson Baldwin of the *New York Times* told him that Ghormley "was really completely defeatist. He was almost despairing. He was heavily overworked and he said [to Baldwin], 'This is a shoestring operation, we haven't got enough of anything. We're just hanging on by our teeth.'" Baldwin, a veteran military journalist respected by senior commanders for his perceptive assessments of individuals and events, added that "here was a time when you needed tough, hard, almost ruthless men. He was a miscast, in my opinion. He should never have been in that job."

When Nimitz's staff at Pearl Harbor unanimously answered in the negative about whether Ghormley exhibited the necessary leadership qualities, Nimitz turned to the most aggressive naval commander then operating in the Pacific, Vice Admiral William "Bull" Halsey, to replace the reticent Ghormley. Nimitz hoped that Halsey's tenacious style of leadership, illustrated by his combative approach after Pearl Harbor and in leading the country's first naval air strikes against Japanese island bases, would energize the men under him, including those marines on Guadalcanal.

Vandegrift received word of Halsey's promotion on October 18. Although he liked Ghormley, "I simply felt that our drastic, imperiled situation called for the most positive form of aggressive leadership at the top. From what I knew of Bill Halsey he would supply this like few other naval officers."

Jubilation replaced gloom in the foxholes on Guadalcanal when word arrived that Halsey had taken over. "I'll never forget it!" gushed Lieutenant Commander Roger Kent, air combat officer on Guadalcanal. "One minute we were too limp with malaria to crawl out of our foxholes; the next, we were running around whooping like kids."

The joy extended to the correspondents and military analysts, who had grown accustomed to filing disheartening reports of the fighting. "The effect on the men of the fleet and those ashore at Guadalcanal was electric," wrote newspaper correspondent Gilbert Cant. "Halsey had the reputation of being the fightingest admiral in the Navy."

From his headquarters in the southwest Pacific, General Douglas MacArthur was effusive in praising the change. "William Halsey was one of our great sailors." MacArthur added that "his one thought was to close with the enemy and fight him to the death."

Halsey's appointment hinted of electric action to come, but before Halsey could arrive and make an impact, the marines first needed to stop the Japanese army on Guadalcanal. Chesty Puller, a marine counterpart to the newly assigned admiral, displayed that brand of ferocity with which Halsey, the man the press nicknamed "Bull," would approve. Like Halsey, Puller would play a crucial role in the next few days.

———

Halsey needed Puller's aggressiveness, as Maruyama had placed his men into position to strike directly at Chesty's sector. During the afternoon of October 24, while Puller's marines attached additional ration cans to the barbed wire, lines of Japanese snaked along four separate jungle paths to their jumping-off positions facing Puller. Torrential rains impeded their movement, but they slogged forward, knowing that the same rain also tormented the marines.

Late in the afternoon an observer in Puller's line south of the airfield saw a Japanese officer looking through field glasses at their sector. Later, a patrol spotted smoke swirling from a large jungle bend two miles from Puller's front, indicating the possibility of a Japanese bivouac. "Puller would never have made that mistake," said Colonel Twining about Maruyama allowing his men to cook rice so close to an enemy.

Those rice fires and the officer scouting Puller's sector with field glasses were the first indications that Maruyama had crossed the Lunga River and gathered south of Chesty's line. Puller was convinced that the Japanese were about to launch an attack against his battalion, but Vandegrift maintained his focus on the west.

Darkness brought additional rains that, besides making the defenders more miserable, made it harder to detect oncoming Japanese infantry. Fearing that Briggs's forty men stationed on the knoll would be overwhelmed at any moment, Puller again asked Sims for permission to draw them back to the perimeter, but Sims once more declined. Believing that shooting would erupt at any moment, Puller ordered all the field telephones in his sector opened so that every company and platoon leader could hear each message to and from Puller, and he alerted del Valle that he would soon require fire support.

Word spread among Puller's foxholes that the Japanese were assembling in the jungle growth just beyond the open fields to their front. Marines checked their ammunition, sharpened their bayonets, and kept a close watch ahead, knowing that they had to hold. If the enemy punched through their thin line, the path to Henderson Field would be wide open and Japanese dominance on the island would be all but assured.

"Shep, we'll probably get mixed up in a scrap tonight," Chesty said to Sergeant Major Frank Sheppard. "The weather is right, and the moon won't be much. It'll rain like hell, and Nips are out there."

Sergeant Briggs could attest that the Japanese were, indeed, out there. Around 9:00 p.m. Briggs and his forty men at the knoll, masked by the jungle foliage, watched Japanese infantry silently wind through the jungle toward their hummock. He telephoned Puller and, since the enemy had already advanced so near to his men, whispered to his commander, "Colonel, there's about three thousand Japs between you and me." As Japanese soldiers filtered to the right and left of the still undetected Briggs, Chesty told Briggs to remain at the knoll until the Japanese had passed by, and then he should "take your men to the left—understand me? Go down and pass through the lines near the sea. I'll call 'em to let you in. Don't fail, and don't go in any other direction. I'll hold my fire as long as I can."

At almost the same time, one of Puller's company commanders reported that the Japanese had already begun cutting the barbed wire to his front. "Hold fire until you get an order from me," replied Puller, trying to give Briggs as much time as possible to exit the area before the shooting started. Puller then told his company officers, "If the bastards break through, use the bayonet. And keep someone at every phone."

Chesty called Vandegrift's command post to relay information that his outpost reported enemy troops skirting around them. A few minutes later he again checked in with Vandegrift with an update that "the outpost has called in and said, 'We are being overrun, hundreds of Japs around us,' and then silence."

Puller could only give Briggs a few additional moments before he ordered his marines to open fire, forcing Briggs to divide his men into small groups and tell them to make their own way back to the perimeter. Briggs's groups headed eastward toward the shore, then through thick jungle facing the army's 164th Infantry sector on Puller's left flank. Some men lost their bearings in the rain and became separated, but most were able to sneak through the jungle to the open ground between the perimeter and the jungle.

Briggs stepped onto the open field for a quick reconnaissance but quickly pulled back when he heard Japanese. He and his men slumped down to hide in the foliage, pulled branches and leaves over them, and again prayed as a battalion of Japanese infantry paced by, some coming so close that Briggs could have reached out and grabbed their ankles. One brushed against the edge of Briggs's bayonet and a second tripped on the helmet of another prone Marine, but the soldier continued toward the perimeter without glancing down. "I don't know why they didn't stop to get us," Briggs said later. "It was the most unreal experience I've ever had—like a dream. That whole battalion of Japs swinging by—singing, jabbering, shouting 'U.S. marines, you going to die tonight.'" Briggs's men hid in the jungle all night, waiting for a chance to break out and join Puller, but the presence of so many Japanese in their area forced them to remain where they were for the time being.

"They Kept Coming and We Kept Firing"

Puller put down the phone to make a final check of his men on the perimeter and prepare them for what might be the bloodiest encounter they would ever face. Nervous marines stared into the dark and clutched their rifles in anticipation of what was about to hit them, but Chesty was there, pacing the line to reassure them. As one reporter put it, "The little bantam rooster of an officer" walked "among the forward foxholes with his chest stuck out as if he were on parade, addressing his officers as 'son,' and his troops as 'old man,' excoriating the enemy with language that scars the foliage like a flame-thrower."

Fortunately for Puller's battalion, Maruyama was unable to mass all 7,000 soldiers on the narrow jungle trails for a single, concentrated charge. Forced to maneuver their way through vines, roots, and rain to the front along the four paths, throughout the long, bloody night, units arrived at the jungle's edge in piecemeal fashion, where waiting officers attacked only when they had collected enough men to mount a charge. The forbidding undergrowth that had so often vexed Puller and his men in earlier patrols and actions now helped save Puller's battalion from probable annihilation.

The seconds ticked away as silent privates and corporals watched from their foxholes. No longer the same marines who had shot at every sound and imaginary demon during their initial night on the island, they held their fire and waited for the enemy to come into view.

Shrill Japanese cries of "Blood for the Emperor!" and "Marine you die!" were met at 10:00 p.m. by one marine shouting back, "To hell with your God-damned Emperor! Blood for Franklin and Eleanor." Puller issued the order to commence firing, at which every rifleman and machine gunner streamed thousands of bullets through the heavy rain across the field toward the jungle, and mortarmen poured hundreds of shells on the enemy. Pebbles rattling in the cans attached to the barbed wire alerted Chesty's young marines, who picked off Japanese soldiers as they tried to climb over the razor-sharp apron. Del Valle's artillery ripped into the forces still assembling in the jungle, while the deadly 37mm antitank gun cut swaths through Maruyama's charging ranks with their metallic balls. "It was a wild fight," wrote Colonel Twining of the first of what would be numerous waves of Sendai attacks against Puller that night. Nine Japanese battalions in all hammered at the perimeter, led by "the famed 29th Regiment, against one of ours." A private standing next to battalion surgeon Edward Smith said to the doctor, "Can you beat it! The crazy yellow bastards have attacked Puller's men. They'll have their revenge tonight!"

The ground shook as Japanese soldiers stampeded toward the wire amid mortar shell eruptions, and enemy troops tossed their bodies over the barbed wire to permit the soldiers behind to use them as a path across the razor-sharp barrier. Officers, screaming orders and encouragement, waved their sabers as they ran into Puller's interlocking fields of fire. In various places Japanese soldiers used hand grenades to create openings in the wire, only to be cut down by marine machine-gun fire as they raced through the gaps. Puller's marines locked their foe in hand-to-hand combat, the most frightening, personal form of battle, and when Captain Regan Fuller, the A Company commander, spotted a group of Japanese gathering at the edge of the jungle, he routed them with three direct hits from 37mm rounds.

Each weapon contributed its unique tune in fashioning a vile symphony, a melody one marine described as a "booming, sounding, shrieking, wailing, hissing, crashing, shaking, gibbering noise. Here was hell." The rapid-fire cough of the Browning automatic rifle blended with the staccato of machine guns, the crash of del Valle's artillery shells, and the hailstone-like rhythm created when the 37mm antitank guns sprayed their deadly canister.

Dead Japanese littered the ground before Puller's sector, but despite the carnage, more enemy soldiers took their place. The throngs charged closer to the perimeter and in some places punched through to the interior. In the middle stood Puller, stomping up and down the 2,500-yard line as he encouraged his marines. Chesty barked at his men to fill one gap in the perimeter or to direct their fire to another about to be overrun, all while firing his pistol at the Japanese along with everyone else.

Throughout the draining night, the Japanese threw waves of suicidal banzai attacks against Puller's sector. Survivors of one attack regrouped with fresh troops who had just arrived, shouted support for their emperor, and charged in fifteen-minute onslaughts that threatened to break Puller's line before receding against Chesty's guns and bayonets. Interludes ensued while Maruyama gathered another group and sent it running across the field, only to have the Japanese commander watch as Chesty's line bent but never broke.

Two of the onslaughts targeted Puller's left flank, where Captain Fuller's A Company manned the perimeter. The Japanese rushed from the jungle, screaming as they hurled hand grenades and fired their rifles. Puller called in mortars and artillery to back up the heavy volume of fire maintained by Fuller's riflemen and machine guns, and the combined arsenal slaughtered hundreds of Japanese trying to climb over the barbed wire.

Wounded early in the fighting and unable to use his rifle, Private Theodore G. West ignored painful wounds to remain at his position and supervise two rifle squads near him. West was later awarded a Navy Cross for his actions in helping prevent one section of Puller's line from collapsing. With an already thin line further diminishing from casualties, the regimental executive officer, Lieutenant Colonel Julian Frisbie, dispatched a runner to the back lines field hospital to collect able reinforcements and rush them to Puller's perimeter.

Another charge at 1:15 a.m. smashed into the left center of Puller's line, defended by Captain Marshall Moore's C Company.

Moore's interlocking fields of fire mowed down scores, but other Japanese reached the perimeter to engage in hundreds of one-on-one fights involving bayonets, knives, and fists. Sergeant Basilone, soon to distinguish himself, saw eighteen-year-old Private Cecil H. Evans, only a year out of high school, dare the Japanese to attack. "He had his rifle by him, and was screaming at the Japs to come on," said Sergeant Basilone. "What a guy he is!" When Evans's squad leader and the rest of his crew were either killed or wounded in the mass frontal attack, Evans prevented the Japanese from overrunning his position by pouring a steady stream of fire at the enemy, an action for which he later received the Silver Star.

"That line we were holding was hit by a very large number of Japanese," said Private First Class Gilbert Lozier of C Company. "Our Marines held on for a while, but the Japanese broke through, there was some hand-to-hand fighting in which several members of my squad were killed, but we were able to close the Japanese gain, and kill those who had gone through the gap."

During one frenzied moment, Puller ordered Captain C. B. Cross, a tough, young Oklahoman, to take a group of men to the top of a small rise where several marine machine guns had been destroyed, and hold off the Japanese until replacement machine guns could be brought up. Cross collected a handful of men, told one to grab a gunny sack filled with hand grenades, and rushed through the rain and mud to the hill, but when he opened the sack to start tossing grenades, all he found inside were canned rations. Undaunted, Cross grabbed a can with each hand, stood on the hill's crest, and hurled them at the onrushing Japanese.

Lieutenant Smith and other medical personnel in the battalion aid station worked nonstop under fire to operate on severely wounded marines. At one moment during the fighting Smith asked a jeep driver to take some of the wounded who were moaning in pain back to the field hospital, but the driver declined. "I'm sorry, Doctor. We're going after more ammunition. It's urgent. There may be another attack." Not one of the wounded, Smith noticed, complained about being left at the front. "Our little island fortress had to be defended at all cost."

Redemption came to another marine private who a few days earlier had been charged by Puller with dereliction of duty for tossing away his mortar shells during a skirmish. Puller intended to discipline him, but he delayed carrying out the punishment until the threat to Henderson Field had been neutralized. During the night's fighting that same private, still under arrest, carried jars of hot coffee along the perimeter while Japanese tracers raced by. Impressed with his courage, Puller dropped the charges.

When the regimental headquarters called during the fighting and asked for Puller, the marine who answered replied that Chesty was on the front line. Lieutenant Colonel Frisbie, Sims's executive officer, told the marine, "Find him. Get him on the phone." Frisbie called several more times without result, but when Chesty finally contacted Frisbie, expecting to learn that he would soon receive reinforcements, he erupted when learning that Sims only wanted to find out how matters were going. "What do you mean, 'What's going on?'" Puller bellowed. "We're neck deep in a fire fight, and I've no time to stand here bullshitting. If you want to find out what's going on, come up and see me." He slammed the phone down and thundered to those near him, "Regiment is not convinced we are facing a major attack!"

John Basilone could relate to Chesty's reaction. A marine cut from the same mold as Puller and born into a family of ten children in New Jersey, the Catholic youth enlisted in the Marine Corps in 1940 after a three-year stint in the army, where he had earned the nickname Manila John for serving in the Philippines. The champion boxer, whom Chesty had teased about digging such a deep foxhole, led two sections of heavy machine guns posted to C Company near the middle of Puller's sector. He had just kicked off his shoes to relieve the itching in his soaked feet when the Japanese commenced their attack, and lacking time to don his boots, he turned to face the invaders barefooted. With mortar shells tossing dirt and hand grenades exploding nearby, he and his gunners fired five hundred rounds a minute at the Japanese, a rapid pace that evaporated the water in the water-cooled weapons and heated the muzzles. To keep the machine guns in use, but lacking the water to do so, Basilone and his men urinated on the guns.

Each time the Japanese threatened to overwhelm Basilone's position, he and his gunners mounted a blistering fire that sent Japanese tumbling down the incline before them. "They kept coming and we kept firing," said Basilone. "We all thought our end had come." He at times removed his machine gun from its tripod and lowered himself to the ground so he could fire more accurate bursts at Japanese soldiers crawling toward the perimeter, and so many dead Japanese piled before his machine gun that they blocked his field of fire. He turned back and fired his pistol to eliminate a threat when enemy soldiers penetrated to Basilone's rear, and when gunners in other bunkers fell to enemy bullets, Basilone ran over and covered those firing lanes. He repaired jammed weapons to get them back into the fight, and whenever gunners ran low on ammunition, the barefoot sergeant rushed to the rear, strapped ammunition belts and spare barrels to his back, and hurried them to the front. During the infrequent lulls, Basilone and his men left their foxholes to shove the bodies to the side so they had a clear field of fire ready for the next attack.

Basilone's feats were a few of the many similar deeds that occurred along Puller's line that night in repelling multiple attacks. Because he had trained them, Puller figured his men would mount a stubborn defense, but one question nagged at him—would he have enough men and ammunition to outlast the numerically superior forces Maruyama could keep sending across the field?

Martin Clemens recognized how perilous the moment was. He saw that Puller's "understrength battalion was battling like mad" to halt the Japanese, who wanted to overrun Henderson Field, but wondered if it could hold. "Things looked pretty bleak." Clemens heard talk at headquarters that personnel might have to "go into the line, but we had no time to dwell on possibilities."

Puller had reached a desperate moment in the battle. "Colonel, I'm just about running out of ammo," said Captain Fuller over the phone. Rather than skirt the truth and promise his captain that extra ammunition would soon arrive, Puller responded, "You got bayonets, haven't you, Fuller?"

"Sure. Yes, sir," answered Fuller.

"All right then. Hang on."

Puller was proud of his men, but he needed reinforcements if his battalion was to survive the night and save Henderson Field.

"Puller's Presence Alone Represented the Equivalent of Two Battalions"

By 3:00 a.m. Puller estimated that the Japanese assaults had reduced his battalion to around 500 men. This concerned Vandegrift, who feared that Puller, who had already beaten back multiple savage attacks against the southern line, might be unable to stop the assaults that were yet to storm his rapidly thinning line; should the Japanese rout Puller's defenses, little remained to prevent them from reaching vulnerable Henderson Field. "The Sendai Division was knocking on our door," wrote Colonel Twining of the tense moment.

Puller expressed similar concerns to Lieutenant Colonel Frisbie that the Japanese threatened to overrun his line. He explained that the Japanese had so often infiltrated his perimeter that his bodyguard, Sergeant Sheppard, had organized a small security party for Puller and the two staff members with him. When Frisbie asked if he wanted more reinforcements, Puller replied, "Sure, we could use help. But if it's coming, for God's sake don't hold it back. Send it on in."

Vandegrift ordered the closest reserve unit, the army's 3d Battalion, 164th Infantry under Colonel Robert K. Hall, to move to Chesty's aid. Puller would have to hold until Hall navigated through rain and mud a half mile to Puller's line, but according to Twining, a close friend of Puller's since the 1920s, "I never had a moment of doubt. I did not feel we were outnumbered that night. To me, Puller's presence alone represented the equivalent of two battalions."

When Sims informed Puller that Hall's battalion would be led to the front lines by Father Matthew F. Keough, a Catholic chaplain from Philadelphia, Chesty asked to speak to the priest to ascertain whether Keough could handle the task. A chaplain did not normally become involved in military movements such as this, as the action violated the norms for noncombatants established by the Geneva convention. These regulations stipulated that corpsmen, surgeons, and chaplains were to refrain from taking up a weapon or assisting in any fighting. Puller hardly cared whether Keough broke the rules of war, but he needed to know that the priest possessed the skill and guts to quickly guide the sorely needed reinforcements to his line. After a brief conversation with the chaplain, Puller concluded that Keough, whose constant visits to the front lines during the heaviest of fighting had earned him the respect of every marine, exhibited the courage and knowledge of the terrain to lead the army battalion forward.

Father Keough could have been Chesty Puller's best friend, for the marines he tended considered him to be a marine in chaplain's garb. He was familiar with every inch of the perimeter because of his frequent visits to men scattered along the line, and the enlisted became accustomed to seeing the priest, who had been wounded at the Matanikau, patrolling both in the daylight, searching for wounded marines in need of religious consolation, and at night, when Keough visited the hospital. No matter where he went the chaplain, standing over six feet tall, always carried a loaded pistol and a cartridge of extra bullets. "The boys loved him, because he was a real man," said fellow chaplain Father Thomas Reardon.

As Keough guided the battalion from its bivouac, an army officer, unaware of what was occurring, tried to stop the priest, but Keough stormed by, directing a torrent of profanity at the officer as he left for Puller's sector. Keough arrived near the front to see Puller waiting along a rough road one-quarter mile behind the front lines.

"Here they are, Colonel," said Keough.

"Father, we can sure use them," replied Puller.

Puller turned to Hall, who commanded the inexperienced army battalion, and said, "Colonel, I'm glad to see you. I don't know who's senior to who right now, and I don't give a damn. I'll be in command until daylight, at least, because I know what's going on here, and you don't."

Hall said, "That's fine with me. You lead on."

"I'm going to drop 'em off along this road," Puller explained, "and send in a few to each platoon position. I want you to make it clear to your people that my men, even if they're only sergeants, will command in those holes when your officers and men arrive."

"I understand you. Let's go," said Hall.

With a Japanese charge again threatening to break the line, Puller, Hall, and Keough led small groups of Hall's battalion toward the perimeter. About every hundred yards, Puller delivered squad-sized units to runners who had raced back from the front to meet Puller and take the army infantry to the fighting.

The reinforcements arrived just in time to help stop three successive Japanese charges. "The Japs continued to assault our lines throughout the night of October 24 until 8 a.m.," Puller said later. "We would break up one assault and another would come. Probably ten altogether. Army reinforcements arrived about 3 a.m. and, believe me, I was damned glad to see them. But even so the Japs managed to wedge into the left center of our lines and wiped out some of my men. There was no such thing as falling back."

When Puller left his command post to check the line, he saw that his marines and the freshly arrived army infantry maintained a tenuous grip on the perimeter but had blended together well. "Old Lewie, he was the same Lewie," said Colonel Thomas. "He was fighting and the 164th was just the strength he needed, and he just fed them in the line all along his foxholes, a few doughboys and a few marines, and they fought there."

Some of the automatic weapons had been fired so continuously that the rifling was worn smooth. When Puller telephoned del Valle with a request to bring everything he had into the battle, saying, "We're holding on by our toenails," del Valle agreed to the request but doubted that he would then be left with enough ammunition to provide support the next day. "If we don't need it now, we'll never need it," warned Puller. "If they get through here tonight there won't be a tomorrow."

The final assault occurred just before dawn. The inexperienced army infantry battling next to Puller's marines gave a good account of themselves, but the line buckled. The Sendai killed every marine in one gun position, and in Chesty's center, one hundred Japanese punched a temporary salient 150 yards wide and 100 yards deep. "It looked ominous for a while," wrote Colonel Twining, but with the dawn Puller, in the final action of a long, arduous night, placed mortarmen on either side of the salient and wiped it out.

The Japanese had mounted at least seven major charges, and numerous smaller forays, against Puller's line throughout that bloody night. The marines fought saber-wielding officers and soldiers who jumped into their foxholes; they thrust bayonets into Japanese trying to do the same to them; they grabbed, clawed, and scratched in one-on-one deadly contests.

Dawn thus revealed a gruesome result. Bodies littered the open field in front and lay mangled along the perimeter, while in some foxholes, the intertwined bodies of both marine and Japanese combatants indicated how personal this battle had been. Captain Regan Fuller, who earlier in the fighting resorted to using bayonets when his men ran out of ammunition, noticed layers of Japanese bodies piled high in front of marine machine guns and along the jungle's edge.

─────

The October 24–25 battle for Henderson Field terminated with the return of the missing members from Sergeant Briggs's scattered platoon. After spending an anxious night in the jungle, trying to avoid enemy soldiers and marine artillery, the next afternoon Briggs and a handful of his marines entered the perimeter.

Over the next two weeks, thirteen missing men from Briggs's platoon trickled into the perimeter, either singly or in small groups. They had survived by playing dead to trick the enemy, hiding in jungle foliage, lying prone during American artillery barrages, squeezing water from rotted wood, and skinning and consuming birds raw. Of Briggs's forty marines, twenty-four emerged unscathed, but the sergeant had lost three killed, ten wounded, and three missing in action.

"The Sendai Was Destroyed"

The morning after the attack, Puller walked the battlefield. Craters pocketed the open land, and in places Japanese bodies were stacked two and three deep. He guessed that at least 300 Japanese had perished in front of his guns, and many more had died in the fields and jungle from marine gunfire and del Valle's artillery.

He strolled among his marines, congratulating them on their courageous stand, and told them that their deeds would earn them medals and accolades from a grateful nation. He was proud of the bravery and discipline displayed that exhausting night by every officer and man, but especially by his "Pearl Harbor marines," young men who only a few weeks ago had not even fired their rifles in combat. They had shed the trappings of home and donned the accoutrements of war to safeguard their country, and had emerged triumphant.

Signs of combat branded every marine. Blood that marked their faces and matted their hair mingled with the grime and gore coating their uniforms. In the immediate aftermath of combat, when the adrenaline that had pumped so furiously through their bodies during the fighting had at last subsided, the marines, newly enlisted and veterans alike, appeared to be on the verge of collapsing. Puller made certain to extend a few words to as many as possible.

"I rested my head on the ledge of the emplacement, weary, tired and grateful the Lord had seen fit to spare me," said Sergeant Basilone. "Then I heard my name being called. Looking up I saw Lieutenant Colonel Puller, my commanding officer, standing with his arm outstretched. He shook hands with me and said, 'I heard you came back for ammunition. Good work.'"

Perplexed at why Maruyama never varied his tactics that night instead of throwing his Sendai against Puller's perimeter in piecemeal charges, he asked a captured warrant officer to explain the strange moves. "That is not the Japanese way," the prisoner replied. "The plan had been made. No one would have dared to change it. It must go as it is written." Puller would have improvised a speedy substitute for faulty plans, as he had in Nicaragua and in rescuing Rogers's men at Point Cruz, but he counted himself fortunate that did not occur here. If his counterpart had been able to mass his Sendai for one or two mammoth attacks, which admittedly the jungle would have made more difficult to execute, Chesty's outnumbered force, no matter how bravely they defended the perimeter, would most likely have been overrun.

That same morning the commander of the army's 164th Regiment, Colonel Bryant E. Moore, located Puller to extend his gratefulness. "Colonel," Moore said to Puller, "I want you to know how happy I am to have had my men blooded under you. No man in our outfit, including me, had ever seen action, and I know our boys couldn't have had a better instructor. I wish you'd break in my other battalions." Puller praised the army infantry's performance and added, "They're almost as good as Marines, Colonel."

General Roy S. Geiger, in charge of marine air units, also walked the battlefield that morning and was stunned at the Japanese bodies stacked in rows in front of Puller's line. He saw marines, still covered in blood from the overnight confrontation, recovering the dead and helping their wounded buddies, some bleeding from multiple bayonet stab wounds, to aid stations. The plasma jars strung on tree limbs and on bloody bayonets painted an image of how frightful the fighting was in Puller's sector, and symbolized the courage and sacrifice that Puller's men extended throughout the battle. Geiger, moved by the scene before him, returned to headquarters impressed with what Chesty and his battalion had accomplished the previous night.

Geiger was not the only one so affected, for Puller and his marines conducted a heroic defense that matched other celebrated stands. The bodies of 300 Sendai lay draped over the barbed wire or within the perimeter, more than 1,000 fell in the firing lanes to Puller's machine-gun and rifle fire, and an estimated 1,500 lay scattered in the jungle just beyond the open field. Captured Japanese documents showed that Puller's battalion had withstood attacks from three Japanese regiments and part of one brigade, the equal to almost a Japanese division. "By the morning of the third day the Sendai was destroyed," wrote Colonel Twining of the once-proud Japanese unit.

In the savage fighting, Puller and the army battalion suffered losses of 53 dead and 98 wounded, but aided by del Valle's artillery, they had saved Henderson Field from being overrun and kept Vandegrift's perimeter intact. While the courage of the young marines and army infantry determined the successful outcome, Japanese blunders contributed to their defeat. Whether due to the jungle or to some other factor, they had committed the Sendai piecemeal, and they had badly overestimated their own abilities while underestimating the fighting talents of their American opponent. This action terminated their October counteroffensive and, according to Colonel Twining, "The Japanese suffered a severe blow to their morale when their blue-ribbon, semi-sacred Sendai warriors were stopped in their tracks by Puller and his understrength, malaria-ridden battalion."

Puller attributed victory to the bravery of his men, sturdy defensive positions, the efficiency of machine guns and mortars, and del Valle's support. "We held them because we were well dug in, a whole regiment of artillery was backing us up, and there was plenty of barbed wire," he subsequently said.

Chesty was so effusive that he even extended credit to the army battalion. "I was damned glad to see them," he said later. He frequently visited the wounded in hospitals, talking, as correspondent Robert Sherrod wrote in *Time* magazine, "in his Virginia drawl with a pipe clenched between his teeth," joking and congratulating them for stopping the Japanese cold. Sherrod, impressed with Puller's interactions with his marines, added for

home front readers, "They will follow him to hell." The correspondent wrote, "Devoted to his men, he watches over them like
an old hen. Said a sergeant: 'You're afraid to talk about the old
man because likely as not he'll be right behind you whether
you're in a foxhole, on the line during an attack, or standing in
line for chow.'"

One day after the battle, Puller arranged for his dirt-covered
and bloody marines to bathe in a river as guards scanned the
jungle for Japanese. They refreshed themselves in the cooling
water, and were delighted when Chesty stripped and hopped in
the river to frolic with privates and corporals. Captain Regan
Fuller claimed the incident was yet another example of why
Chesty was so beloved, as he displayed "a common touch the
men liked. Though a few of the Clausewitz-type officers in the
rear ranks snickered behind his back, the men knew he was real,
that he never put on an act, and they loved him."

Puller made certain that his malaria-ridden men received
rest, arranged for mail to be brought in, and eliminated unnecessary work so they could rebuild their strength. On one of his
walks about the sector, Puller came upon a young officer supervising while his men picked up debris. Puller strolled over and
whispered, "Let the boys get in their sacks and leave them the
hell alone. They're half dead from fever and fighting, and they'll
have to hop to it again any day now."

One day Colonel Thomas called Puller back to headquarters,
and when Chesty arrived, waiting to greet him was none other
than Admiral Nimitz, Puller's commander from *Augusta* days,
who had flown in for a quick visit. Thomas introduced Puller to
the commander of Pacific forces, but Nimitz halted him. "You're

ten years too late. Puller and I were shipmates, away back there in China station days." Nimitz complimented Puller for his superb defense along the perimeter and chatted about their time together aboard the heavy cruiser.

While Puller appreciated Nimitz's words, praise from his marines meant more, a phenomenon Robert Sherrod captured in his magazine profile of Chesty. "Marines," Sherrod wrote, "will always remember the day when Puller and his outfit, standing one man to every five yards, held a line 2,500 yards long in the jungles of Lunga sector, mowing down charging Japs for four frenzied hours. Puller was everywhere. All through the rain-drenched night Puller coolly kept his thin line intact." Sherrod then allowed a machine gunner to have the final word. "I gave thanks to God and Puller."

Puller recommended various individuals for awards, including a Medal of Honor for Sergeant Basilone. He placed Father Keough's name on the list for leading the army battalion to meet Puller's sector, but superiors, much to Puller's chagrin, removed the chaplain from consideration. His anger subsided when Captain Fuller and the other company commanders were awarded Silver Stars, and when his 1st Battalion, 7th Marines, received a commendation for "its determined and vigorous defense against an attack conducted by numerically superior enemy forces." The citation explained that after the assault began, the battalion held their line for five hours until the 164th Battalion arrived, at which time the combined force battled throughout the night while inflicting heavy casualties. The commendation concluded that "the high combat effectiveness demonstrated by the 1st Battalion, 7th Marines is a tribute to the courage, devotion to duty and high professional attainments of its Commanding Officer, Lieutenant Colonel Lewis B. Puller and to the Company Commanders, Captain Charles W. Kelly, Jr., Captain Regan Fuller, Captain Robert H. Haggerty, Captain Marshall W. Moore and Captain Robert J. Rodgers."

Puller's battalion, and many fellow commanders, believed Puller deserved his own Medal of Honor for that night. Colonel Edson had received that award after his courageous stand at the ridge the previous month, and Puller's October defense seemed to be its equal. Colonel Frisbie recommended Puller for the award, which was seconded by Colonel Sims and by headquarters officers, but the matter went no further. "I recommended that Lieutenant Colonel Puller also receive this award but was overruled," wrote Twining. "Why, I cannot imagine." Vandegrift may have been upset with Puller for what the general considered Chesty's sporadic communications with headquarters, and with Puller's penchant for criticizing headquarters personnel while favoring his enlisted.

Private First Class Robert Leckie, who fought at Guadalcanal in the 2nd Battalion, 1st Marines and later penned a classic memoir about combat on the island, thought Puller might have been overlooked because Chesty could not abide playing the political game. Leckie wrote that "for in him there was none of the guile that slips up the ladder of promotion. Chesty had become notorious among brother officers for insisting that regimental staffs were too large and the distance between command posts and front lines were too long." Leckie claimed that while Puller's demeanor and salty tongue earned no favor with higher-ups, it made him beloved by the enlisted.

As consolation, Puller received his third Navy Cross, which mentioned that while Puller's battalion manned a lengthy front in a heavy downpour of rain, "a Japanese force, superior in number, launched a vigorous assault against that position of the line which passed through a dense jungle." The citation added, "Courageously withstanding the enemy's desperate and determined attacks, Lieutenant Colonel Puller not only held his battalion to its position until reinforcements arrived three hours later, but also effectively commanded the augmented force until late in the afternoon of the next day. By his tireless devotion to duty and cool judgment under fire, he prevented a hostile penetration of our lines and was largely responsible for the successful defense of the sector assigned to his troops."

As long as his marines received recognition, Puller was happy and wasted little time fretting about which award he deserved. Besides, he needed to keep his focus on any combat that lay ahead. At least he would then enjoy the collaboration of a new admiral at the helm. Bill Halsey, a commander who displayed many of the same traits as Puller, made a quick imprint on Chesty and the marines on Guadalcanal.

CHAPTER FIVE

"COLONEL PULLER LOOKS TOUGH, TALKS TOUGH, ACTS TOUGH, AND IS TOUGH"

Final Guadalcanal Action, November 1942–March 1943

The day before Puller's battalion stopped Maruyama at the perimeter, General Vandegrift had flown to Nouméa to discuss the situation at Guadalcanal with Halsey. The capital city of French-controlled New Caledonia, Nouméa would develop into one of the most important naval bases and command centers in the Pacific war for the Allies. American ships, whether shuttling troops and equipment to the South Pacific, entering port to take on fuel and supplies, or steaming in for repairs, became a constant presence while supporting the effort to wrench Guadalcanal from the Japanese and in the subsequent drive northward up the Solomons.

Vandegrift hardly noticed the island's more moderate climate and improved accommodations, for he was focused solely on convincing Admiral Halsey that he needed help for his fatigued marines on Guadalcanal. Time for relaxation would come later; he needed assurances that he had the backing of a commander who was willing to throw in every resource and turn to any alternative to ensure that Puller and the other men at Henderson Field had at least a fair shot at defeating the Japanese. Vandegrift, Puller, and the Guadalcanal marines had witnessed enough of Ghormley's timidity. Give them an admiral who delivered the tools of war, and they would get the job done.

"I impressed on him the poor physical state of my command—the inevitable result of two and a half months of restricted diet, sleepless nights and disease." He mentioned the frightening effects of naval bombardments that prevented his weary men from obtaining sorely needed sleep, the shortage of planes and supplies that placed them at a monumental disadvantage to an enemy that could freely rush in fresh provisions and men to the island, the hundreds of cases of debilitating malaria that each week sapped his ranks every bit as much as battlefield wounds, and the negative impact on morale created by watching the daily stream of Japanese men and supplies pour ashore. "I told him that to hold we simply had to have air and ground reinforcement, that our people were practically worn out."

Halsey, given the post to inject optimism and fighting spirit in the Guadalcanal forces, listened, weighing his navy's urgency to protect warships against the marine need for men and supplies, and handed Vandegrift an early Christmas present. "Gray eyebrows bristling, the compactly built Halsey drummed the desk a moment with his fingers. He abruptly turned to me. 'Can you hold?'" Vandegrift replied, "Yes, I can hold. But I have to have more active support than I have been getting." Halsey answered, "You go on back there, Vandegrift. I promise to get you everything I have."

Vandegrift returned from Nouméa three days later, after Puller's late October win, with the good news that Admiral Halsey had pledged to divert every possible man and resource to the island, precisely the boost that Vandegrift and the marines on Guadalcanal needed. Vandegrift said that the flow of men, supplies, and reinforcements that Halsey tapped "gave me riches beyond the dreams of avarice. Tactically my situation resembled the period following the battle of the Ridge when we had beaten the enemy but could not pursue. This time I could pursue. We turned west."

Puller's marines regarded Chesty's leadership as a blessing, and now they had an admiral who exhibited the same grit as their commander instead of duplicating the hesitation and uncertainty that had plagued earlier operations. "They had no doubts either about Admiral Halsey," wrote battalion surgeon Lieutenant Smith. "He was a fighter who understood them and talked their language." The combination of Halsey at headquarters and Puller in the field should, his battalion marines concluded, produce additional victories that would seal their enemy's fate.

"Hell, These Are Just Band-Aid Wounds"

As November opened, both sides on Guadalcanal had been worn down from combat, disease, and lack of nourishment. In October alone, the division reported almost 2,000 cases of malaria, a number that would double in November. The strain of jungle patrols and constant alerts exhausted the marines, causing Vandegrift to conclude that "the cumulative effect of long periods of fatigue and strain, endless labor by day and vigilance by night were aggravated to an alarming degree by the growing malarial rate."

The Japanese suffered in equal measure. Lieutenant Keijiro Minegishi wrote in his diary three days after their failed attempt to crack through Puller at Henderson Field, "I never dreamed of retreating over the same mountainous trail through the jungle we crossed with such enthusiasm." He added: "On the up hill my body swayed around unable to walk. I can't imagine how the soldiers carrying the artillery are doing. I must take a rest every two meters. It is quite disheartening to have only one tiny teaspoon of salt per day and a palmful of rice porridge."

Japanese military strategists assembled a mid-November assault that they hoped would finally deliver the knockout blow against the stubborn Americans. The same military forces that had shocked the world with their audacious attack at Pearl Harbor and had swept across much of the Far East and Pacific in the eight months since had embarrassingly been stymied by Vandegrift's forces on Guadalcanal. Despite engaging the Americans for three months, the Japanese had failed to dislodge the marines, a lapse that irate superiors in Tokyo had brought up with alarming frequency. They admonished their commanders at Rabaul and Guadalcanal to reverse that trend or face removal from their posts.

General Hyakutake intended to halt that slide and retake the initiative on Guadalcanal. While his ground units, bolstered by reinforcements and 10,000 tons of supplies, assaulted the marine perimeter, the Imperial Japanese Navy would lure Halsey's fleet into a decisive battle in the narrow waters separating the island from Florida Island and Tulagi, a short distance to the north. By vanquishing both Halsey at sea and Vandegrift on land, the Japanese would establish sole possession of the island, register a victory that would make their southern perimeter, stretching from the Solomon Islands westward to New Guinea, all but impregnable in the foreseeable future, imperil American supply lines to Australia, and put that island continent into play as a potential target.

To that end, Hyakutake shifted an infantry regiment from the western side of the perimeter to Koli Point, ten miles east of Henderson Field, to mount an assault from that venue. After failing to crash through from the west, Hyakutake hoped that an offensive staged from the opposite side of the perimeter would shift the momentum to his side. On November 2 the Japanese landed 300 fresh troops, two field guns, ammunition, and provisions at Koli Point and began assembling for yet another attempt to seize the airfield.

Hyakutake was not the only commander to alter his plans. After Halsey's intelligence warned Vandegrift of another imminent attack against the perimeter, this time from the east, Vandegrift dispatched Puller's counterpart, Hanneken's 2d Battalion, 7th Marines, to Koli Point with orders to break up the enemy before they could threaten the airfield from that direction.

Hanneken left the perimeter on the first day of November, and within twenty-four hours he clashed with the enemy where the Nalimbiu River flows into Koli Point. After a violent fire-fight Hanneken, running out of mortar ammunition, and unable to contact Vandegrift's headquarters due to faulty radios, conducted a fighting withdrawal to the river and dug in on the west bank for the night. The next day Vandegrift ordered Puller and an army battalion to his aid. After Puller led his battalion away from Henderson Field and joined Hanneken, landing craft transported both battalions from the Nalimbiu to a strip of beach near Koli Point, where they passed through army lines and continued toward the Metapona River a few miles away.

The next morning Puller and Hanneken crossed the mouth of the Metapona and headed toward Gavaga Creek, 1,500 yards east of the Metapona, with Puller advancing along the beaches while Hanneken took the inland path. When the two battalions reached their jumping-off points, Puller and Hanneken attacked the Japanese while the army's 2d Battalion, 164th Infantry launched a corresponding assault from the south.

Within the first few minutes, Japanese artillery shells and machine-gun bullets ripped into Puller's command post. Shrapnel from one shell knocked Chesty off his feet, piercing his side, left leg, and left foot. For the first time in a twenty-three-year career that included combat against rebel forces in Haiti and Nicaragua, patrols on Guadalcanal, the miraculous rescue of Rogers's force at Point Cruz, and the bloody October fight to protect Henderson, Puller had been wounded in battle.

Bloodied but conscious, Puller attempted to inform Vandegrift about the situation but was unable to reach his superior because his communications lines had been severed during the fighting. Though hobbled from his injuries, Chesty shrugged off assistance from others and crawled to the beach to help his communications man repair the line. The two worked while bullets pinged only feet away and mortar shell explosions coughed up dirt on both sides, situations Puller had faced many times before without being harmed; but this time his luck ran out when a Japanese sniper shot Puller twice through the fleshy part of his arm. As word spread through the battalion that Chesty had been hit, two sergeants lifted Puller onto a poncho to prevent sand from filtering into his open wounds, while other men shoveled a foxhole for their wounded commander.

While the small group tended Puller, the battalion fought its way toward the west bank of Gavaga Creek, where the combined marine–army force pinned the Japanese against the sea and sealed off any escape route. Puller tried to remain in charge, but later that night he concluded that, because of his wounds, he was no longer able to move around and command his troops the way he felt he should. Incapable of operating along the front line with his troops, he reluctantly contacted headquarters and requested that they send a replacement.

Surprised to read this message from one of his most effective commanders, an officer who would never leave his men in the midst of battle unless it was absolutely necessary, Vandegrift replied that another officer, Major John C. Weber, would immediately leave the perimeter to fill in for Chesty. Determined that his marines would not see him carried away, Puller, with blood-soaked bandages covering his arm, leg, and foot, slowly rose from the poncho and limped to the beach, where he again collapsed.

A handful of amtracs arrived at dawn to remove the wounded and dead. Puller lingered on the beach until the final marine had been evacuated, after which he staggered unassisted to a landing craft. The amtrac conveyed him to the perimeter, where Puller eased into a jeep for a painful ride to the field hospital, which was then little more than canvas stretched above the wounded to block out the sun and rain. Colonel Edson watched his fellow commander arrive and walked over to ask if Puller needed anything. "Nothing to it," Puller answered. "Hell, these are just Band-Aid wounds." When Colonel Twining stepped over from Vandegrift's headquarters to see how Puller fared, Chesty dismissed his concerns as well. All he had was, as Twining quoted Puller, "a fanny full of 'scrapnel.'"

Surgeons removed six small pieces of metal from Puller's body but lacked the equipment and training to extricate a larger chunk deeply embedded in his thigh next to the bone. When they explained to Puller that the more complicated surgery would have to be done in an Australian hospital, Chesty balked at being separated from his battalion. Doctors suggested that leaving the jagged metal in his leg could result in irreparable damage, but Puller laughed off their concerns. "Hell, when I was a boy in Virginia half the old men in the county carried around enough Yankee iron in their bodies to open junkyards. I can't go to Australia while my men are fighting." The physicians dropped the issue and acceded to Chesty's wishes.

A Japanese battleship, three cruisers, and two destroyers interrupted Puller's stay in the field hospital when they bombarded Henderson Field and the adjacent areas. As the vulnerable field hospital offered sparse protection from the shelling, corpsmen and other marines hurriedly moved Puller and the other patients to sturdier shelters. With their commander barely evading harm from Japanese shells, in three days of combat his men at Gavaga Creek helped defeat the Japanese and force the survivors to retreat into the jungle, where an inland patrol by a group of marine Raiders pursued and sent them fleeing piecemeal to their lines. After securing Henderson from Hyakutake's western assaults, Puller's battalion had now helped clear Vandegrift's eastern flank.

The same day that Puller was wounded, Admiral Halsey arrived from his headquarters on New Caledonia, intent on bolstering morale on Guadalcanal and at home still recovering from Japanese victories that dominated the war's first half year. Accompanied by Vandegrift, Halsey freely mingled with the infantrymen who gathered around the admiral each time his jeep stopped. Marines responded to Halsey because they sensed, as they did with Puller, that Halsey felt a kinship with privates and corporals.

"On November 8 Admiral Halsey flew in like a wonderful breath of fresh air," wrote Vandegrift. "During a tour of the area he showed extreme interest and enthusiasm in all phases of the operation, concurring with my existent positions and future plans. More important, he talked to a large number of Marines, saw their gaunt, malaria-ridden bodies, their faces lined from what seemed a nightmare of years."

Had Puller been able to attend, he would have loved listening to Halsey as he regaled the group of war correspondents that accompanied him. Better than most senior commanders, Halsey knew how to use the press to convey messages to home front readers and, more importantly, to the marines, army infantry, and sailors then in the South Pacific. He relied on brief quotable phrases, many replete with profanity and current wartime stereotypes, to convey his message.

While Puller lay wounded near Gavaga Creek, one correspondent asked Halsey his formula for winning the war. Halsey replied, "Kill Japs, kill Japs and keep on killing Japs." To wild laughter and applause from marine audiences, Halsey claimed that one of America's soldiers was the equal of twenty Japanese, and vowed that the enemy's next move would be a retreat that would not halt until American forces occupied Tokyo.

The next morning—the same day an amtrac brought Puller to the field hospital—Halsey decorated thirteen marine officers and men. The thirteen rejoined the front lines as soon as the ceremony ended, but they returned with praise for their new commander who credited privates and corporals in an attempt to let them know he appreciated their labors. Like Puller, Halsey engendered devotion among his men and forged a bond that built unity of purpose and a willingness to exert extra effort.

That same concern for the men from Puller had enabled his battalion to stage its noteworthy defense of the Henderson Field perimeter. In subsequent months, that unbreakable link would produce additional victories elsewhere in the Pacific.

"A Lot of Them Grew into Men Here"

As Thanksgiving neared, Puller rejoined a battalion that, after two months of combat, badly needed a break during which to recuperate. Physically and mentally exhausted marines, some on the brink of nervous collapse, suffered chills, high fevers, and tremors from malaria. Dengue fever and other tropical diseases wreaked havoc with their bodies, and inadequate diets and dysentery sapped strength from the already tired men.

Although recovering from his own wounds, Puller did what he could to assist his men. He wrote letters to the families of each marine evacuated due to injuries or illness, taking time to praise the efforts of their son, brother, or husband and vowing to continue the fight until the Japanese were vanquished. He took his place in the food line with privates and corporals, and washed his clothes in the river with the enlisted. On the rare occasion when he received a bottle of fine liquor from friends in the rear, he shared most of it with the men.

According to Sergeant Briggs, Chesty was "an inspiration, and a man whom any guy in the battalion would have unquestionably followed anywhere." Captain Marshall Moore, C Company's commander, said that his men loved Puller because "he was an outstanding leader and had that rare gift which few people have of having an outfit which would follow him to hell and back and enjoy every moment of it." Even Vandegrift, who bristled at some of Chesty's gruff comments, called Puller "one of the best combat patrol officers I know."

Puller and his battalion remained at their post along the

147

perimeter until Christmas Eve, when they withdrew from the line and prepared for evacuation. On New Year's Eve, a group of chaplains conducted a ceremony to honor those who had been killed in the months since marine forces had landed on Guadalcanal. Navy Seabees constructed a large altar in the middle of the American cemetery, and a catafalque symbolizing the dead rested on a platform with a marine honor guard about it. Rows of plain white crosses and Stars of David for the 1,400 slain surrounded the altar, while beyond stood 7,000 marines, in gear, soon to leave Guadalcanal.

Three Catholic priests, including Father Keough from the October battle along the perimeter, celebrated a Solemn High Mass of Requiem. After the ceremony two other chaplains, a Protestant minister and a Jewish rabbi, spoke, followed by single marines from each platoon walking forward to place a palm frond in front of a cross honoring a slain friend. The ceremony ended fittingly with a bugler sounding "Taps," and as every marine stood at attention, the powerful, simple notes wafted over the crowd.

On January 5 Puller led his battalion aboard the liners *President Hayes*, *President Adams*, and *President Jackson*, the same ships that had brought them to the island. The fever-ridden, tired marines, who a few months before could have navigated the cargo nets up the transports' sides with ease, now labored with each rung. Some had to be helped to the ships, or even carried aboard, but no one minded, for these vessels were transporting them away from the hell that was Guadalcanal.

Puller later explained that Guadalcanal changed his young marines. They had enlisted as civilians unfamiliar with the ways of war, raw but willing to learn. Training had begun their transformation into marines, but they could only count themselves fully initiated once they had been in the fire, had killed to avoid being killed, and had seen their buddies, slashed and bloody, dying on the battlefield. Guadalcanal had been their final exam in that education, and in the process, they had learned much about themselves. Most had been wrenched from civilian lives and dumped into a world diametrically opposite from the peace and calm offered at home, yet when matched against a military machine to which some had attributed super powers, they had not simply held their own but had bested their foe. The men detested combat and were ecstatic to steam away from Guadalcanal, but they also left with a satisfaction that comes only with victory. "It's the reaction from the discovery that they're finally leaving this damned place," said Puller, "and yet, a lot of them grew into men here."

Puller's battalion suffered 89 dead, 156 wounded, and 3 missing in its two months on the island, but they also received 80 percent of the medals and commendations handed out to the 7th Marine Regiment. Puller added a third Navy Cross for his defense of Henderson Field, a Bronze Star for his rescue of Major Rogers's unit, and a Purple Heart for his November wounds.

The performance of Puller's battalion, alongside other marine and army units as well as the navy in the waters off Guadalcanal, gained a crucial airfield for the United States, kept open the vital supply lines to Australia, gave American factories time to produce weapons, tanks, aircraft, and the other items of war, and provided military strategists a staging area for future advances up the Solomon chain. Halsey, Vandegrift, Puller, and their soldiers and sailors, in the words of American correspondent Ira Wolfert, had turned Guadalcanal into "a 'this far and no further' line drawn around the well-fanged Jap where he has bit into the toothsome Pacific, and it is hoped the line will one day turn into a strangler's cord around his neck." He added that "one thing seems rather clear—the Japs who started the war with a slam-bang rush have been slammed back into caution. They are no angels but they seem to fear to tread."

The marines and army infantry recorded their first land triumph of the Pacific, an initial win in an unbroken catalog of victories that would occur over the next three years as the ever-expanding American military juggernaut stormed across the Pacific to Tokyo. On Guadalcanal, they had busted the myth of Japanese military superiority, causing Japanese naval planner Captain Toshikazu Ohmae to tell American interrogators after the war, "After Guadalcanal I knew we could not win the war," and allowed President Roosevelt to believe that Guadalcanal, combined with the American efforts in North Africa, had fashioned a turning point in the land conflict.

This first American ground offensive of the war boosted a home front weary from losses suffered at Pearl Harbor, Wake Island, Guam, and the Philippines. The navy had already countered enemy advances in the Battles of the Coral Sea and Midway in midyear, but the public wanted evidence of a land assault that proved their military was as good as Japan's, especially in jungle warfare. "People had come to believe that the Japs were supermen, that maybe our American boys really weren't as rugged as the Japs," said one officer. "What people wanted, back in

Second Lieutenant Lewis B. Puller in 1926, during his time at the Marine Barracks, Pearl Harbor.

From the Lewis B. Puller Collection (COLL/794) at the Marine Corps Archives and Special Collections, Marine Corps History Division, Quantico, Virginia

Lewis Puller (*second from left*), poses in Nicaragua with his close friend, Gunnery Sergeant William A. Lee (*second from right*), and two members of the Guardia Nacional in 1931.

From the Lewis B. Puller Collection (COLL/794) at the Marine Corps Archives and Special Collections, Marine Corps History Division, Quantico, Virginia

Lewis Puller (*saluting*) marches in review with Company M in Nicaragua in 1932.

From the Lewis B. Puller Collection (COLL/794) at the Marine Corps Archives and Special Collections, Marine Corps History Division, Quantico, Virginia

As shown in this photograph of Lieutenant Colonel Lewis B. Puller during the early days on Guadalcanal in 1942, Puller often shed nonessential items, including uniform parts, while in combat on jungle islands.

From the Francis Farrell Collection (COLL/4708) at the Archives Branch, Marine Corps History Division, Quantico, Virginia

Marines cautiously advance through one of Guadalcanal's streams, wary of what might be hidden in the thick jungle foliage to either side.

From the Frank Cannistraci Collection

Marines cross a field of kunai grass, which could often grow as high as four feet or more. Before the Battle for Henderson Field, Puller had fire lanes cut into the grass to prepare the marines' defense.

From the Kenneth McCullough Collection

Chesty's brother, Lieutenant Colonel Samuel D. Puller, also served in the Pacific. His 1944 death on Guam affected Puller, who had shared a happy childhood with his brother despite the loss of their father.

From the Samuel D. Puller Collection (COLL/769) at the Marine Corps Archives and Special Collections, Marine Corps History Division, Quantico, Virginia

At Cape Gloucester, Puller and his marines battled nature as well as the Japanese. Here you see the results of one of the island's frequent downpours.

Cape Gloucester, USMC Photo No. 8, from the Frederick R. Findtner Collection (COLL/3890) at the Marine Corps Archives and Special Collections, Marine Corps History Division, Quantico, Virginia

The "green hell" of Cape Gloucester's dense jungle foliage impeded operations and slowed vehicles as they attempted to reach the fighting.

Cape Gloucester USMC Photo No. 12, from the Frederick R. Findtner Collection (COLL/3890) at the Marine Corps Archives and Special Collections, Marine Corps History Division, Quantico, Virginia

At Peleliu, in September 1944, Puller's marines fought on the miserable coral rocks and ridges to pry the enemy from pillboxes and caves.

Peleliu USMC Photo No. 2-10, from the Frederick R. Findtner Collection (COLL/3890) at the Marine Corps Archives and Special Collections, Marine Corps History Division, Quantico, Virginia

Marines at one of the many coral hills and ridges that turned combat into a nightmare.

Peleliu USMC Photo No. 2-14, from the Frederick R. Findtner Collection (COLL/3890) at the Marine Corps Archives and Special Collections, Marine Corps History Division, Quantico, Virginia

Marines scale ladders during their landing at Inchon on September 15, 1950.

From the Photograph Collection (COLL/3948) at the Marine Corps Archives and Special Collections, Marine Corps History Division, Quantico, Virginia

In September 1950, General Douglas MacArthur (*third from left*) visited Chesty Puller (*second from left*) to award him a medal for his actions in the war.

From the Oliver P. Smith Collection (COLL/213) at the Marine Corps Archives and Special Collections, Marine Corps History Division, Quantico, Virginia

Lewis Puller in Korea, November 1950.

From the Oliver P. Smith Collection (COLL/213) at the Marine Corps Archives and Special Collections, Marine Corps History Division, Quantico, Virginia

In December 1950, marines halt during their withdrawal from the Chosin Reservoir. Puller remained with the final unit before departing just as enemy forces closed in.

Chesty Puller with his family in 1949. From left to right are Puller, daughter Martha Leigh, daughter Virginia Mac, wife, Virginia, and son Lewis B., Jr.

Chesty Puller talks to marines in 1961 at celebrations marking the twentieth anniversary of the 2d Marine Division's formation.

After he retired, Chesty Puller enjoyed the many visits made to his home by young marines seeking advice or simply to meet the famous commander. Here he shows a Japanese samurai sword to Corporal John F. Andrews.

Throughout his life, Puller loved reading biographies and histories. He spent hours in retirement, reading and puffing on his pipe in front of the fireplace.

From the Lewis B. Puller Collection (COLL/794) at the Marine Corps Archives and Special Collections, Marine Corps History Division, Quantico, Virginia

Chesty Puller often spoke to reunions and other gatherings of marines. At this August 1968 1st Marine Division reunion, he shouted one word, "Marine!," which induced a thunderous greeting from the assembled marines. Among them was the master of ceremonies and retired marine, Ed McMahon (*behind Puller*), from *The Tonight Show Starring Johnny Carson*.

From the Jacob Vouza Collection (COLL/3328) at the Marine Corps Archives and Special Collections, Marine Corps History Division, Quantico, Virginia the summer of '42, was a hand-to-hand battle royal between some Japs and some Americans to see who would really win." By engaging in such combat week after week, and in successfully defending the airfield, Puller's battalion and other units handed their countrymen a resounding reaffirmation of their abilities.

Halsey emphasized the point with his praise of the marines "who have performed such magnificent deeds for our country." He said that because of their contributions, the marines had "written your names in golden letters on the pages of history and won the undying gratitude of your countrymen." Halsey ended with the wish, "God bless each and every one of you."

Before leaving the island earlier in December, Vandegrift issued a letter to his officers and men in which he spoke of his pride in their performance and his admiration for their courage. Vandegrift wrote that the marines and other forces on Guadalcanal "have made the name 'Guadalcanal' a synonym for death and disaster in the language of our enemy," and said, "At all times you have faced without flinching the worst that the enemy could do to us and have thrown back the best that he could send against us. It may well be that this modest operation begun four months ago today has, through your efforts, been successful in thwarting the larger aims of our enemy in the Pacific."

Correspondents echoed Vandegrift's words. Ira Wolfert mentioned that before the war, some social commentators had accused the younger generation of being too soft to go to war, but that oft-rebuked generation had demolished those criticisms at Guadalcanal. He wrote that "this generation, the so-called 'soft' generation, 'softened up,' according to experts, by this and that, WPA, boondoggling, youth administrations, automobiles, labor-saving devices, and so forth, had a chance to prove them-selves."

The proof for Puller's men and for their fellow marines, how-ever, came with a price. Lieutenant Commander E. Rogers Smith, a naval physician at Mare Island, California, discussed the Guadalcanal campaign with marines recovering from their wounds. After interviewing them, Smith wrote about the valor of "a group of healthy, toughened, well-trained men" who had endured unspeakable conditions at Guadalcanal. He said each man had lost weight, and "rain, heat, insects, dysentery, malaria, all contributed" to what he called "a disturbance of the whole organism" and a painful "aching fatigue that they felt could never be relieved. And this in men trained to such an extent that they had known no fatigue during most of their periods of training."

Despite these ills, these veterans of the Guadalcanal fighting, including Puller, returned to the United States, where they spread uplifting tales of courage and sacrifice that spurred other young men to enlist. They also contributed to a publication that disseminated combat advice from the Guadalcanal veterans to the rest of the Armed Forces. Puller's teaching skills would once again benefit the Marine Corps.

"You Have Saved the Lives of a Good Many Soldiers"

Chesty did not accompany his battalion to Australia. On the last day of 1942, he instead received orders to fly home, with the assurance that he would rejoin his 1st Battalion before it returned to the war zone. With that promise in his pocket, on January 9, 1943, he flew into Washington, DC, to a warm welcome from his wife, Virginia. The pair drove to their home in Saluda for a happy reunion with his two-year-old daughter, Virginia Mac, and for the next few days Puller relaxed, ate good food, and spent time with his wife and child. Neighbors shouted their greetings to the colonel as he strolled along the sidewalks with Virginia Mac and enjoyed witnessing the domestic side of a man so widely viewed only as a warrior.

Business matters intruded on their holiday, but even then, Puller tried to include his wife. He and Virginia enjoyed two weeks in a luxurious Washington hotel and ate at fine restaurants while Puller attended meetings at Marine headquarters. One evening he and his wife drove to the home of Major Otho Rogers, the officer who had been killed at Point Cruz. He extended his sympathy and consoled the widow, praising the service her late husband had given him, and then humbly accepted a box of cigars from Mrs. Rogers, who explained that not long before he died, Otho had asked her to purchase them as a Christmas gift for his colonel.

With three months of Pacific combat under his belt, Puller felt justified in pointing out a few shortcomings that had impaired operations and impeded the efforts of his men. He took advantage of a booklet printed by the War Department, a tour arranged by George Marshall, and discussions with the press to air his recommendations on how to improve those combat conditions.

At the request of General Marshall, Lieutenant Colonel Russel P. Reeder, Jr., of the Operations Division of the War Department General Staff flew to Guadalcanal before Puller's departure to obtain the views of officers and enlisted about the successes and failures of their jungle tactics against the Japanese. In his foreword to the 1943 booklet, *Fighting on Guadalcanal*, a publication printed for and restricted to servicemen, Marshall wrote that "the American Marines and Doughboys show us that the Jap is no superman. He is a tricky, vicious, and fanatical fighter. But they are beating him day after day. Theirs is a priceless record of the gallantry and resourcefulness of the American fighting man at his best." Marshall ended by urging each officer and enlisted man to read the pamphlet and learn their lessons. "We *must* cash in on the experience which these and other brave men have paid for in blood."

Marines ranking from General Vandegrift to lieutenants and sergeants contributed their thoughts. Vandegrift suggested that each marine, especially those currently in training, should "go back to the tactics of the French and Indian days," especially "the tactics and leadership of the days of Rogers' Rangers," a special scout unit organized and trained by Major Robert Rogers that fought for Great Britain in the American colonial wars. Mirroring Puller's experiences in Haiti and Nicaragua, Marshall believed that jungle warfare required combining the tactics of eighteenth-century warriors with the power provided by modern weapons.

Twenty-three pages of the sixty-nine-page booklet offered the advice of Puller and the men of the 7th Marine Regiment. Colonel Reeder interviewed Puller the day he left the hospital on Guadalcanal, and Puller, as usual, held nothing back in lengthy responses that criticized headquarters staff blunders more than it did the Japanese. "In order to get a true picture of what is going on in this heavy country," he said, "I make my staff get up where the fighting is. This Command Post business will ruin the American Army and Marines if it isn't watched." He claimed that if the platoons and squads saw their commanding officers in their midst, close to the shells and explosions, they would fight with more determination, but "as soon as you set up a Command Post, all forward movement stops."

Puller claimed that headquarters staffs were twice as large as needed. He easily made do with five staff officers, and "I could get along with less." While the Japanese operated in the jungle with superior walkie-talkies, his marines had to hope their faulty devices worked, and he asserted that communications wire should be scrapped. "To HELL with the telephone wire with advancing troops. We can't carry enough wire. We received an order. 'The advance will stop until the wire gets in.' THIS IS BACKWARDS!"

Puller selected five of his noncommissioned officers to provide comments from the enlisted men's point of view. One of the five (none were named in the booklet) explained that the Japanese "hit hell out of our points" and when the point falls, the men behind should immediately take cover. They advised that "if you shoot their [Japanese] officers, they mill about," and "when we cease firing, they cease firing. When we fire, they open up. They do this to conceal their positions."

Puller's conclusions made few new friends among headquarters staff, but their opinion mattered little to him. His message was intended to improve conditions for the privates, the sergeants, and the young officers under his command. Puller expounded these views because he considered his actions a continuation of the teaching duties he had displayed with the Gendarmerie in Haiti, the Guardia in Nicaragua, the Basic School in Philadelphia, and while training his marines in camp. Puller believed that an officer must not only lead his men into battle, but he must also teach them. Instruction first began during training, but he contended that too many officers abandoned the educational tool once training ended. At each step along the way to a battle zone, from boot camp straight to the battlefield, Puller imparted lessons. That is why Army Colonel Moore was grateful that Chesty took command of his regiment's battalion when Father Keough guided it to the perimeter in late October. In their first action, Moore's infantry learned more about combat from a marine colonel than they had from their army instructors in training camp.

Puller also took advantage of a speaking tour to spread his message. Puller was surprised when a Pentagon aide telephoned him with a request to meet the army's chief of staff, George Marshall. When he arrived, the aide explained that Marshall would like Puller to join a handful of other senior officers in a speaking tour to the nation's military camps. "The General has known you for many years and he believes that no one can do the job better than you," said the aide. He pointed to the notion held by many people in the nation that the Japanese were invincible, and Marshall hoped Puller could dispel those anxieties. Chesty, fearing that the military command would muzzle him and dictate the message they wanted, asked what Marshall wanted him to say. "The General wants the truth, Puller. There will be no wraps on you. Say what you like about command, men, performance, or anything that you think will be helpful. But the one idea he wants you to get across is that we will whip the Japanese in the end." The aide explained that Marshall had asked the Marine commandant, Lieutenant General Thomas Holcomb, to lend him Puller for six months, but Holcomb balked at keeping one of his best battalion commanders away from the combat zone that long and agreed to only three. "We know you're impatient to get back into action, but try to remember that if we don't do this job, it's going to be so much harder out there in the Pacific." Puller, confident that Marshall was a man of his word in allowing him to speak his mind, agreed.

The aide took Puller into Marshall's office, where the army chief of staff moved straight to the point. "Puller, it'll only take about ten minutes to talk to you, because there's only one thing I want you to get over with to the army. The army people believe that the Germans and Japanese are invincible. What are your ideas on it?"

"Well, I don't know anything about the Germans," Chesty replied. "But from my opinion the Japanese are just a little bunch of yellow sons of bitches, and any American can lick three of them if you give them a half a chance."

"That's exactly what I want you to get over to them," said the general.

Puller embarked on what he described as a three-month

"Chatauqua trip to every division that they had and all their schools here in the United States." He visited training centers throughout the nation, telling audiences about Sergeant Raysbrook at Point Cruz and John Basilone at the perimeter, always putting the focus where he thought it belonged—on his men, not on himself. He explained to young soldiers soon to head to the Pacific to face the Japanese that "they're not supermen, and we can whip hell out of 'em, and you'll be helping to do it soon, I suppose. If you take your training seriously there's nothing to worry about. But you'll have to be hard—and you can be hard when you write to your families, too. Try to convince 'em we're in a war to the finish, and that all these [labor] strikes and softness and confusion will have to go."

Giving the impetuous Puller free rein to speak on any issue all but assured fireworks. At a press conference arranged by the Navy Department on January 22, Puller claimed that the marines had so thoroughly checked the Japanese offensive at Guadalcanal that, if the commanding officer on the island staged a full-scale offensive, the enemy could be defeated in ten days. "Of course," he said, "I can't say what the plans of the commanding general down there now are, but I believe that in a ten-day operation, using the available men there, we could clean the Japanese out."

A reporter covering the press conference portrayed Puller as a man "with a ready smile" and soft voice. "Tanned and rugged in appearance, although he was wounded seven times in a single battle," according to the reporter, Puller never once mentioned his own injuries but shined a light on the bravery of his men. He also boasted that his battalion had been out of battle long enough and is ready to transport "anywhere they want us to go ahead."

The reporter ended his article by describing Puller's reaction on Guadalcanal when a doctor tried to pin a casualty tag on him and suggest he be taken off the field of battle. "Colonel Puller rose from his foxhole," related the reporter. "There were blood-soaked bandages on his arm, leg and foot." In a voice that had lost none of its vigor, Puller said, "Evacuate me, hell! Take that tag and label a bottle with it. I will remain in command." Undoubtedly Chesty used more profane words than the reporter was permitted to print, but newspapers around the nation ran the article, which helped spread the image of Puller as a fearsome warrior who could lead men to victory against any foe.

His March address to the 1st Cavalry Division at Fort Bliss in El Paso, Texas, typified Puller's message at each stop. "Before the assembled Cavalry Division in Howze Stadium at Fort Bliss Saturday afternoon," an *El Paso Times* article began, "a Marine Corps lieutenant colonel, veteran and hero of Guadalcanal, exploded the myth that the Jap soldier is a 'superman' with the unequivocal statement that 'he is not only stupid, but is mentally and physically inferior to the American.'"

The article explained that General Vandegrift had recommended Puller for a Medal of Honor for his stirring defense of Henderson Field, and in introducing Puller, Major General Innis P. Swift, commanding officer of the division, said, "Colonel Puller looks tough, talks tough, acts tough and is tough. And he just told me that he wanted to get back to his outfit as quickly as possible as there was only one person he hated worse than a Jap and that was a blankety blank 'gold brick.'"

In his talk, Puller said that Americans should expect a long war that demanded sacrifice and loss, and cautioned the young soldiers before him that to defeat the Japanese, they would have to develop a killer instinct. "Our enemies do not know the meaning of the words 'chivalry' and 'sportsmanship,'" Chesty emphasized. "They are out to kill, to exterminate, to annihilate, by any manner or methods. We must remember that, too. If we do not learn to hate, and to kill, well, it will just be too bad."

He did not shrink from criticizing conditions even when addressing the men responsible for creating those circumstances. To a group from the War Production Board in Washington, DC, tasked with collecting and sending equipment to the soldiers on the front line, he moved directly to his point. "I want to ask you why American troops shouldn't have the world's best fighting equipment." He mentioned that when his men's trenching shovels broke at Guadalcanal, they grabbed Japanese shovels from enemy bivouac areas or battlefields because the Japanese version was more reliable. Puller told the audience that he discarded his field glasses because they were "not worth a damn in the tropics. They fog up because they are improperly sealed, and once they get damp, they're done for."

He repeated his concerns about staff officers lacking combat experience who issued unrealistic orders, and said the Corps must not be too proud to learn from their mistakes. When asked by the Marine commandant, General Holcomb, about Raider battalions, he replied that they were superfluous and no better than an ordinary marine battalion. "I must be getting old," whispered Holcomb to another officer upon hearing the blunt assessment. "I ought to know better than ask Puller a question like that."

The tour was a success. Military audiences loved the no-nonsense talk from a battalion commander who, because he had confronted an enemy they would soon face, had much wisdom to impart. He inspired those young soldiers, much as did the fabled football coaches, from Knute Rockne at Notre Dame to Stanford's Pop Warner. As General Marshall had asked, wherever he spoke Puller was able to puncture the myth of Japanese superiority and provide a realistic picture of the fighting in the Pacific. On a more personal level, the tour had the added benefit of cementing Chesty's heroic reputation among the American public.

George Marshall admitted as much in a thank-you letter to the Marine colonel. "You were given a very heavy and tiring schedule," Marshall wrote, "but reports from every organization you visited indicate that your inspirational talks and first-hand information which you have brought from actual combat with the Japanese have been of tremendous value in preparing our soldiers for the type of enemy they will soon face. Undoubtedly you have saved the lives of a good many soldiers and have given the veteran's touch to some of our training. I am sure every soldier is grateful."

Puller disrupted norms at home much as he had against the Japanese on Guadalcanal or during his time in the 1920s and 1930s while fighting rebels in Haiti and Nicaragua. His remarks to young soldiers around the country conveyed Marshall's messages, but he also proved effective when speaking from the heart in question-and-answer sessions with the press or when queried by personnel at the Navy Department. As General Holcomb recognized, Puller never hesitated to step on toes when necessary, especially when it involved fighting for better equipment for his marines or educating military trainees in what to expect from the combat zone. At home or on the battlefield, Chesty Puller fought for his men.

———

Less than three weeks after his presentation in El Paso, Puller again said goodbye to his family and boarded a plane for the long journey back to the combat zone. Puller the family man now shrank to the background and yielded center stage to Puller the combat leader.

Conditions in the Pacific had improved while Puller was home. As he had predicted in his late January press conference that the Japanese could be defeated in ten days, the final enemy troops left Guadalcanal two weeks after he uttered those prophetic words. In early March more than 150 American and Australian bombers and fighters attacked a Japanese convoy in the Bismarck Sea north of New Guinea as it steamed toward Lae with 9,000 reinforcements and supplies for Japanese units fighting on New Guinea. The loss of eight transports and four escorting destroyers, as well as the deaths of almost 3,000 sorely needed reinforcements, hamstrung the Japanese effort on New Guinea.

While Puller had been vacationing with his family and completing General Marshall's tour, Halsey had begun the slow march up the Solomon Islands chain from Guadalcanal. Using Henderson Field as a base from which to drive north, Halsey gathered men, war materiel, and ships for a campaign that gradually swept northwestward and eliminated Japanese concentrations on New Georgia, Kolombangara, Vella Lavella, and Bougainville before closing in on the main enemy bastion at Rabaul, located at the eastern tip of the large island of New Britain, seven hundred miles from Guadalcanal.

On New Britain's western end stood another Japanese base. The "green hell" of Cape Gloucester awaited Chesty Puller.

★ CHAPTER SIX ★

"THE JUNGLE EXPLODED IN THEIR FACES"

Cape Gloucester, April 1943–February 1944

With military action intensifying in the Pacific, Puller expected to rejoin his 1st Battalion and soon be in combat. When he instead learned that he had lost command of his battalion for a headquarters post as operations officer in charge of coordinating movements and exercises, Puller vehemently objected. His response reached a sympathetic audience, and two months later, headquarters named him the executive officer, or second in command, of the 7th Regiment. He still remained posted to staff headquarters, but since part of his duties now required him to observe units in training and maneuvers, Puller used that to spend more time with marines in the field than he did with headquarters personnel.

The shift from his battalion came with a promotion to full

colonel, but despite the elevation, Chesty considered his headquarters post a demotion. Active combat was occurring throughout the Pacific, and Puller believed that his place was at the front, not behind the lines with headquarters personnel.

"I Get Around a Little Bit"

On September 27, 1943, Puller and the regiment departed Australia for Oro Bay, New Guinea. When they arrived, they disembarked into the island's humid, sweltering climate to continue training for the upcoming marine assault against the Japanese at Cape Gloucester, New Britain.

The 7th Regiment conducted field exercises at Oro Bay on New Guinea's coast while the other marine units involved in the operation, the 1st and 5th Marine Regiments, trained at Milne Bay and at Goodenough Island off New Guinea's coast. As executive officer, Puller had a hand in outlining the training, and consequently could be in the field to observe the troops as they conducted their maneuvers.

Puller and other headquarters staff designed a rigid schedule with two main purposes—to so often repeat the maneuvers that the marines could execute their roles without thought and to develop unit cohesiveness. "They tried to teach us through constant repetition to do all the little things without thinking about them," said one marine. "Also, out of this monotonous going over and over things, you came to think nothing could go wrong. You and your buddies did it so often together that you got to have a lot of confidence in the business of doing the thing with the group, whether it was a squad, a platoon, or a company."

Chesty raced about the training area as if he were twenty years younger, ignoring the pain from the shrapnel still embedded in his leg. His jeep driver, Private Dick Rowland, a former high school football star, figured he was in for a tumultuous, and most likely dangerous, time when he applied to be Puller's permanent driver. "You don't have to take it," said Puller in an effort to give the young man a chance to back out. "Eight others before you have been killed or wounded. I get around a little bit." Rowland wanted the job, but the athletic Rowland found that he could only with effort keep up with the man double his age. "I chased him all over New Guinea and twenty-eight days on the long patrol on Cape Gloucester," said Rowland, "and him with all that shrapnel still in his leg!"

The young driver had heard tales of Puller's devotion to his Marine Corps, but Rowland was equally as impressed with the colonel's love for his wife. Rowland said that Puller, like most officers, had chances to date nurses and Red Cross ladies, but he politely declined each invitation. "He kept a picture of his wife in a little case and looked at it often," added Rowland.

Officers of Puller's stature were permitted to censor their own letters home, but Puller declined and asked a captain from the intelligence section to censor his mail as if he were reading a private's letter to his girlfriend or mother. The officer agreed, and like Rowland, was surprised to see a man with a reputation as a rough combat leader so frequently express his love to Virginia, even though he knew another officer would read it. The captain said that they "were the most sensitive loving letters that one could imagine."

————

The regiment's target for the upcoming assault, Cape Glouces-ter on the large island of New Britain, lay 200 miles northeast of the New Guinea coast. Japanese installations at Rabaul on New Britain's eastern end, with its 90,000 troops, funneled re-inforcements and supplies to the Solomons and serviced the warships that guarded the waters at the southern edge of Japan's vast expansion. Two crucial airfields 350 miles away at Cape Gloucester on the opposite end of New Britain protected Ra-baul's western flank and threatened General Douglas MacAr-thur's advance along New Guinea's northern coast. The general needed those airfields in American hands if he was to continue his steady march toward his eventual target, the Philippines.

New Britain's terrain made Guadalcanal's jungles seem tame. Towering trees one hundred feet high fashioned leafy canopies shading jungle growth so dense that marines three feet apart might not see one another. The only open terrain denting the rain forest stood at Cape Gloucester, where the Japanese had constructed two airfields on the level ground. Temperatures hovered around 100°F, and the near-daily torrential rains that deluged the island intensified in December, exactly when the marines' landing was scheduled.

Almost 11,000 Japanese troops under the command of Lieu-tenant General Yasushi Sakai defended the western sector of New Britain, with a third of them stationed at Cape Gloucester. The marine plan called for the 7th Regiment and two battalions of the 1st Marine Regiment to land on Yellow Beaches 1 and 2 at Borgen Bay, seven miles southeast of Cape Gloucester. While Puller and the 7th Marines solidified the beachhead, the 1st Regiment would swerve westward along the coast and secure the airfields. A smaller operation mounted to the southwest by the third battalion from the 1st Marines would block any Japanese attempt to move men and supplies northward to assist their comrades defending the Cape Gloucester area.

———

With training at an end and the departure date drawing near, Major Raymond Davis remained stuck at headquarters, with no prospects of being involved with the Cape Gloucester operation. His repeated attempts to land a combat post ended in frustration, and he now faced being left out of a battle in which most of his fellow officers would be involved.

On the day the marines started filing onto the transports bound for New Britain, Davis walked to the beach so he could observe the proceedings. As he shuffled along the sand, he spotted Chesty Puller overseeing his regiment and boldly walked up to the colonel. Davis had attended the Basic School in the 1930s, when Puller was such a highly regarded instructor that his students often asked Puller to keep teaching even though class had ended. Davis recalled that Chesty would walk into the classroom with his lesson plan in hand, but immediately place it on a table, pick up a cue stick to use as a pointer, and begin talking.

"They made me make up a lesson plan," Puller would say, "but we are going to talk about the real things. We are going to talk about the fighting, the war." Chesty shared stories of the battles in Haiti and explained the lessons he absorbed in Nicaragua. He dissected the tactics that worked and those that failed, and highlighted those battlefield moments during which soldiers either met the challenge or crumbled under the pressure.

Davis loved learning from Puller at the Basic School, but he also discovered that Chesty excelled as an instructor outside the classroom as well. During Puller's time aboard *Augusta* as commander of the marine detachment, Davis served nearby in a similar detachment aboard the USS *Portland*, then also posted to the Far East. Puller enjoyed the reputation for having the best unit in service, and when Davis met Puller on liberty a few times, he made certain to ask for advice. "It's been years since we had a war," Puller said in one chat. "Might be years before another, so you are being judged in your peacetime roles—perfection in drill, in dress, in bearing, in demeanor, shooting, self-improvement. But more than anything else, by the performance of your Marines." Davis admired Puller's emphasis that no matter what one did, one should strive for perfection. He told Davis, "Every waking hour Marines are to be schooled and trained, challenged and tested, corrected and encouraged, with perfection as the goal."

With that shared background, Davis figured he had nothing to lose in now approaching Puller to complain that on the eve of the Cape Gloucester operation, he was about to be left behind when everyone else he knew headed to battle. He gambled that Chesty would be impressed with Davis's desire to be in the fight and hoped that their times together in Basic School and on liberty would help smooth the way.

He was right. When he explained his predicament, Puller immediately replied, "It's a hell of a note when a man wants to go to war and no one will let him. Get in that ship over there!" Davis happily assented and became a part of the assault.

———

While loved ones back home celebrated a day devoted to peace and family, on Christmas morning Rear Admiral Daniel E. Barbey led the invasion convoy out of New Guinea's Buna Harbor, 200 miles south of Cape Gloucester. Due to the stifling heat belowdecks, men slept topside as the convoy steamed northward toward its destination. A marine who enjoyed a civilian career as a vaudevillian singer tried to lead others in Christmas carols, but his attempt failed when the religious tunes touched too close to home. He adapted by turning to the popular song, "Pistol-Packin' Mama," recorded three months before by crooner Bing Crosby and the Andrews Sisters, and soon had the throng of marines joining in.

The singing helped take their minds off the coming assault, but no one could block out every troubling notion. The Japanese added to the tension by taunting over the radio their knowledge of the marine operation and vowing to annihilate the invaders. "Our soldiers are fully prepared to repulse this insolent attempt," announced Radio Tokyo. "The jungles will run red with the blood of the butchers of Guadalcanal."

That night the convoy passed through Vitiaz Strait separating New Guinea and New Britain and swung around Rooke and Sakar Islands to approach Cape Gloucester from the northwest. Before dawn of December 26, the ships bearing the single battalion of the 1st Marines broke away for its smaller attack to the southwest.

Shortly before daybreak, the main force carrying the bulk of the 7th Marines steamed east of Cape Gloucester toward the landing areas. Puller watched two cruisers and eight destroyers open the operation with a thunderous bombardment, after which army Liberator bombers droned above to blast Japanese defensive positions near the airfield. Some of the inexperienced marines thought that no one could live through that one-two punch, but Puller and the battle-hardened men knew better.

"Make 'Em Scramble"

When the bombardment halted at 7:45, and landing boats packed with marine riflemen churned shoreward, masked by the smoke created by their naval and army cohorts, marine combat correspondent Samuel Stavisky huddled in his landing craft as it plowed toward the beach. He could not help but think of Tarawa where, a month earlier, Japanese artillery, mortars, and machine guns had slaughtered hundreds of marines as they landed on the tiny Pacific islet, but at Cape Gloucester he splashed ashore without any Japanese resistance. Whether the lack of a shoreline defense resulted from an effective bombardment of Japanese positions or was part of an overall enemy plan mattered little to the correspondent. He was alive and had avoided a repeat of the Tarawa bloodbath. "I breathed an audible sigh of relief," wrote Stavisky, "and I could hear 'Thank God!' ringing in my ears from dozens of tightened lips around me when we jumped off the launches onto the strip of beach." In twenty minutes, landing craft placed ashore all three battalions of the 7th Marines.

They had arrived unopposed because Major General Hori Matsuda, the commander of the ground forces on New Britain, never dreamed the Americans would land where they chose. The narrow beaches, only six feet wide on average, led directly into impenetrable jungle and swampland so miserable that neither man nor machine could move without great effort. Matsuda, expecting the enemy to skirt the soggy terrain, had deployed his forces on both flanks of the swamps, and while the marine landing placed Puller's 7th Marines in the correct spot to drive a wedge between the two enemy concentrations, they would have to operate in nightmarish territory.

The marine advance bogged down as soon as they crossed the six feet of sand and disappeared into Cape Gloucester's rain forest and swamp. One company commander had to abandon his jeep when it became hopelessly mired, and trees felled by the pre-invasion bombardment stitched a crisscross pattern impeding their path.

Disappointed that he was not among the initial assault units, Puller at least had the chance to talk to his former battalion before they left the transport. He instructed them that as soon as they hit the beach, they needed to quickly exit the amtrac and assault their first day's objective—Target Hill 600 yards to their right—before the enemy had a chance to react from the bombardment. "As soon as the bombardment lifts," Chesty said, "make 'em scramble."

The battalion did just as Puller ordered, moving inland and

brushing through Japanese fire on both flanks to swerve east toward Target Hill, a 450-foot mound with a commanding view of the landing beaches. They destroyed two enemy guns but encountered a surprise obstacle when, according to Stavisky, they moved "into an unexpected, unmapped swamp that reached to our ankles, then rose to our knees and higher, while we struggled to keep our weapons high, dry, and ready to fire."

Areas that maps had mislabeled as "damp flat" were in reality marshes so deep that some men caustically commented that it was "damp up to your neck." Submerged logs and tree limbs tripped men and twisted their ankles, and marines who stumbled into invisible sinkholes had to be helped out by their buddies. Machete-wielding marines hacked their way through the thick underbrush, and while they encountered only sporadic fire, they suffered their first casualty when one of the enormous trees, its roots weakened from the bombardment, crashed down and killed a marine. After the incident, Puller's men nicknamed the trees "widow-makers" because of the lives lost from similar mishaps. Despite the grueling conditions, however, by noon the battalion had secured Target Hill.

Even though amtracs struggled to maintain a flow of supplies across the swamp, by dusk the 7th Marines had established a perimeter only a mile wide and nine hundred yards deep, while their companion battalions from the 1st Marines had landed to their rear and were steadily advancing west along a coastal road toward the airfield. The first day cost the marines twenty-one killed and twenty-three wounded, mostly to the troops battling along the coastal road, but the navy absorbed higher casualties when Japanese dive bombers from Rabaul sank the destroyer

USS *Brownson* (DD-518), killing 108 officers and men. The lack of concentrated enemy opposition facing the marines that day proved to be an ill predictor of what would soon unfold.

One of New Britain's trademark torrential rainstorms swept in from the Bismarck Sea that afternoon. Brisk winds lasting into the night toppled trees, and lightning painted a ghastly hue over the swampy terrain. General Matsuda organized a night-time banzai charge at marine lines, but he underestimated marine strength and threw only 1,000 men against the numerically superior marines.

In the rain and wind, Major Shinichi Takabe's 2nd Battalion, 53rd Infantry charged the perimeter's center, manned by Lieutenant Colonel Odell Conoley's 2nd Battalion. Lightning blinded men and wind whipped rain into their faces, forcing marines to fire randomly into the dark at where they hoped the enemy would be, and so much rain gushed into their foxholes that marines moved out when water levels rose to uncomfortable depths. "It was a choice of drowning or getting shot," said Colonel Conoley of the bizarre night.

A regiment's executive officer normally remains behind the lines with staff personnel, but Puller's superior, Colonel Julian N. Frisbie, gave Chesty free rein to prioritize his duties, almost assuring his frequent absence at headquarters. Puller often visited the front, checking on defensive positions and seeing that supplies reached the men doing the fighting. During the banzai charge, Puller returned to headquarters, only to strip it of non-essential personnel to carry ammunition through the swamp and remain on the line to help throw back the enemy assault.

The nightlong fighting ended at dawn when Matsuda's men withdrew, leaving 200 dead on the field.

Combat in the first week at Cape Gloucester settled into a numbing sameness. Morning mists brought a suffocating heat made more intense by the looming trees' interlocking branches, which trapped the air and allowed only the dimmest of light and breezes to penetrate. Monsoon rains flooded the swamps, creating quagmires that clutched men and vehicles and hampered resupply efforts. Socks rotted within a week, wallets molded, and watches and pocketknives rusted. Soggy uniforms never dried, further burdening men laboring under the weight of their equipment. Rations turned to mush, and if marines wanted to protect cherished items such as letters from girlfriends and family from dissolving, they placed them in prophylactics and knotted them at the end to make them watertight. Even sparse breaks in the rain brought no relief, as water from prior downpours dripped on them from a thousand branches above. One marine wrote in his diary, "It had rained very hard all night. At times it seemed as though a solid sheet of water was descending." Adding insult to injury, a December 28 earthquake shook the Cape Gloucester area.

The 1st Marine Regiment progressed along the coastal road heading to the airfields, but conditions inland, where the Japanese staged daily attacks on the 7th Marines in the miserable terrain and weather, impeded every step taken by the regiment. The marines moved ahead a few yards at a time, battling the enemy as well as nature as they fought to gain ground.

At one stage of the fighting Frisbie, concerned with a gap in his regiment's line, dispatched Puller to fill the 1,000-yard space between the 1st and 2nd Battalions. When he arrived, Chesty ignored the hazards from enemy fire to inspect the entire open stretch before realigning the battalions and closing the gap.

The first time Private Rowland, Puller's driver, accompanied Chesty on a tour of the front lines, a Japanese machine gun opened fire at them. Rowland dropped to the ground, but Puller stood erect, as if he walked and talked in a protective bubble. "I hit the deck and looked up to see him looking down at me," he said of Puller. "He told me never to do that again. He said I could scare half the men on the line, and they were spooky enough without me helping." Rowland had reacted the same way Puller had in his first action in Haiti, when Sergeant Major Lyautey had cautioned the young officer that if he wanted to gain his men's trust, he must never flinch under fire. Puller had remembered that advice and now, as he had done with actions in the early days at Guadalcanal, passed it along with words to Rowland the same way Lyautey had done with him.

Each night the men waited in their foxholes, hoping that additional banzai charges would not occur and praying to escape injury from one of the frequent Japanese air raids. Puller barely avoided serious injury on December 30 when a bomb from an enemy aircraft smashed into the regiment's command post, killing four of the staff and wounding another seven.

While the Japanese, the terrain, and the weather conspired to block Puller's men, the units along the coastal road, supported by a group of Sherman tanks, wore down opposition blocking their path to the airfields. They overran the main enemy line on

December 28 and within two days had pushed on to seize both airfields.

The 7th Marines had cleared Cape Gloucester's coastal areas, but the regiment still had to pry the Japanese from their jungle bunkers to the south and seize control of the inland areas if the airfields were to be secure from attacks from that region. That mission would bring the marines, and Puller, into contact with a river and a ridge made infamous for their horrors.

"Their Blood Kept Flowing into Our Faces"

Once the Marines established a defensive line protecting the Cape Gloucester area, senior commanders turned to clearing two ridges overlooking the eastern portion of their perimeter. To secure their lines and ensure that they possessed a base from which to expand operations inland and to the west, marines needed to first sweep Japanese forces off Aogiri Ridge, and then advance to Hill 660 and grab control of that elevation. Intelligence, however, had failed to discover the presence of a narrow stream that would impede their progress and pose a grave risk to their success. That the marines afterward labeled this stream Suicide Creek indicates the price they paid to snatch that natural barrier from the Japanese.

At first glance, the creek one mile northwest of Target Hill hardly seemed like a formidable obstacle, no more a threat than any of the other lazy rivulets intersecting the jungle beyond the beaches. "The creek is swift, two or three feet deep, perhaps

CHESTY PULLER

twenty feet across at the widest, twisting between steep banks,"
wrote Asa Bordages, a newspaper correspondent who accompanied the marines on this assault. "It flows over rocks that make
footing difficult, and here and there a tree has fallen into the
stream. The banks rise steeply from ten to twenty feet, up to
little ridges in the jungle."

At midmorning on January 2, 1944, two battalions from Puller's 7th Marines joined another from the 5th Marines and
plunged deep into the jungle toward the creek and Aogiri Ridge.
The jungle vegetation hampered their route to the stream, but
they expected to easily ford it and advance 1,200 yards to engage the Japanese.

While the marines closed in on Suicide Creek, across the
water a crack battalion under Major Shinichi Takabe dug in
along the stream to prevent the Americans from breaking
through to the ridges beyond. They burrowed into bunkers and
foxholes so thickly camouflaged by jungle vines and branches
that unsuspecting marines would walk straight into a trap. "All
the Japs had to do was wait in hidden pillboxes so well camouflaged you might walk over them without knowing they were
there," wrote Bordages. At the appropriate time, they could
open fire at the marines from point-blank range and "cut them
up without the Marines ever seeing a target to shoot at." Hundreds of fields of fire, designed to slaughter their foe as they
waded across, crisscrossed the stream, which in effect formed a
moat protecting the Japanese defenders entrenched on the
other bank and beyond to Aogiri Ridge.

Cautious marine scouts posted in front of the column approached the gurgling sounds of the stream's fast-moving

178

waters. Immediately behind, communications crews strung wire connecting the front area with the command post, while marine infantry tightened their grips on rifles and scanned the jungle for telltale signs of the enemy.

Lead scouts reached the near bank of Suicide Creek in early afternoon. Twenty-five feet of water, containing hundreds of treacherous, slippery rocks, separated them from the far side, but they crossed without incident and signaled the main body to follow. When the first elements had joined the scouts and began climbing the steep bank on the other side, Japanese fire ripped through their ranks. "Then they got it," wrote correspondent Bordages. "The jungle exploded in their faces."

Snipers, many using rifles with scopes, took a heavy toll in the opening moments. Marines fell to the ground or slumped lower into the water, firing at invisible targets they could only locate from the crack of rifles and the staccato bursts of machine guns. Gunnery Sergeant Thurman Miller saw a massacre unfolding but felt helpless against the bullets slicing through the air. "When we reached the creek, one by one marines began sliding down the banks, their rifles held high over their heads. One by one they were picked off by snipers." Platoon Sergeant Jack Buckley started out with a group of thirty-nine men, but after an hour of fighting, only nine remained.

The stream so narrowed in some spots that marine mortar shells exploding on the enemy showered shrapnel back into marine lines. Survivors retreated across the stream, dragging their wounded buddies with them, as other marines maintained a covering fire against targets they could not see.

A few men on the bank rushed into the creek to grab fallen

buddies, only to be killed by a sniper. Some of the wounded lay in the water, battling the swift current to avoid being swept downstream while hoping that an enemy bullet did not finish them. Other clusters of marines angled sideways along the creek to uncover a weak point through which to cross, but each time murderous Japanese fire turned them back. A gruesome four-step pattern appeared throughout the long day—a group of marines advanced into the stream, came under heavy fire, retreated, and probed for another location. One platoon crossed the stream three times that day but pulled back without seeing the Japanese who had so lethally blocked their way. Some marines purposely waded into the water and drew machine-gun fire to provide a target for their buddies hidden on the bank behind, and while here and there a few men reached the far side, as Bordages said, they then engaged in hand-to-hand combat, fighting "one by one in desperate little battles."

Anxious to be with the troops, Puller felt underused and out of place at headquarters. He pestered Frisbie for permission to take charge of a unit at the front, but his commander felt Puller was too valuable to take that risk. Even then, Puller found ways to join the action. "He could not stand it when Colonel Frisbie would make him stay in the command post," said Dick Rowland, "and every chance he had, off we would go, checking the line companies."

On one of those trips to the front, Puller arranged for half-tracks to bring supplies to the 3rd Battalion, and he noticed that many of the wounded and dead had been shot through the head and chest. "Most wounded, you see, are shot through the leg—lower part of the body," he later said. "Well I wondered why so many of our Marines were killed and badly wounded by being shot through the head and chest. When we finally picked up our marbles and went forward, practically all the Japanese had telescopic sights on their rifles."

When he thought that K Company, in particular, lacked aggression along the creek, Puller lingered awhile with the unit to inject some fighting spirit. In midafternoon Puller returned to the regimental command post, but shortly afterward Frisbie, upset with the same company, ordered Puller to race back and take any necessary steps to invigorate K Company. When Chesty arrived, he relieved its commander and remained with the company until he was certain that the executive officer had matters in hand.

With dusk, the marines dug in, waited for the inevitable counterattack, and hoped to wrest control of Suicide Creek from the Japanese the next day. After resorting to hand-to-hand combat to repulse a charge from fifty Japanese, they settled in for the night.

After an uneasy night at the front lines, shortly before dawn on January 3, marine platoons again tried to cross the barrier, but each time enemy snipers, machine-gun fire, and mortars threw them back. Snipers forced one group of marines to seek shelter in water up to their necks, and one marine, hit multiple times, cried for help, but no one was able to reach him. Sherman tanks moving up from the beach might have tipped the scales in favor of the Americans, but the lumbering vehicles had to wait for engineers to lay down logs to fashion a "corduroy road" before they could progress through the swampy terrain.

Asa Bordages saw bullets zip barely over prone bodies as

marines rolled down the banks or crawled on their stomachs. Once back in the water, the marines squatted low to make a smaller target and inched back to friendly lines. Some, Bordages noticed, pressed themselves against the far bank, hugging the ground to avoid the bullets that kicked up the dirt about them. Wounded marines in the creek cried for help, but every time a buddy tried to reach them, enemy fire drove him back. One wounded marine haunted a sergeant named Wills. "He was calling me, and I couldn't help him. All of them were guys we knew, but we couldn't do a thing. We had to lay in the water and listen to them." He added, "Their blood kept flowing into our faces."

A veteran of Guadalcanal, Staff Sergeant Kerry Lane, believed he had seen the worst during the fall 1942 defense of Henderson Field, but he now realized that it had been a meek foreshadow to Suicide Creek. "Marines who fought at Guadalcanal thought they had seen every imaginable horror of war," wrote Lane. "But we watched the Battle of Suicide Creek unfold with disbelieving eyes" as buddies slumped in the water, bullets shredded vines and branches, and the shriek of mortar shells and rhythmic fire of machine guns masked the moans of the wounded. "Blood flowed as copiously as the rain, turning the jungle floor into slimy mud littered with the bodies of the dead and wounded Marines, who were trampled by men fighting for their lives."

An impatient Frisbie, upset with a second day of stalemate along the creek, again dispatched Puller to the 3rd Battalion with orders to prod the unit into action. His presence at the stream stabilized the weary marines, who were bolstered with the knowledge that Chesty had a knack for salvaging victory out of hopeless situations, and figured that if anyone could lead the marines successfully across Suicide Creek and start them on their way to Aogiri Ridge, it was the forty-five-year-old veteran. Upon arriving, Puller called headquarters to request bulldozers to flatten the creek's banks and allow tanks and men to reach the other side, and then passed word to everyone in the battalion that they should prepare for an attack early the next morning. "We have enough power here to drive," he asserted, "and we are going to drive."

Engineers completed the corduroy road, which opened a path for the tanks Chesty needed to reach the front lines, but the armored vehicles were unable to navigate the steep banks. To create a level path upon which the tanks could cross to the Japanese side, Chesty ordered his bulldozer forward to scrape dirt from the banks and shove it into the water. As Puller directed the operation, marines maintained a covering fire to safeguard their exposed commander as well as the bulldozer driver, Corporal John E. Capito, operating in his exposed seat. Capito nudged dirt into the creek to level a twelve-foot-high bank, but within a few minutes a Japanese bullet smashed into the corporal's teeth and knocked him out of the battle. "He sat up in the open like a shooting-gallery target for all the enemy's fire," wrote correspondent Bordages of the heroic scene. Staff Sergeant Lane jumped into the seat to continue the operation, but a bullet felled him as well. Finally, Private First Class Randall Johnson crept forward, hugged the water, and kept the bulldozer between him and the Japanese as he operated it by moving the controls with a shovel and an axe handle. His actions enabled three tanks to cross to the Japanese side, where they used their cannon to demolish log-and-earthen bunkers while marines reduced the smaller pillboxes and foxholes.

The next morning Colonel Frisbie took more drastic action by relieving the battalion commander, Lieutenant Colonel William Williams, and putting Puller in temporary command. Puller arranged a meeting with his company commanders to let them know they would waste no time in hitting the enemy. When one officer objected that they required additional tanks to support the effort, Puller reminded him that as marines, all they needed were rifles, grenades, and bayonets to attack the Japanese.

After a fifteen-minute artillery bombardment, at 8:00 a.m. Puller's men, behind the tanks and two half-tracks, crossed Suicide Creek and disappeared into the Japanese-dominated jungle. Obliterating pillboxes and bunkers along the way, and spurred on by Puller, by nightfall the battalion had moved forward 1,000 yards.

During the fighting, an amtrac lumbered up with hot coffee for Puller and the officers, but he refused the treat until his men had been taken care of. "If that S.O.B. can get that up here to me," Chesty exploded, "he can get a hot meal up to these troops!" He handed the coffee container to marines nearby, and then ordered the battalion rear echelon to transport hot coffee and chow in time for the men to enjoy something in the morning.

Two days of bitter combat ended with forty marines killed and two hundred wounded, but Puller had helped clear the path to the southeast. Aogiri Ridge waited beyond, but it was now defended by Matsuda's weakened units. Puller's performance again illustrated the difference a commander can make to a battle's outcome. Under Williams's direction, the 3rd Battalion had underperformed and yielded the initiative to the enemy, but once "the famous Chesty Puller," as one marine called him, arrived with his bulldog demeanor, during the two days he helmed the battalion he imparted fresh vigor into the unit. His actions provided further evidence that Puller performed best when leading a frontline company or battalion in combat rather than wasting his time at headquarters.

After the battle ended Staff Sergeant Lane, whom Puller watched leap onto the bulldozer and operate it until a bullet ended his day, collapsed from exhaustion and loss of blood. As stretcher-bearers took Lane to the rear, Puller halted them and told the corpsman, "Take good care of this sergeant. He's one hell of a Marine!" Word of that small token of appreciation spread throughout the battalion, adding yet another reason why the marines so respected the officer.

In the battle at the aptly nicknamed Suicide Creek, men had fought and died to traverse a distance in the jungle that, according to correspondent Bordages, "a man might stroll in an hour. It was on Cape Gloucester, New Britain Island. It may not have been as bad as the later battle of Iwo [Jima] but it was worse than the worst of Guadalcanal." Platoon Sergeant St. Elmo Murray Haney, a longtime veteran who had served with the same regiment in World War I and fought at Belleau Wood, said, "I never saw anything worse than this." Younger marines, offering their own descriptions of the battle, told the correspondent that while Guadalcanal was a place they would like to forget, "This time we bought a corner lot in hell."

"Every Foxhole Was a Battle to the Death"

Aogiri Ridge stood only 1,200 yards southeast of Suicide Creek, but the march through Cape Gloucester's jungle, terrain, weather, and Japanese defenders seemed like miles. Rains saturated them every step of the way, torrents that Bordages compared to "savage, slashing, torrential rain that struck hard enough to hurt. If you faced it, it made you gasp." Men fought in mud above their knees, and in the blinding rain they could not hear shouts from the man next to them. "They were wet, chilled through, twenty-four hours a day," wrote Bordages, "every day."

According to marine correspondent Stavisky, monsoon winds toppled trees "as if they were bowling pins, maiming and killing a number of marines. We were deluged by torrents of water. Our foxholes, dumps, emplacements were swamped." With no way to keep dry, "we did what we could to cover ourselves but were wet most of the time, and had to put up with it, officers and men alike."

Wet, and alone. A marine said that after he walked ten paces, he turned to speak to his buddy, but he could not see him because of the thick vegetation. If the jungle could so suddenly swallow a marine, men wondered how many Japanese might be hidden only yards away. "Ah, I can tell you," the marine said, "it was a very small war and a very lonely business."

If the enemy did not get them, Cape Gloucester's insects and animal life might. Large black mosquitoes plagued them each step of the way, and ants swarmed over marine boots and pants. Nine-foot pythons, centipedes, and enormous spiders infested their jungle route.

The Japanese needed to hold Aogiri Ridge to control northwest New Britain because the ridge protected their main supply route, a path called Government Trail. The two-hundred-yard-long ridge looked hardly menacing, small enough that it did not even appear on marine maps. The ground gradually rose from its base until fifty feet from the top, where it angled sharply to the crest, but every yard offered another piece of an intricate collection of bunkers and gun positions.

For two days, marine units probed through dense jungle hiding enemy machine-gun nests. Chesty assumed temporary command of the 3rd Battalion, 5th Marine Regiment, when both its commanding officer and executive officer were wounded, comforting news to marines who had just lost their top two commanders. "He loved the Marine Corps, he loved the 1st Division, and he loved the enlisted," wrote Gunnery Sergeant Thurman Miller. "He was one of us, and our morale lifted somewhat."

A permanent commander, Lieutenant Colonel Lewis W. Walt, arrived on January 8, but any unease the men felt by losing Puller dissipated when they learned he was another version of Chesty. Asa Bordages wrote that the marines who had already fought with the thirty-year-old Walt emphasized that "when Walt attacks, he attacks with everything he's got—including himself."

Walt first queried Puller for an update. As they talked, enemy bullets from what appeared to be the base of a heavily defended hill shredded the foliage near them. Walt sent patrols, including one with Puller at the helm, around the left flank to locate a way up, but the Japanese checked every move and forced Walt to dig in for the night after taking heavy casualties.

Along with Puller's 7th Marines, Walt moved forward the next day. Cleverly concealed, the Japanese, including veteran soldiers who had defeated American infantry in Bataan, forced the marines to battle for every yard in the thick jungle. When a young officer complained that his weary men could not continue, Walt ordered him to either advance or he would relieve the man. Fighting in front of enemy foxholes and bunkers included hand-to-hand contests, causing Bordages to conclude that "every foxhole was a battle to the death." In some, Bordages inferred from the body positions that both the marine and his Japanese opponent had bayoneted the other to death.

The battle's tide turned when Walt and his men managed to push a 37mm antitank gun to the summit. Marines behind bushes and trees mounted a thick covering fire to pin down the Japanese while their buddies slowly nudged the gun upward. Noticing his men struggling to advance the weighty weapon up the slippery hill, Walt said to his runner, Corporal Lawrence H. Larson, "Come on, Larson. Let's lend a hand." By evening, Walt's men stood atop Aogiri Ridge, where they dug in and prepared for the inevitable nighttime banzai.

The first of five attempts came shortly after midnight. Shouting "Marines, you die!" the Japanese charged toward Walt's unit, hoping to seize the deadly 37mm gun and turn it against the Americans. Walt ordered his men to hold fire until the

Japanese rushing from the reverse slope had drawn within yards of the marine line, at which time the marines opened a murderous fire that decimated the Japanese ranks.

Once again, hand-to-hand combat ensued in the dark and rain, with opposing combatants using rifles, bayonets, fists, and teeth to kill their foe. After the fourth banzai, Walt's men were almost out of ammunition, but fortunately, as the enemy prepared for a fifth attack, a detail from headquarters arrived to replenish their stores.

Walt called in artillery to break up the fifth charge. The shells first exploded 200 yards from the marine line before gradually moving closer until only fifty yards separated friendly shells from the marines. A Japanese major broke through the shell bursts, wielding a sword in one hand and a pistol in the other, and ran straight toward Walt's foxhole. Walt raised his .45 to fire at the major, but an artillery shell exploding in a tree above the Japanese officer did the job for him. "He actually died three paces from where I crouched, .45 in hand, waiting for him," said Walt afterward.

Dawn saw the Japanese retreat for good, leaving bodies littering every yard of the slope. Correspondent Bordages wrote that these young marines, from small towns and cities, mounted a noble defense at a ridge soon to be renamed Walt's Ridge, where "the conquerors of Bataan backed down before the victors of Guadalcanal."

Marines from the 7th Regiment secured the final stronghold in the vicinity of Aogiri Ridge on January 11. Behind the landform meandered the narrow road cut through the jungle to rush troops and equipment to the front. With the ridge in American hands, Puller and Walt had now denied that vital path to the Japanese.

Colonel Frisbie, impressed with Puller's work along the front lines, recommended his executive officer for the Distinguished Service Cross. Chesty had taken temporary command of two battalions and, as Frisbie's recommendation specified, "Without regard for his own personal safety, while under the fire of riflemen, machine guns, and mortars of the determined enemy in well-entrenched positions, he moved from company to company along his front lines."

Next up was Hill 660, another landform in the vicinity of Aogiri Ridge. Puller again joined the 7th Regiment before they attacked the hill, shouting encouragement and making sure they were ready. "He come down the line, walking amongst his men," said Leonard Kovar. "Wore a little old peashooter pistol on his hip. Didn't carry any other weapon. Smoked a damn pipe and chewed on it and looked at you. And everybody was Old Man. I was sitting there with some of the other guys along the trail, waiting to move up, when Puller stopped and looked at me.

"He said, 'Old Man, how you doing?' But here he was, about 50, and I'm 21.

"It's a little tough, Colonel," answered Kovar.

"It'll be all right," said Chesty. "Tomorrow we'll secure this place, and we'll go down to the airport and we'll get some tents."

The regiment's 3rd Battalion attacked the next day, but when sniper fire drove them back, Puller told Frisbie he was going to walk down to the battalion and evaluate the situation. Knowing that Puller would probably want to intervene, Frisbie warned his executive officer, "Now Lewie, remember you are no longer a battalion commander. Look in on them but don't take over." Puller agreed, but a few minutes after Chesty arrived at the front, Frisbie received a report that his second in command was already out front of the forward line, spurring the men on. One marine said that this was an example of "loyal troops rushing forward to protect their beloved commander," who "was just as wet and mud-covered as all the rest."

With the battle raging, Puller walked the length of the marine line, halting at each gun emplacement and asking how the marines were doing. At one foxhole, a frightened young marine looked up at Puller and said, "Colonel, we got to get the hell out of here." Puller asked the boy to step out of his position and walk with him a few yards to the rear. When Puller asked what was on his mind, the young man replied that he was weary from the fighting and wanted to go home. Chesty paused a few seconds and then answered. "Look, Old Man, I want to go home, too. I'm not getting any younger." Puller added that he, too, had a family at home and understood that combat offered only hardship and fighting, "but neither of us is going home until we lick these bastards. We've got to help make our folks safe back home." Those few minutes alone with a scared marine boosted the boy's spirits and enabled him to return to his position better prepared to meet the challenges to come.

The three-day assault on Hill 660, which ended in a rout of the Japanese defenders, marked the end of Japan's defense in western New Britain. Only a few scattered posts to the south existed, but here, too, Puller would play a major role.

"Puller Couldn't Sit Still"

Now that the Japanese had been pushed back from Suicide Creek, Aogiri Ridge, and Hill 660, Matsuda ordered his forces in western New Britain to pull back through the jungle and retreat east toward Rabaul on the opposite end of the island. Major General William H. Rupertus, the commander at Cape Gloucester, had the enemy on the run and only had to clean out isolated pockets of Japanese, and after studying maps, he concluded that his major effort should be made to the south, where an eighteen-mile trail led to Japanese enclaves.

Rupertus turned to his most trusted commander, Chesty Puller, who, despite constant pain from the shrapnel in his leg, had rallied marines to action in the previous encounters. Rupertus also thought that a 400-man patrol plunging deep to the south would benefit from Puller's experiences in jungle warfare and his knowledge of Japanese tactics. "I can depend on him to push the attack," Rupertus said. He ordered Puller to advance eight miles south to Agulupella, from where he was to continue along the trail to Gilnit, a village on the Itni River, which flowed toward the southern New Britain coast.

After selecting his team, Puller gathered his company officers and emphasized that he did not want to see them at the command post once they were on the trail. Their place, he asserted, was with the men on the patrol. Besides, he said, if they had a relevant reason to communicate with him, they only had to wait a short time before they would see Puller moving along the formation.

They left in three columns, each starting from a different location near the northern coast and moving inland to meet at the village of Agulupella. After converging on February 1, Puller and his company commanders finalized the plans to move twenty miles southeast to the Itni River.

Before leaving the village, Puller met Stavisky. The combat correspondent, who had arrived on Guadalcanal with Puller in September 1942, wanted to accompany this Itni patrol because, as Stavisky wrote, Chesty was "a figure of heroic proportions in the Corps." Always hunting for a good story, Stavisky believed that Puller would provide him with plenty of material. Even though as executive officer of the 7th Marines he was no longer a frontline commander, Puller "continued to insert himself into the battle lines along with, and often out in front of, the grunts. He took his command post with him, at times to the consternation of his higher command. In Puller's public opinion, there were too many officers on staff and they were too far from the action to make quick, effective responses to the changing battle conditions."

Puller had often balked at dealing with the press, whom he considered a necessary evil, but Stavisky's and other reporters' coverage on Guadalcanal, where they frequently exposed themselves to Japanese fire while working on their stories, softened Chesty's stance. He gave Stavisky free rein to interview any marine and accompany any scouting mission that occurred along the way.

Stavisky had met few officers like Chesty Puller, who, despite being middle-aged, walked with an erect posture and still maintained a slender physique on the five-foot-ten frame. "Chesty was a Marine of extraordinary strength and endurance because he never let up on his own rigorous training," Stavisky wrote. "He was easily recognized by his jutting jaw, powerful chest, and the pipe clenched in his teeth—and, close up, by searching green eyes."

According to Stavisky and others, Puller's peers called him Lewie, the enlisted men called him Chesty, and he called every enlisted marine Old Man unless angry, when he used their official designation. "Then his low voice transformed from a unique mixture of soft growl, Virginia drawl, and an outlandish Brooklynese into a blast of wrath that murdered the King's English and devastated the transgressor," wrote Stavisky.

Unlike some other officers, who sought promotions and acted as if they were better than their men, "On Guadalcanal, on Cape Gloucester, he ate the same meager meals his grunts ate, slept on the wet ground when the grunts had to, and refused comforts of any kind when his men had none," said Stavisky. Puller's whirlwind style of command impressed the correspondent, who had witnessed enough officers to know they often bunkered down behind the lines and rarely visited the men up front. "Puller couldn't sit still. He paced back and forth in his tent, pondering a problem, awaiting a report. He walked swiftly along the battalion perimeter, meticulously checking every position both day and night, once, twice, three times."

Puller led the patrol out of Agulupella and headed southeast. Since they operated a distance from the main marine force to the north, air drops supplied them along the way. Piper Cubs had earlier shuttled in smaller loads to villages dotting the trail, and during the trek, 5th Air Force B-17s dropped tons of rations and equipment to Puller's marines below. The column learned to take cover, however, when some of the crates in the first few drops smashed into their lines, with one crate demolishing Puller's empty hut.

Some at division headquarters wondered why Puller, known for his toughness, requested that the aircraft include several hundred bottles of mosquito lotion in their drops, but he had a reason for what seemed an unusual appeal. "Hell, the colonel knew what he was about," said one marine. "We were always soaked, and everything we owned was likewise, and that lotion made the best damn stuff to start a fire with that you ever saw."

The marine column killed seventy-five Japanese stragglers along the Itni River on their way to the village of Gilnit. However, they mostly came across rotting bodies or emaciated soldiers dying from a tropical disease. One officer spoke of the ever-present "stench of death" that accompanied the patrol, or as Puller more harshly summed it, "The pig-sticking was fine." Stavisky, accustomed to brutal battlefield conditions from Guadalcanal, wrote, "We kept running into Jap stragglers, and there being no request from HQ for more prisoners, they were killed in the brief encounters."

Japanese medic Ogawa Tamotsu treated many of the soldiers perishing in western New Britain. With limited medical supplies and almost no food, he felt helpless to combat the complex diseases that weakened the men already succumbing to wounds and starvation. As Puller's unit pursued him in the jungle, some of his patients, sapped from dysentery, malaria, and malnutrition, stumbled into the jungle to die alone in the wilds. Trained to treat his men, Tamotsu had no choice but to leave behind those soldiers who were unable to walk, handing them a few rations and telling them they must make it on their own. Until he exhausted his supply, for the most serious cases Tamotsu injected a shot of opium and a solution of corrosive sublimate into their veins, which caused death in a few seconds. He hated acting in this manner, but neither Puller nor the native islanders the Japanese had harshly suppressed gave them any respite. "It was a hell's march," Tamotsu said of their attempt to avoid the Americans and natives.

From Agulupella, Puller led the column over harsh terrain twenty-eight miles south to Turitei. The bank of the stream became so precipitous that engineers had to rig a line so marines could slide down to a bridge the same engineers had earlier put in. They next moved to Gilnit nine miles away, advancing cautiously along the banks of the crocodile-infested Itni River, until they came to Gilnit and set up camp. Puller ordered one of his commanders, Captain George P. Hunt, to lead a reconnaissance team into Gilnit but stipulated that Hunt, a Guadalcanal veteran, return before dark. When Hunt failed to materialize by nighttime, according to Stavisky, Puller "exploded and ordered Captain Hunt arrested for disobeying orders to return that same day. He dressed down the captain for all to hear."

After reaching Gilnit and making contact with an army patrol operating from the Cape Merkus beachhead, Puller, convinced that the southwestern region of New Britain was clear of Japanese, turned the column north for its return to Cape Gloucester. On February 16, after completing the fifteen-day patrol, Puller returned to the perimeter.

The Itni patrol marked the end of Puller's involvement at Cape Gloucester. During the campaign for New Britain, the 1st Marine Division lost 438 killed and 815 wounded, including 25 deaths caused by falling trees. Although he was present at the front lines for only a part of the operation, Puller made such an impact that he received his fourth Navy Cross. The citation commended him for his role as temporary commander of the 3rd Battalion, 7th Marines, when he "quickly reorganized and advanced the unit" to seize their objective, and of the 3rd Battalion, 5th Marines, where he "unhesitatingly exposed himself to rifle, machine-gun and mortar fire from strongly entrenched Japanese positions to move from company to company in his front lines, reorganizing and maintaining a critical position along a fire-swept ridge."

Puller feared that Cape Gloucester might be his final command. When he heard a rumor that one-third of the Guadalcanal veterans would be rotated home now that they had been in two bloody campaigns, Puller wrote the Marine commandant. He had no desire to return home until the Japanese had been defeated, and in his letter he requested that his assignment to a combat unit be extended for the duration of the Pacific fighting. Rupertus forwarded it to Washington with his approval.

Puller's actions in Cape Gloucester reaffirmed his excellence in commanding a company or battalion-sized unit. The smaller numbers of men in those components allowed him to operate closer to the marines on the front lines, where Chesty's courage and his willingness to fight at their side stiffened the men's morale and contributed to victories. His proximity to combat, which rarely occurred with senior commanders at the regimental or division level, had also eliminated some of those irritating command barriers that might have stood between Puller and his marines.

His request to remain in the fray until war's end, however, combined with his impressive Pacific record, meant that he would soon merit his own regiment. With three battalions then under his command, he would find it more difficult to leave headquarters and be up front, the most effective arena for someone as energetic as Chesty Puller. That desire to be in the middle of a fight would inevitably clash with the increased demands put on a senior commander operating in the rear.

The island of Peleliu offered more than another blood-soaked field of battle. It presented Puller with his most challenging times.

CHAPTER SEVEN

"I'M JUST A PLATOON LEADER AT HEART"

Assault at Peleliu, March–September 15, 1944

Developments moved quickly after the Itni patrol. Puller received a promotion to temporary colonel in mid-February and, more significantly, he assumed command of the 1st Marine Regiment. Puller had excelled while guiding platoons, companies, and battalions, but at this level he would now supervise a regimental headquarters section, three battalions, as well as their supporting units, more than three times the size of his largest previous command.

Some senior officers had reservations as to whether Puller could handle a military organization this size. No one doubted his effectiveness in leading smaller units, where his undisputed bravery in combat and the personal touch he brought to his command produced top-quality outfits that found ways to win. A regiment, however, required its commander to remain at headquarters, where the constant flow of information from three different battalions provided the data he needed to form educated decisions. Could Puller rein in his impulse to rush to the front, where he had always felt comfortable and had been able to rally his men, and was his bombastic style of leadership suited for the more structured, restrained role required by a regimental commander?

Brigadier General O. P. Smith, a Puller admirer and the assistant division commander of the 1st Marine Division for the upcoming assault of Peleliu, questioned whether Puller could coordinate the diverse elements comprising a regiment and feared he lacked the diplomatic skills required to work with the larger regimental staffs Chesty had always criticized. Puller's disdain for staff personnel was well documented, a point Puller loved emphasizing by tapping his uniform pockets and boasting that he carried his filing system with him.

The questions intensified before Chesty departed for Peleliu when Smith left headquarters to visit Puller's sector. When he could not locate Chesty's command post, one of Puller's battalion commanders informed Smith that Puller was near the front. Smith "went up ahead a piece, and here was Lewie with his regimental CP [command post], ahead of these two battalion CPs." Smith joined Puller and commented to his elusive officer, "Look, Lewie, you know according to the book that the regimental CP is supposed to be behind the battalion CPs."

"Yes, I know," Puller replied, "but that's the way I operate. And if I am not up here they'll say, 'Where the hell is Puller?'"

Smith concluded that he could do little to stifle Puller's enthusiasm for operating at the front but inserted Lieutenant

Colonel Richard P. Ross, Jr., a highly regarded staff officer, as Chesty's executive officer. Smith hoped that Ross could assume management of some of the administrative details and paperwork normally handled by the regimental commander.

Puller held no such doubts about his new post. He had used each stage of his career to prepare for the next step, and while he admitted his fondness for the enlisted men, he had never shied from claiming that his ultimate goal was to occupy the top Marine job. He had often remarked that since his days in Haiti, he had treated every posting as a platform to the highest command job, and in the Marine Corps, that journey ended at the commandant's house in Washington, DC, the residence for every commandant since 1806. In his view, his desire to ascend to that office was no different than a young manager who hoped to become his business's top executive.

Puller had also been dogged by a recent controversy contending that at Guadalcanal and Cape Gloucester, his aggressive command style emerged from his desire for victories, which in turn had overshadowed the welfare of his own men. He had at times irritated other commanders by asking how many Japanese they had killed, and when O. P. Smith served with Puller on a board to determine whether marines who had received letters of commendation for their heroics deserved to be upgraded to Bronze Stars, he observed that Puller invariably favored the most bellicose men. "And Lewie, of course, unless a citation was written to show that the Marine was advancing in the face of the enemy, he would have no part in giving him a Bronze Star!" said Smith.

After the war Second Lieutenant George L. Haggerty, an

officer with Puller's 1st Marine Regiment, was asked about the issue. Haggerty had often praised Chesty's ability to motivate his marines, but he hedged on this topic. Haggerty answered that Puller was interested in the safety of his men during training, but "I'll go no further than that. He believed in saving the men for battle; not in saving them from battle; saving them for battle."

The majority of marines either had no opinion or scoffed at the criticism, but the percentage of detractors increased with the ghastly number of casualties Puller's regiment was about to suffer in the ridges of Peleliu.

"KILL JAPS!"

To ensure his regiment was ready for its next action, Puller started training his men before they left Cape Gloucester, even using patrols as teaching tools to sharpen their skills. Near the end of April they left New Britain for Pavuvu, an island near Guadalcanal, where he instituted a more thorough training schedule.

No one in the regiment missed Cape Gloucester's dreary conditions, but Pavuvu was no idyllic isle either. The heat and rains were not as oppressive compared to what they had just endured on New Britain, but beyond that, the marines saw little that endeared them to the island. "Pavuvu was terrible," said Lieutenant Haggerty. "The main thing I remember about Pavuvu was the land crabs and the coconuts falling. We had several casualties from men being hit in the head with falling coconuts. We were bivouacked at a coconut plantation. We had land crabs and rats all over the place."

Puller again stood in the food line along with the enlisted and glared at any officer who attempted to cut in at the front. If a private or corporal glanced his way, surprised that a colonel stood in line behind him, he had the same ready answer. "What's the matter, son? Officers gotta eat, too."

To clean up after maneuvering for hours under the hot sun, Puller's enlisted men improvised a shower by attaching a 55-gallon drum of water to the top of a shed standing on a nearby hill. Puller made it available to every marine in the unit, and since additional water for the shower had to be painstakingly carried up the hill, each man who used it, including Chesty and every officer, was responsible for grabbing a bucket and replacing the water he had just used so that the next man could clean himself.

One day Puller watched a 2nd lieutenant step out without refilling the water supply. "Enjoy the shower, young man?" Puller asked the officer. When the lieutenant assured his commander that he had, Puller added, "Good, now get two buckets, fill them with water and take them back up the hill. And keep doing that until you've replaced all the water you just used."

In the field, Puller trained his men with the latest equipment and weaponry, but he also stressed that since the Corps' founding in 1775, marines had relied on guts and rifles. When an officer showed him the newly introduced flamethrower, for instance, Puller instinctively grasped how the weapon would benefit his regiment but asked the man, "Where's the bayonet fit on?" He was all for progress in battlefield tactics and weapons but never wanted his men to forget that success in combat boiled down to the courage and marksmanship of the individual marine.

He held evening sessions with his officers, where Puller tossed out theoretical tactical situations and asked for solutions. He reminded them that classroom knowledge often bore little resemblance to the twists and turns of battlefield events, which called for the ability to improvise and to trust in one's judgment.

As always, he emphasized that officers led from the front, in plain view of their marines, rather than issue orders from behind. He said that they might be criticized for following that advice but that he had always ignored the detractors because "I'm just a platoon leader at heart." He added that the only way a field commander could knowledgeably lead men in combat was to be in the thick of the action, where he could form conclusions based on what he observed, not on what he heard secondhand. As evidence, he turned to two of the Civil War idols, Robert E. Lee and Stonewall Jackson, whom he had read about since youth. That pair, famed for their battlefield talents, had often exposed themselves to enemy fire to better assess a situation. "I recommend it to you," Puller said. "It has nothing to do with bravery. I can feel fear as much as the next man. I just try to keep my mind on doing my duty."

One officer questioned Chesty's wisdom of stationing colonels on the front lines. When that officer argued that high-ranking commanders were more valuable to the unit than a private, Puller replied, "No officer's life is worth more than that of any man in his ranks. He may have more effect on the fighting, but if he does his duty, so far as I can see, he must be up front to see what is actually going on with his troops. They'd find a replacement for me soon enough if I got hit. I've never yet seen a Marine outfit fall apart for lack of any one man." However, Puller cautioned the young officers at Pavuvu. "I don't want you to go up under the guns just for show. It's only the idiots and the green kids who think they're bullet-proof. But if you don't show some courage, your officers won't show it either, and the kids will hang back. It's that kind of an outfit that always has trouble."

Training included a few practice landings on Cape Esperance and Koli Point, a place Puller, still pained from the shrapnel wounds, would as soon forget. The Guadalcanal locations lacked a coral reef for the marines to surmount, but the exercises provided excellent opportunities for the units to perfect their timing and smooth out any wrinkles that appeared.

His regiment enjoyed a special appearance on Pavuvu when comedian Bob Hope brought his live show to the island. For more than an hour, the songs and comedy routines made the men forget the war and all its hardships, and allowed them to be kids again. Men laughed at Hope's jokes, no matter how corny they were, and ogled the gorgeous females that were a staple of Hope's wartime shows. Puller, however, did not attend, and wrote Virginia that he was not interested in glancing at Hope's female performers when he had someone like her waiting at home.

Puller received unfortunate news on Pavuvu when he learned

that his brother, Lieutenant Colonel Samuel D. Puller, the executive officer of the 4th Marine Regiment, had been killed by machine-gun fire on July 27 during the assault on Guam. Puller deflected conversation from the topic whenever someone mentioned the loss, but he shared his feelings in a handful of letters. He wrote a friend that "my brother's death was a blow but a man has to die and he went out in a good manner and I am proud of his performance of duty."

Only a few months earlier, Puller had taken a three-day break from Pavuvu when Sam informed him he was now stationed on Guadalcanal. The brothers visited the sites of Puller's 1942 battles, both the conflicts along the Matanikau as well as where his marines had prevented the Japanese from smashing through to Henderson Field. Puller feared that the jungle's growth might have obliterated most signs of the October 1942 perimeter clash, but barbed wire and battle debris, including a few Japanese skeletons, marked the location where Chesty had so gallantly defended the airfield. Puller glanced over what remained of that battle and remarked to Sam that now, without the gunfire and explosions, the site no longer had the same effect.

On the way to Peleliu, a reporter for *Newsweek* magazine, Bill Hipple, was able to provide Puller with details of his brother's death. He told Chesty that he was standing next to Sam when his brother, without uttering a sound, had suddenly slumped dead in Hipple's arms. "He died painlessly," Hipple told Puller, "didn't even know he was hit." Hipple wrote that "this seemed to comfort Chesty, who then, with a trace of tears, removed a corncob pipe from his clenched lips and began a half-smiling reminiscence of their happy boyhood in the faraway days and hills of Virginia, and their boisterous times together as young enlisted Marines in the 1920s."

Puller never forgot Hipple's thoughtfulness in relating the story. Even though he shared only pleasant childhood memories with the correspondent, reality was a bit different. In light of their father's death, he and his brother had to lean on each other to fill the gaps left by the missing parent, not merely during their youth but as they wound through high school years and beyond as well. He was proud that Sam had achieved the high rank he enjoyed, and that if his brother had to die, it happened on the battlefield while in a marine uniform.

He also never forgot that the Japanese had killed his brother. Only days after learning of his brother's demise, Puller had two words painted on a sign that he posted near the mess tent. The words, similar to those that had been splashed across a huge sign at Tulagi by Admiral Halsey, were "KILL JAPS!"

"We'll Catch Hell Is My Guess"

The fighting on Peleliu differed from the late 1942 combat that had marked Guadalcanal when Puller's battalion and their fellow marines had fought desperate clashes that could easily have swung either way. On Peleliu, however, the Japanese battled out of desperation, trying to win violent confrontations on Pacific islands far from Japan to prevent the American intruders from continuing their high-powered march toward Tokyo.

Since the victory at Cape Gloucester, American forces had

notched additional triumphs in demolishing the Japanese defense lines. Two months after annihilating Japanese infantry on Tarawa, in January 1944 American forces invaded the Marshall Islands. Five months later another military armada assaulted Saipan in the Mariana Islands, highlighted by the "Marianas Turkey Shoot," in which American carrier aircraft splashed more than three hundred Japanese planes. Landings on Guam and Tinian in the same island chain followed the next month, while MacArthur continued to dismantle Japanese forces in New Guinea. In a stark indication to Japan that their war had taken a turn for the worse, in June American B-29 bombers conducted the first bombing of the Home Islands since the 1942 Doolittle raid when Jimmy Doolittle's bombers blasted Japanese steel factories at Yawata.

The newspaper headlines Virginia read at home had changed to reflect the promising outlook. Whereas 1942 publications had highlighted the destruction at Pearl Harbor, the American surrender in the Philippines, and the August-to-November difficulties on Guadalcanal, they now focused on Pacific victories at places American civilians could not locate without a map. Betio, Kwajalein, and Eniwetok entered the nation's vernacular, grabbing headlines alongside New Guinea and Cape Gloucester, and newspapers large and small ran stories about the U.S. Navy's newest weapon, the fast carrier task force, which combined a powerful collection of aircraft carriers and surface warships with carrier air groups able to reach targets heretofore beyond their range. Month by month the Japanese could feel the American noose tightening about their necks, and if they were to protect their homeland from total destruction, they had to somewhere halt that inexorable march across the Pacific.

———

The next American target, Peleliu is one among a string of volcanic islets comprising the Palau Islands. Six miles long and two miles wide, it rests at the chain's southern end and contained an airfield a brief distance inland from its southern beaches. Famed aviatrix Amelia Earhart was rumored to have landed on the island before mysteriously disappearing. Commanding the airfield and running two miles north stood a series of steep coral ridges called the Umurbrogol Mountains, a harsh terrain of jagged coral outcroppings that sliced clothing, scuffed boots, and bloodied anyone who tripped on its hard surface. After being instructed about those conditions, some marines thought combat on Peleliu would be similar to what combat on the moon might be like, and Peleliu reminded one marine of "a place that might have been designed by a maniacal artist given to painting mathematical abstractions—all slants, jagged, straights, steeps and sheers with no curve to soften or relieve."

Resting 430 miles east of Mindanao in the Philippines, Peleliu held strategic importance for both combatants. Japanese aircraft based on Peleliu airfields could threaten General MacArthur's upcoming Philippine invasion, but in American control, those airfields could provide aerial support for that same assault.

Three marine regiments would land on Peleliu's southern beaches. While the 7th Marines waded ashore to secure the right flank of the 1.5-mile-wide zone, the 5th Marines would hit their beaches and advance inland to seize the airfield.

Puller and his 1st Marines faced the toughest task. After landing at two beaches on the western flank, the regiment was to swing immediately left toward high ground dominating that portion of the landing zone. The task required the regiment to attack between a heavily defended coral bluff on the left and a small peninsula to their right, both from where the enemy could direct murderous enfilading fire. Rupertus purposely selected Puller for this demanding objective because he thought Chesty's hard-hitting style was the best guarantee of success against the stiffest sector facing the invasion.

Puller never shied from a tough fight, but he objected to plans that asked his regiment to land between well-entrenched Japanese forces. Headquarters dismissed his comments, however, and replied that the pre-invasion naval and air bombardment would eliminate a significant portion of the defenses facing Puller; but Chesty doubted that a three-day bombardment would inflict enough damage to adequately hamstring the Japanese.

The Japanese commander, Lieutenant General Sadae Inoue, had started fortifying the islands five months earlier. He took advantage of the coral ridges to construct elaborate caverns and tunnels protected by hundreds of sniper positions and foxholes. Interlocking fields of fire would punish the marines as they moved forward, and Inoue designed his defenses so that when marines attacked one bunker, they would come under fire from other camouflaged positions.

Openings in the terrain ranged from tiny cracks holding single Japanese defenders to 500 caves, some sizeable enough to house entire companies. The Japanese bored tunnels a few feet into the hard surface, then cut sharply to the side as a way to blunt the effects of dynamite charges and flamethrowers. Caverns up to six stories deep protected Japanese soldiers from the impact of the American bombardment and sheltered them until the marines left the beaches and headed inland. At that point the Japanese defenders, which included among its number the Manchurian Imperial Guards, who had never been defeated in battle, would man their posts and gun down the invaders.

Inoue prepared to greet the American landing with artillery and mortar fire extending from shore to a coral reef 500 yards out, and he sprinkled hundreds of wire-controlled mines beneath the surface to mutilate the marines as they waded toward land. Machine-gun positions, antitank ditches, and rifle pits cut into beaches bristling with barbed wire, while antitank and antiboat guns positioned along the northern and southern flanks provided enfilading fire.

Inadequate knowledge of Peleliu hamstrung the 1st Marine Division commander, Major General William H. Rupertus. Pete Ellis, a marine spy sent to collect information on the Palaus, had mysteriously disappeared in the 1920s, and aerial reconnaissance had revealed little due to the thick vegetation that covered much of the western side of the island, where the Umurbrogols housed the enemy's multiple caves and interconnecting tunnels.

As the invasion group steamed toward Peleliu, a major strategic alteration disrupted Rupertus's plans and diminished the significance of seizing Peleliu. Admiral Halsey, whose carrier aircraft had encountered surprisingly light opposition in attacking Mindanao, an island in the southern Philippines, recommended bypassing that island and leapfrogging directly to Leyte Island to the north. Since the main justification for invading Peleliu was to obtain an airfield to support MacArthur's attack on Mindanao, there now no longer existed a reason to seize the island, but Admiral Nimitz declined to cancel an operation that had, in effect, already begun. Since intelligence had predicted a relatively simple operation, Nimitz believed the possession of another airfield would be worth the risk. General Rupertus agreed with Nimitz and told his staff that "we're going to take some casualties, but let me assure you that this will be a short one. Rough but fast. We'll be finished in three days. It might only take two."

Puller did not buy it. The Japanese had inflicted severe losses on marines invading other Pacific islands, and he expected the same here. He told First Lieutenant Frank Sheppard, a platoon leader, "We'll catch hell is my guess. One of these days we're going to be caught on an amphibious operation and be driven into the sea."

The Japanese had no intention of driving them into the sea, for they had changed their defensive tactics since earlier in the war. Instead of destroying the Americans at the shore, they planned to delay them at the beaches as long as possible, then allow them to move inland, where prepared defenses in the Umurbrogols waited with the major response.

Inoue instructed his 11,000 men, many of them veterans of combat in China, that if the Americans outflanked their positions, they were no longer to commit suicide, as had been the case in prior confrontations, but to remain hidden until the enemy passed by, then emerge and kill their foe from behind. That defensive strategy perfectly suited Peleliu's harsh coral terrain and set the stage for another bloody contest on a Japanese-held island.

"There Are Amtracs Burning on the Reef"

Puller, concerned that his superiors had underestimated the Japanese defenses, had spoken to his regiment at an outdoor movie theater before leaving Pavuvu. He reminded them of the surprise attack at Pearl Harbor that started the war, of Japanese atrocities in Bataan, and of the horrors his Guadalcanal veterans had witnessed in the Solomons. He told them that they were most likely facing expert defenders willing to die for their country but that he had no doubt the regiment would add to its already admirable record of battlefield laurels.

Four days of naval air attacks on the island preceded a three-day naval bombardment starting on September 10. Thirteen battleships and cruisers, escorted by fourteen destroyers, poured salvos into every inch of terrain on and beyond the beaches, so thoroughly covering the southern end of Peleliu that the naval commander announced that he had run out of targets and planned to halt the bombardment. Puller placed little stock in the naval assessment. When a naval officer asked for his opinion, Puller scoffed and considered any cessation in the barrage an asinine move that would only help kill his men.

Events proved Puller correct. The bombardment did little more than put a dent into Inoue's sturdy defenses, and once the three-day bombardment halted, his entrenched men emerged unfazed and ready to repel the marine invaders. Inoue posted a battalion south of the airfield, another along the landing beaches, and withdrew the rest of his men to the Umurbrogols to wait for the culminating battle.

Unfortunately for Puller's regiment, the bombardment also failed to scratch a key defensive position dominating the left flank of his landing zone. Despite the hundreds of shells that rocked the island, none hit the location to the left called The Point. This oversight would cost Chesty some of his finest marines.

In the early hours of September 15, Puller walked to the bridge to thank the ship's captain for conveying his men to Peleliu. Standing nearby, the fleet's commodore overheard Chesty and said, "Puller, you won't find anything to stop you over there. Nothing could have lived through that hammering." Remembering Tarawa and other earlier island assaults where high-ranking officers boasted that the pre-invasion bombardments had wiped out the enemy, only to have marines walk straight into a firestorm, Puller replied, "Well, sir, all I can see is dust. I doubt if you've cleaned it out." He said that he had been studying the maps for weeks, "and I believe they'll have pillbox stuff and fortifications like we've never seen before. They've been at it for years."

The navy captain wished Puller luck but, agreeing with the commodore, said he would see him for dinner, as "everything's done over there. You'll walk in." Restraining his desire to reply in more caustic terms, Puller simply added, "If you think it's that easy why don't you come on the beach at five o'clock, have supper with me, and pick up a few souvenirs?"

Amtracs soon began bearing three marine regiments toward shore. Chesty's 1st Regiment, with Puller and his small staff accompanying the third wave, churned to the left end of the zone, while the 5th Marines hit the center and his former regiment, the 7th Marines, proceeded to the right flank.

He had done everything he could to prepare them for this moment. The rigorous training he had imposed on his marines had instilled confidence in veterans and youngsters alike. He knew they were frightened; he would have been more concerned if they were not. Until they reached land and fought the enemy with their rifles and machine guns, however, he tried to convey a sense of calm that might ease their jitters, figuring that serenity and courage, combined with luck, forged powerful tools that would bring them safely through.

Puller's premonitions of a deadly landing materialized before the first amtracs had reached the halfway point to the beach, when shells ripped into the landing craft and drenched marines as their amtracs inched closer to shore. "We were half a mile from the beach when a shell landed twenty yards behind us," said Private First Class Harry Dearman. "I knew they were plotting our range and I held my breath while waiting for the next shell. It came so close it sent spray all over us in the amtrac.

They had our range now, and I figured the third shell would be fatal. For some reason, it never came." An aerial observer watched the carnage unfold below and radioed, "There are amtracs burning on the reef."

In the first wave of Puller's regiment, Lieutenant Haggerty worried because "it was a long ways to go in." Once his amtrac crossed the coral reef 500 yards out, "the Japanese started opening fire on us with all kinds of artillery and mortars and machine guns. It took us about half an hour more to get that last 500 yards. We finally got in but we lost a lot, we lost a lot of them." Some wondered how they or any marine could survive the gauntlet of fire and explosions through which they had to advance.

Eighteen-year-old Private First Class Fred Fox safely reached the shore, but one of his sergeants died before firing his weapon. As they were about to embark in the landing craft, the veteran of both Guadalcanal and Cape Gloucester combat had told Fox that, although he had survived those prior assaults, he could not now shake the feeling he was going to be killed on Peleliu. Fox tried to assure him that he was not alone in grappling with those fears but that they would most likely dissipate once they had landed. Within the first two minutes of their amtrac hitting the shoreline, the sergeant lay dead.

Tom Lea, an artist-correspondent covering the assault for *Life* magazine, glanced back at the reef after reaching shore and saw one of the landing craft disintegrate from a direct hit. "Pieces of iron and men seemed to sail slow motion into the air." He witnessed Japanese machine guns zero in on the reef, "and marines fell with bloody splashes into the green water," creating a strange, almost surreal reddish-green hue. "As bursts began to creep steadily from the reef in toward the beach, the shells from one mortar rustled through the air directly over our heads at intervals of a few seconds, bursting closer, closer. Then a flat cracking flash nearly buried me with sand."

While training for this operation, Puller had emphasized to his marines the necessity of leaving their amtracs as quickly as possible and moving up the beach. In the first moments of a landing, amtracs attracted the heaviest fire, and any man who lingered gambled with his own life. Once Puller's amtrac hit the sand, Puller, his leg smarting from the Guadalcanal wound, leaped over as bullets ricocheted off the amtrac's side and hurried to a coconut grove thirty yards inland, where he set up a temporary command post between his two landing beaches. Platoon leaders prodded their men to form a line, young privates dug in wherever they could, and wiremen followed closely on Puller's heels, setting up the communications system. Japanese fire dropped several of the wiremen only yards from Puller before they had a chance to finish their jobs, but others quickly filled in.

He looked back at the amtrac he had abandoned only moments before to see several shell explosions simultaneously pulverize it and kill those marines who had been tardy in exiting the craft. His was not the only amtrac to suffer such a fate. "I looked down the beach and saw a mess—every damned amtrac in our wave had been destroyed in the water by the enemy, or shot to pieces the minute it landed," Puller said.

A Japanese 47mm antitank gun opened fire on Puller's men from The Point, the dangerous coral bluff to his left, while machine guns on both flanks decimated the ranks of marines scrambling for cover. Not far from Puller, Lieutenant Haggerty ran across the sand while enemy machine-gun bullets kicked up the sand near him, and he leaped into a tank trap dug to impede American tank movements. Within seconds he scrambled out when Japanese mortar and artillery rounds crashed down on that spot. "We had to get out of there in a hurry and move inland, which we did. But we lost quite a few people doing it. The casualties were beginning to mount up quickly."

The heaviest action occurred on the outer left flank, where Captain George P. Hunt's K Company assaulted The Point, a plot of land rising thirty feet that jutted twenty-five yards into the water. From foxholes dug into the jagged coral, sharp pinnacles, and crevices, Japanese machine gunners and snipers brought down murderous enfilading fire on Hunt's men as soon as they left the amtracs. "It surpassed by far anything we had conceived of when we studied the aerial photographs," wrote Hunt, who was stunned that the naval bombardment had hardly damaged the area. They maneuvered in what Hunt called "a deathtrap, swept by flanking fire at point-blank range," but if they wanted to survive and complete their mission of protecting Chesty's left flank, his company had to seize The Point.

Private First Class Fox, who had witnessed the veteran sergeant die on the beach, thought The Point, with its concentration of enemy guns that enjoyed a clear view of the landing beaches, looked like a smaller version of the famed Little Round Top at Gettysburg, where in July 1863 Civil War colonel Joshua L. Chamberlain mounted a dramatic defense against Confederate infantry charging uphill. Even though outnumbered and running out of ammunition, Chamberlain reorganized his men and, in a daring downhill bayonet counterattack, won the day. Fox could not help but notice that here, at Peleliu, his unit resembled the Confederate forces while the Japanese stood in Chamberlain's position.

Hunt sent two platoons to take it, but when they fell back against withering fire, he contacted Puller, who immediately directed reinforcements to Hunt's sector. Finally, after eight hours of brutal combat, Hunt and thirty survivors reached the summit, where they dug in and fought off repeated enemy counterattacks to regain control of the vital hill. For eighteen additional hours, alone on top of The Point, Hunt and his band fended off the numerically superior Japanese defenders.

While Hunt's company assaulted its objective, on Hunt's right Puller moved inland to the southern end of a series of jagged coral ridges collectively called the Umurbrogol Mountains. Japanese hidden in thick brush at the approaches to the ridges slowed Puller's pace, which forced the marines to conduct a turtle-like tempo of advancing a yard or two, ducking for cover, and jumping up moments later to repeat the process.

Puller's marines operated under a blistering sun that took temperatures above 100°F. Hundreds of explosions sprayed shrapnel and chunks of coral into marine faces and cast a smoky pall over the battlefield, causing some men to whisper hasty prayers as they sprinted from one rock pile to another, hoping simply to keep one step ahead of the machine-gun bullets that smacked near their feet.

While Puller battled the Japanese on one side of an outcropping, the 5th and 7th Marines fought on the other, making it more difficult for either to assist the other. However, Puller dismissed it as a minor nuisance that, in one way, benefited him. As one marine said, "The fact that we were, for all practical purposes, cut off from the rest of the division didn't bother the Old Man at all. In thinking back, it was a made-to-order situation for Chesty. He liked nothing better than to do things his own way, without the brass breathing down his neck."

At division headquarters, O. P. Smith waited for updates from Puller about his landing against some of Inoue's most elaborate defenses, but in the hazardous opening moments of the assault Chesty, a habitual offender of the need to keep his superiors informed, concentrated on moving his men off the beach. For two hours Smith remained in the dark about events on his left flank. Finally, in midafternoon, one of Puller's officers entered Smith's headquarters with the information that Puller was under heavy artillery, machine-gun, and mortar fire at the foot of a ridge three hundred yards northeast. When a team of marines finally installed ground wires connecting the two command posts, Smith asked Puller for an assessment. Typically using as few words as possible, Chesty answered that his regiment, despite suffering severe casualties fighting its way through the Japanese, had made progress.

In late afternoon Japanese infantry, following fifteen tanks, burst from the Umurbrogols to attack Puller's right flank. Puller's men drove off the assault, but significant losses there and on his left side forced him to filter in his reserve company and any staff he could spare.

By the end of the first day, Lieutenant Colonel Russell Honsowetz, commanding Puller's 2nd Battalion, had advanced through swampy terrain to the edge of the airfield before a Japanese counterattack halted their progress, while Puller's units on the left struggled to make headway toward the Umurbrogol Mountains. His regiment had lost more than 350 men during the bloody landing, and its exhausted and hungry survivors had yet to encounter Inoue's main defenses in the Umurbrogols, where battle-tested infantry waited for Puller to advance into the ridges.

The expected Japanese banzai hit marine lines on the crest of The Point around midnight, with Hunt and his men alternately hurling their grenades toward the Japanese and tossing back enemy grenades that landed near them. "The fight became a vicious melee of countless explosions, whining bullets, shrapnel whirring overhead or clinking off the rocks, hoarse shouts, and shrill-screaming Japanese," wrote Hunt. The Japanese harassed Hunt's line throughout the night, and although they rebuffed each charge, when dawn brought a cessation to the fighting, Hunt commanded fewer than twenty healthy men.

While this unfolded, Puller tried to balance the more complex responsibilities of running a regiment with his desire to leave the command post to fight with his marines at the front. If he lingered at the command post, he could not rally the marines with his presence, but if he abandoned his command post to be with his men, he risked being out of touch with the rest of his regiment and thus being unable to adequately direct their movements.

The combat marine always came first for Puller, and despite

facing the demands of commanding a regiment, Chesty visited the front more than other senior commanders. For a person who admitted to being a platoon leader at heart, the impulse to join the men who risked their lives for their country was as natural as breathing. At the same time, that instinctive yearning clashed with the duties of commanding units at the regimental and division levels. For the rest of his career, Puller struggled to successfully blend those dual strains.

CHAPTER EIGHT

"THE OPPOSING FORCES WERE LIKE TWO SCORPIONS IN A BOTTLE"

In the Umurbrogols, September 16–October 2, 1944

G eneral Rupertus's plans for the second day tasked the 5th Marines with seizing the airfield and the 7th Marines with securing the area immediately to its east, while Puller's three battalions moved northward from the landing beaches to approach the Umurbrogols. After arranging for supplies and reinforcements to be sent to Hunt at The Point, Puller launched his morning attack following a thirty-minute bombardment from air, sea, and marine artillery.

Three Japanese-occupied hills and a fortified blockhouse with four-foot-thick walls obstructed the progress inland. Hills 200, 205, and 210—so named after their elevation in feet— guarded the pathway to the Umurbrogols, where the bulk of Inoue's soldiers manned a sturdy defense line anchored in the coral ridges. While Lieutenant Colonel Stephen Sabol's 3rd

Battalion cleared enemy forces from level terrain adjoining the beaches left of the Umurbrogols, in the middle of Puller's advance, Major Raymond Davis, the officer who had asked Puller to include him in the Cape Gloucester landings, and his 1st Battalion slowly chipped away at enemy resistance, laboriously knocking out each cave and pillbox on their way to destroying the concrete blockhouse standing between them and the Umurbrogols. Lacking room to swerve around the flanks, Davis ordered his men to attack straight into the complex of pillboxes that protected the blockhouse. Japanese defenders inflicted heavy casualties on the battalion, which stalled until tanks with their extra firepower arrived in the afternoon. Backed by those weapons, Davis overwhelmed the blockhouse and continued toward the ridges.

Before starting that day's offensive, Puller made clear to Lieutenant Colonel Honsowetz, operating on Davis's right, that after seizing the airfield, Honsowetz was to continue north to take Hill 200, another fortified landform guarding another approach to the Umurbrogols. "Look, Honsowetz, I want that sonofabitchin' ridge before sundown. And I mean, goddammit, I *want* it!"

Honsowetz's 2nd Battalion swept across the airfield with ease but, like its companion battalions, butted into heavy opposition as it executed a movement north to Hill 200 and its complex of pillboxes and tunnels. Charging through the coral terrain, Honsowetz's men clubbed their way up Hill 200 to the crest, losing marines each yard of the way to machine-gun bullets and mortar shells. By late afternoon, however, after suffering 200 casualties, Honsowetz reached the twenty-yard-wide crest and prepared to repel the expected nighttime banzai charge. Unable to dig foxholes in the hard coral surface, his marines piled rocks in front of their positions and prepared for a long night repelling Japanese attacks.

While his three battalion commanders carried out Chesty's orders, Puller raced back and forth from the front lines to his headquarters, which, to correspondent Bill Hipple's dismay, stood dangerously close to the fighting. "You could never feel secure when you were around Chesty," Hipple wrote. "He wasn't ever satisfied to just sit back and command the action, he wanted to be as close as he could to it—and lend a personal hand, even firing a few shots himself, at the slightest opportunity. He wasn't content to have his CP [command post] a few hundred feet behind the front. He wanted to be right at the front, and, so help me, that's where we were on D plus one [September 16]."

During the second day of battle, Puller had abandoned the beaches to establish an irregular line facing the pathway to the Umurbrogols. Honsowetz's and Davis's zones in the middle and right registered the largest gains, but even that pair advanced no more than half a mile against Inoue's sturdy defenses. To their left, Hunt and his small force continued to fight for their lives at The Point.

That evening Puller contacted Colonel John T. Selden, the division chief of staff, and requested replacements for the 1,000 dead and wounded—a third of his regiment—that he had lost in two days of combat. Rupertus, who had expected the assault to end within a few days, angrily reacted to what he concluded was a measured advance in Puller's sector. Reluctant to call on an army reserve unit and face the ignominy of being "rescued" by their military comrades, he denied Chesty's request.

"Can't they move any faster?" Rupertus surprisingly asked Puller, a man known for his aggressive advances. "Goddammit, Lewie, you've gotta kick ass to get results. You know that, goddammit!" Also concerned about Puller's excessive rate of casualties, Rupertus mulled the possibility of relieving the commander but postponed that controversial decision for the time being.

During the night, 500 Japanese again struck Puller's line. While Honsowetz repelled one banzai charge, Hunt's K Company on the crest of The Point bore the brunt of the attack. A Japanese mortar barrage before midnight preceded the onslaught, with Hunt shouting, "Give 'em hell! Kill every one of the bastards!" He and his depleted unit battled the Japanese for four hours, turning away the oncoming enemy soldiers with machine-gun bursts, rifle fire, and bayonet thrusts. By 2:00 a.m., the Japanese wave receded, leaving 350 bodies dead along the sides and crest of The Point. When Puller relieved Hunt and K Company in the morning, Hunt had lost most of the marines he had led ashore the day before. With the failed banzai charge, the Japanese pulled back to their main defense line in the Umurbrogols, filtered into their prepared positions, and allowed marines to walk straight into their trap.

Rupertus's battle plans for September 17 were startling carbon copies of the previous day. With control of the airfield firmly in hand, the 5th and 7th Marines were to finish securing Peleliu's eastern side, while Puller advanced closer to the series of ridges that dominated the island's western terrain.

Puller jumped off at 8:00 a.m. after an artillery and naval bombardment, but stalled in front of a complex of ridges that wove an intricate rocky maze. Only a handful of ridges rose as high as 200 feet, but every ridge, large and small, housed hundreds of Japanese fortifications. Puller could only approach that elaborate labyrinth by penetrating into the deep ravines and charging up slopes infested with machine-gun nests, snipers, and mortar positions. The Japanese had emplaced their large artillery in caves, which forced the marines to scale perilously close to either burn out the positions with a flamethrower or demolish them by hurling demolition charges into the openings. A maddening repetition ensued. When Puller's men finally reached the summit of one ridge, they came under fire from Japanese artillery situated on another, which meant that marines would have to mount another deadly uphill charge to destroy that position. Beyond the second ridge lay a third, fourth, and fifth ridge, each requiring the marines to stage time-consuming assaults that reminded some of prying hundreds of ticks from an animal's skin. "We're up here," reported one frustrated officer after reaching one summit. "But we're knee-deep in Purple Hearts."

In the middle of Puller's drive, Davis's 1st Battalion attempted to take Hill 205, and as elsewhere, they measured their progress in feet and yards. After suffering exorbitant losses, thirty men reached the hill's crest in late afternoon, where they maintained a toehold while Japanese entrenched on adjoining ridges poured more fire onto them.

Newspaper and magazine reporters, who knew that action followed Puller and that the colorful colonel would provide good copy for their stories, often asked to be assigned to Chesty's unit. Correspondent Robert Martin stood near Puller when division headquarters, claiming they had exhausted their supply, denied Chesty's request for reinforcements. Puller threw his field telephone at a coral bank, shouted a string of profanities, and stormed out. "He then went out and personally led his marines deeper into that sun-baked hell where every Japanese had to be killed with a bayonet or a flame thrower," wrote Martin.

Two days of grueling combat moved Puller's line to the base of the Umurbrogols. The savage fighting on Peleliu had so far tested his men, but they would learn in the next few days that the hellish combat for which Peleliu would become synonymous had only begun. The nicknames bestowed on the ridges by the Marines—Death Valley and Bloody Nose Ridge—indicated as much.

"The Whole Area Was Littered with Marine Bodies"

Now perched at the entrance to the main system of fortifications embedded in the Umurbrogols, Puller had to navigate a series of coral ridges running from northeast to southwest in the island's left half, while the 5th and 7th Marines advanced along relatively flat terrain in the eastern half. From above, the ridges resembled an outstretched hand, with three avenues of approach lying in the valleys and ravines that separated the ridges. Japanese infantry manned each slope, ready to pour a devastating fire on Puller's exposed marines as they wound through the ravines. Atop the ridges and on the reverse slopes, Japanese artillery waited for Puller to move into preregistered fields of fire, at which time they would direct a deadly barrage onto their exposed foe. Puller had to grind his way past each ridge in the deadliest fashion—by sending his men straight up the slopes directly into machine-gun and rifle fire while artillery and mortar shells exploded in their midst. With Lieutenant Colonel Sabol's 3rd Battalion racing along open land outside the Umurbrogols near the western beaches, Davis's 1st Battalion entered the mountains on Sabol's right, and Honsowetz's 2nd Battalion battled its way through the eastern entry to the Umurbrogols. They filtered into the valleys and ravines, feeling isolated and vulnerable as the enemy-controlled flanking heights closed in on them.

Over the next two days, frontline marines ran into two major obstacles. On the right, point-blank cannon fire from Hill 100 inflicted heavy casualties and halted Captain Everett Pope's company. Pope quickly reorganized his ninety men and, despite facing withering fire from machine-gun, mortar, and sniper fire, led them to the summit. Now down to twelve men and one wounded officer, Pope held the crest, even though his machine guns had been destroyed and his men were dangerously low on ammunition and water. Throughout the night Pope's dwindling force beat back repeated assaults from three sides, at times resorting to hand-to-hand combat, once even throwing rocks when they ran out of ammunition. By dawn, Puller ordered Pope, who was later was awarded the Medal of Honor for his heroics on Hill 100, to withdraw when the Japanese commenced another artillery barrage.

The principal attack unfolded to Pope's left, where the regiment ran into Bloody Nose Ridge. This southern end of Inoue's fortifications contained battle-hardened veterans of Manchurian combat, backed by mammoth guns emplaced in caverns that could be wheeled out to fire on the marines and then wheeled back in to avoid return fire. Men scaling the ridges saw their groups quickly reduced to one or two as marines fell to the punishing fire streaming from Japanese caves and pillboxes. When the defenders refused to abandon their positions, marines had to scale each ridge and destroy them in costly attacks with flamethrowers, bazookas, or demolition charges.

"'Bloody Nose' is a denuded coral and limestone ridge pitted with caves and bulwarked by concrete emplacements," wrote correspondent Richard Johnston during the assault. "The First Regiment, under much decorated Col. Louis [sic] 'Chesty' Puller, is assailing the ridge after pushing its salient into a narrow valley on its eastern flank."

At one cave, three times the marines tossed in a demolition charge, only to see the enemy grab it and either pull out the fuse or throw the charge back at them. Sergeant Peter Abdella said fighting in the ridges at Peleliu "was the screwiest business I ever saw. Marines were on one side of the ridge, Japs on the other. Marines were throwing grenades over the top. Japs were throwing grenades from their side."

At another time during the fighting for Bloody Nose Ridge, Second Lieutenant George L. Haggerty and First Lieutenant Joseph Fournier planned an assault on a position that had withstood numerous marine attacks. "We've only got about twenty men," Fournier said. "I've been trying to get up on that ridge there across the little plateau in front of it. We've lost a lot of men trying to do it." They hesitated to ask their men to again charge into that deadly fire, but Puller had issued orders to keep attacking until they had knocked out the offending gun. Fournier told Haggerty, "If you can get half a dozen men to volunteer to go with you, there is a field-piece up there which is on tracks because they run it in and out of the caves. There are all kinds of machine gun nests around it and the Japanese are entrenched around it."

Haggerty agreed, gathered six volunteers, and set out on his mission. To pull within range of the gun, they traversed 150 yards of open territory up the slopes, all the while exchanging fire and grenades with the Japanese. "They had been firing mortars and hand grenades and in fact, some of the grenades that we threw up there they threw back down at us." When Haggerty's group scaled the slopes, they found "the whole area was littered with Marine bodies" from the previous unsuccessful attempts, but the young officer kept moving. "We crawled our way up the field and they were throwing hand grenades. We threw several hand grenades up there and I think we got it because it stopped firing." Haggerty had only two men left, but he had fulfilled Puller's order and knocked out that gun.

"The Japanese Are Dying Hard"

Even though the casualties to Puller's units had soared to alarming numbers, Rupertus inexplicably ordered a repeat of the same attacks for September 18. Puller again confronted the enemy in the ridges, while the other regiments cleared the eastern portion of Peleliu. Brigadier General Smith questioned whether

Rupertus realized that Puller had lost more than 1,200 marines in the first three days battling in that harsh coral terrain and believed that a change of plans was needed.

The 5th and 7th Marines steadily advanced in the east, but as Smith feared, Puller encountered stiffer resistance the deeper he plunged into the Umurbrogols. Under fire from multiple positions, marines bypassed single snipers and machine-gun pillboxes, which they left to a company of reserve infantry, so that the marines could eliminate the more intricate, deadlier complexes. As a result, enemy fire hit some marines from both front and rear.

Puller continued to strip nonessential personnel from his command post and send them forward to assist the frontline marines in destroying an enemy that begrudged each yard. Correspondent Howard Handleman described Peleliu as "this unknown blob of coral sand where the Japs are fighting for the first time as though directly protecting their homeland." He wrote that the Japanese "have fought as if Tokyo were 20 miles behind them," and that rather than relying on a battle-ending banzai, "Fanaticism has taken a different course with the Japs dying in prepared positions rather than in hopeless heroic charges." Peleliu's combat was "the kind of fighting men do to protect their homes, not a tiny island outpost." Handleman explained that on more than one occasion Chesty Puller reported instances where Japanese soldiers holed up in caves or bound themselves to trees "so they were unable to retreat. Some were tied to rocks and trees on sheer cliff faces which were difficult to reach." Enemy snipers periodically took positions so close to

Puller that they could fire almost straight down into his command post, requiring Chesty to dispatch patrols to kill them.

Puller looked the part in the 115°F heat, downing salt tablets and water to maintain his strength. "It was a hot day and Puller was stripped to the waist," wrote a correspondent who visited him at his command post. "He was smoking his battered pipe; characteristically he held the pipe between his incisors and talked out of the side of his mouth. His CP [command post] was located where the bluffs came very close to the road. This defilade [cover] was necessary because the Japanese were laying down considerable mortar fire, and considerable small-arms fire was passing overhead."

After stalling against fierce resistance at one ridge, Lieutenant Colonel Honsowetz contacted Puller and expressed doubts that he could seize the hill unless he received reinforcements. Puller replied that he had no men to spare, and repeated his original order to take the hill. "Christ, we can't do it," objected Honsowetz. "The casualties are too much and we've been fighting all day and all night."

"You sound all right," Chesty bellowed. "You're there. Goddammit, you get those troops in there and you take the goddamn hill." By evening Honsowetz's men stood atop Hill 210, but the trail of marine bodies littering the slopes behind offered grim evidence of the toll Puller's men suffered in Umurbrogol combat.

Frontline units disintegrated into clusters of four or five marines attacking a pillbox or mortar position. "It's down to rifle, bayonet and grenade," Puller told Howard Handleman. "We've got to kill every Jap or be killed ourselves. The Japs are making us pay for every man we kill." His marines ascended ridges, only to fall back against heavy resistance, regroup, and try again. Lieutenant Colonel Lewis W. Walt, who had fought so gallantly with Puller on New Britain, visited Puller during the drive into the Umurbrogols and said Chesty "was absolutely sick over the loss of his men; he thought we were getting them killed for nothing."

To the surprise of no one, Puller was often closer to the front than his battalion commanders. Brigadier General O. P. Smith left headquarters to check on conditions near the fighting, but he had trouble locating Chesty. When he asked for Puller's whereabouts, a few marines pointed toward the combat ahead. Smith and his aide continued toward the sounds of gunfire, at times crawling along the ground to avoid enemy gunfire, "and finally found Colonel Puller and his group in what had been a small quarry." Smith said that "Lewie was stripped to the waist, his battered pipe in his mouth, never bothering to remove the pipe when he was talking. He was in his element, making his presence felt. His battalion commanders could not possibly have been between him and the enemy."

Another costly day of combat had shorn half of Puller's regiment. Progress in the unyielding terrain slowed as marines shuffled on jagged rocks toward their next target, trying to ignore the fine coral dust that covered every man and weapon, filtered into their noses, and coated open wounds and rations. In his classic memoir of combat at Peleliu, *With the Old Breed*, Eugene Sledge, fighting with the 5th Marines in the Umurbrogols, wrote that "the overwhelming grayness of everything in sight caused sky, ridge, rocks, stumps, men, and equipment to blend into a grimy oneness. Weird, jagged contours of Peleliu's ridges and canyons gave the area an unearthly alien appearance."

Because they were unable to scratch out foxholes in the rock, shrapnel from mortar shells killed and wounded exposed marines. Rocks slashed their boots, and whenever they dropped to the ground to avoid incoming shells, the sharp coral shredded their clothing and slashed their arms and legs. "The Japanese are dying hard," wrote correspondent Rembert James the same day that Captain Pope attacked Hill 100. "The Japanese are dug in deeper and closer together on Peleliu Island than on any island the marines have ever hit." He quoted Lieutenant Colonel John W. Scott, staff officer of the 1st Marine Division, as saying the enemy had more defensive positions per square yard than any other island assault and described the afternoon heat as so unbearable that men swallowed twenty salt tablets to replenish the salinity they lost in perspiring.

The wretched conditions affected privates and colonels alike. After spending time with Puller, James wrote of the colonel, "Lounging beside a field phone on a sweltering coral hillside, Puller puffed wearily at a cigarette and said in some places the marines had been able to gain only 75 yards in a day while in others they gained 300 yards." Puller told James, "This is the roughest ground you could ever find to fight over and the heat is causing a number of prostrations." In the sweltering conditions, marines discarded canvas leggings and cut off their trousers below the knees to allow air to circulate, and unnecessary equipment littered the rocky ridges as marines retained only their weapons and canteens of water.

James grasped the ghastly cost of Umurbrogol combat when a battalion commander phoned Puller to ask whether he should bypass one particularly stubborn ridge. Under orders to spur the offensive forward, Chesty told him to "go ahead and smash them," but when he put down the phone, he turned to an aide and said, "Call up fifty stretcher-bearers because we are going to need them."

After only a few days of fighting, a pervasive stench permeated the combat zone. Lacking sufficient dirt to bury their excrement, field sanitation in the coral rock became impossible. Bloated bodies decayed in the tropical sun, attracting huge blue-bottle flies. If a marine opened his rations, flies swarmed from the rotting bodies to infest marine and food alike. Each morning, shortly before sunrise, Eugene Sledge "could hear a steady humming sound like bees in a hive as the flies became active," a signal that swarms of the pesky creatures would soon inundate them. Land crabs feasted on the rotting bodies, and at night the sounds of their crawling among dead marines and Japanese made sleep impossible.

Day after day, men fought and died in the hypnotic, unalterable terrain. "The terrain was so unbelievably rugged, jumbled, and confusing, that I rarely knew where we were located," Eugene Sledge wrote. "One ridge looked like another, was about as rugged, and was defended as heavily as any other." Some men doubted that they would survive the nightmarish combat and figured the fighting would last "until all the Japanese were killed, or we had all been hit." Sledge concluded, "On Peleliu the opposing forces were like two scorpions in a bottle. One was annihilated, the other nearly so."

September 19 offered further carbon-copy attacks ordered by Rupertus. Accompanied by flamethrowers, Puller's marines moved forward, some in units now down to a quarter of their strength. No matter how difficult or how deadly their task became, though, Chesty stood in their midst, shouting encouragement and lending strength with his actions. "His men loved him," said Lieutenant Colonel Honsowetz, "they'd do anything for him, and they'd see him up there poking around where he shouldn't have been." The marines would look at each other and say, "Hell, goddamn, the old man's up there. Let's go," a result that occurred, in Honsowetz's opinion, because of Chesty's "way of leadership."

Peleliu's heat and rugged conditions aggravated his leg wound, and each day's assault compounded the pain for the forty-six-year-old Puller. Keeping up with marines in their teens and early twenties taxed every nerve and fiber of his body, and like their commander, four days of fighting a skilled enemy in unrelenting heat exhausted Puller's men. The regiment's casualty count had risen to more than 1,800 men, and in Major Davis's 1st Battalion, only 350 marines remained of the initial 1,147 officers and men who had landed five days earlier. When Puller noticed a group of men returning from the front, he asked which platoon they were in. "Platoon, Hell, Colonel, this is Charlie Company," one marine replied.

Major General Roy S. Geiger, commander of the III Amphibious Corps at Peleliu and Rupertus's superior, studied the appalling losses suffered by Puller and the other regimental commanders and considered relieving Rupertus. He thought Rupertus had erred in failing to adjust his daily plans, and in declining to bring in available army units to bolster the marine ranks, whom Rupertus boasted were more than capable of handling matters without army intervention.

Other officers shared Geiger's concern over the high casualty rates. Both Honsowetz and Davis in Puller's regiment expressed their shock, as well as battalion commanders in the other two regiments. Some blamed Rupertus for sticking with a ground attack in the ridges that had obviously failed and labeled as foolhardy the bayonet charges against those defenses. The strain took a noticeable toll on Rupertus. One officer saw the commander on his cot, holding his head in his hands, complaining that the tension, the climate, and the battlefield conditions were almost more than he could endure.

Some blamed the exorbitant losses on Puller's desire to seek medals. During the fighting, First Lieutenant Lee P. Stack, Jr., of the 1st Tank Battalion, overheard Chesty and Colonel Harold D. Harris of the 5th Marines discussing their tactics. Puller asked Harris, "How many second lieutenants have you killed so far?" When Harris gave a number Puller considered too low for a combat officer, he bellowed, "What the hell are you doing, having a Sunday School picnic?"

Men in the 5th Marines on Puller's right heard about the slaughter unfolding in Puller's sector. One of Eugene Sledge's buddies said to him, "You know, Sledgehammer, a guy from the 1st Marines told me they got them poor boys makin' frontal attacks with fixed bayonets on that damn ridge, and they can't even see the Nips that are shootin' at 'em. The poor kid was really depressed; don't see no way he can come out alive. There just ain't no sense in that. They can't get nowhere like that. It's slaughter." Another marine added, "Yeah, some goddamn glory-happy officer wants another medal, I guess, and the guys get shot up for it. The officer gets the medal and goes back to the States, and he's a big hero. Hero, my ass; getting troops slaughtered ain't being no hero."

Sledge could have cared less whether the bloodbath in the ridges occurred because of Rupertus's unimaginative assaults or Puller's bellicose ways. All that mattered was that sooner or later, he would be scaling similar heights. He wrote, "Even the most optimistic man I knew believed our battalion must take its turn against those incredible ridges—and dreaded it."

Supporters countered that Puller's consideration and affection for his men outweighed any desire for personal glory and claimed that he would never needlessly throw away their lives. Sledge was not a member of Puller's regiment, but he, too, feared the same menaces that hounded Puller's marines. The issue in the Umurbrogols did not center on one commander wasting lives, for every officer battling in the ridges confronted the same tribulations. Chesty's aggressive methods may have differed from those utilized by others, but the results were still the same—in the Umurbrogols, every unit, no matter who led it, suffered.

Robert Sherrod, who wrote some of the most gripping accounts of marines in battle, featured Puller in an October 1944 article for *Time* magazine. In the story, Sherrod accurately portrayed Puller as a hard-nosed, profanity-laced commander. He related one incident when "a Jap mortar opened up and the men around the colonel flattened out. The C.O. himself did not change his position. He stuck out his chest and spat: 'The bastards.'" Elsewhere, Sherrod wrote, "Weary and unkempt, 46-year-old Chesty watched from under his awning as his men dug the Japs out of their limestone caves." When Sherrod asked the colonel how he planned to get them out, Puller replied, "By blood, sweat, and hand grenades."

When the article appeared on newsstands in the United States, the feature shocked Virginia, who had only seen the romantic side to her husband. She vented her anger in a letter to an old friend from their time in China, Admiral Thomas Hart, who told her to ignore the portions that depicted the profane, martial side to her husband and concentrate on her husband's achievements. "You *must* have a feeling of entire pride that your husband should be so written up in a publication of such wide circulation," he advised. "Now your husband is one of those few who have stood out as superlative in that war in the Pacific. We must thank the Lord that we have a few like him." Hart mentioned that she would soon see her husband, and "I can imagine nothing worse for him, when he returns, than a realization that you look upon his past accomplishments with anything other than pride." He said that once her husband was back home, she would find Chesty unaltered, and that the bombastic personality depicted by Sherrod would quickly fade and be replaced by his softer, domestic side. "Despite what he has been through, you will not find him changed insofar as you are concerned. This other side of him is what he carries to the office, so to speak, and has no part in your daily lives together. Please do your best, Virginia, to effect such mental adjustment as is needed."

In the end, all that mattered was how Chesty's marines viewed the issue. As far as they were concerned, Puller's hard-hitting battlefield conduct brought victory on the battlefield, which in their opinion negated whatever criticism his detractors presented.

"I Brought My Ass Outta There, Swabbie"

After six days of rigorous combat near and in the Umurbrogols, Puller and his regiment needed a rest. Major General Geiger visited his command post on September 21 and was alarmed at Chesty's haggard appearance, his labored, almost awkward walk due to his pained leg, and his confusion in replying to Geiger's queries. Geiger took one look at the casualty figures and concluded that the depleted regiment was no longer an effective fighting unit and had to be pulled off the line. More than 70 percent of Puller's 1st Battalion was either killed, wounded, or sick, while the 2nd Battalion lost 56 percent and the 3rd Battalion 55 percent of their men. A staff officer said, "It became rapidly apparent that the regimental commander was very tired. He was unable to give a very clear picture of what his situation was, and when asked by the corps commander what he needed in the way of help he stated that he was doing all right with what he had."

Geiger returned to the division command post to inform Rupertus that Puller's regiment was finished. Geiger, Rupertus's superior, said that Rupertus needed to remove Puller because Chesty would never willingly withdraw from the line, but Rupertus, still averse to admit that his marines required help from an army unit, hesitated. Geiger overruled his subordinate, inserted the army's 321st Infantry Regiment in Puller's position near Bloody Nose Ridge, and ordered the immediate evacuation of the 1st Marine Regiment for rest and reorganization at the division's camp on Pavuvu near Guadalcanal. As Geiger expected, Puller angrily objected to the move but failed to change Geiger's mind.

When the 321st moved into Puller's position later in the day, Colonel Robert Dark, the regimental commander, understood that he was replacing a Marine Corps legend, but the weary-looking Puller he encountered was far from the energetic, vibrant officer he expected to see. When he reached the front lines, Dark assumed that the spot where he met Puller had to be a forward observation post and asked Chesty where the marine had situated his command post. Rather than pointing to a location behind the lines, as the army officer expected, Chesty indicated that Dark stood in it. "I mean your command post," repeated Dark. "Right here!" Puller replied, chagrined that the army officer refused to believe he would be so close to the combat. As soon as Puller departed, Dark shifted his headquarters 1,000 yards to the rear because he thought Puller's forward location offered too much danger for a regimental commander.

Puller's regiment withdrew to the beach area, where for the next week they conducted daily patrols, rested, ate hot food, and read mail from home. Puller still hoped to return to the front, but his marines had seen enough. "We aren't a regiment," said one marine. "We're the survivors of a regiment." On September 24, O. P. Smith again visited Puller, who repeated his desire to be at the front, but Smith noticed that the shrapnel in Puller's thigh had markedly slowed his friend. Smith informed him that orders for his regiment's evacuation were set and that he should take advantage of his time in Pavuvu to regain his health.

Puller never mentioned his disappointment at being taken out of the action in his letters to Virginia. A few hours after Smith's visit, Puller wrote, "Darling: I am well and safe and there is nothing further for you to worry about." In a subsequent letter, he explained to Virginia, "This operation is practically over and after reorganizing the First and getting it back into shape, I will then only have to await the arrival of my relief. Life with you will then be grand and all that I desire." He added, "You are the loveliest woman in the world and you belong to me and I treasure you more than you will ever know. I am the most fortunate of men and will never forget it."

On October 2, Puller's regiments boarded transports for the journey to Pavuvu. Eugene Sledge was on his way from the beach to the front when he spotted among Puller's unit a few buddies from their mutual training in Pavuvu. He hardly recognized his friends. "I saw some familiar faces as the three decimated battalions trudged past us," he wrote, "but I was shocked at the absence of so many others whom I knew in that regiment." Sledge had heard about the rigorous fighting those marines had endured and had seen wounded men from other outfits, "but the men in the 1st Marines had so many it was appalling."

Sledge asked one of Puller's marines how many men in his company had survived the week in combat. Weary, and staring from bloodshot eyes, the man replied, "Twenty is all that's left in the whole company, Sledgehammer. They nearly wiped us out. I'm the only one left out of the old bunch in my company that was with us in mortar school at Elliott." The marine wished Sledge luck, but he said it in a tone that indicated he doubted Sledge would enjoy little, if any, good fortune. "What had once been companies in the 1st Marines looked like platoons; platoons looked like squads," wrote Sledge. "I saw few officers. I couldn't help wondering if the same fate awaited the 5th Marines [his regiment] on those dreadful ridges. Twenty bloody, grueling, terrible days and nights later, on October 15 my regiment would be relieved. Its ranks would be just about as decimated as those we were filing past."

Puller's men resembled the famous drawing by Tom Lea for *Life* magazine. The picture depicted a marine leaving the front lines, with ridges and charred trees in the background, gazing straight ahead with what veterans called the "thousand-yard stare," as if the glossy eyes set in dark, sunken sockets saw much but comprehended little. Below the drawing, Lea wrote of his subject, "He's Finished—Washed Up—Gone."

They climbed aboard the transports, pale imitations of the refreshed, hearty infantry they had been before Peleliu. As marines shuffled by, a navy officer on one ship asked each man if they brought out any souvenirs. One marine patted his own rear and said, "I brought my ass outta there, swabbie. That's my souvenir of Peleliu."

Puller had lost more than 1,800 men to combat, heat exhaustion, and battle fatigue, but he could hold his head high. In what turned out to be Chesty's final campaign of the war, facing a chilling maze of fortifications dug into punishing terrain, his regiment took 10 ridges while destroying 3 blockhouses, 22 pillboxes, 13 antitank guns, and 144 caves. "It seemed impossible that men could have moved forward against the intricate and mutually supporting defenses the Japanese had set up," said Brigadier General Smith. "It can only be explained as a reflection of the determination and aggressive leadership of Colonel Puller."

———

Due to the painful thigh, now swollen to almost twice its normal size, a member of his staff had to help Puller aboard the transport USS *Pinkney* (PH-2). Medical personnel rushed him to the operating room where the surgeon, Commander Herbert Patterson, operated for two hours to remove a one-inch piece of shrapnel that had lodged next to the bone. Puller spent the next few days in his cabin, recuperating from the operation and from the exhausting days on Peleliu, but when the vessel arrived in Pavuvu a week later, Puller was able to resume normal duties.

He was the Chesty of old. Private John Loomis was walking his guard post outside Puller's tent when the colonel called for him. The young marine, fearing he had done something wrong, and slightly awed by speaking to someone of that high rank, instead found a warm, interested Puller inquiring about his health and background. Standing in a lengthy line a bit later to purchase paper and soap at the temporary post exchange set up in a coconut grove, Loomis was again impressed when Chesty walked over and joined Loomis and other privates at the end of the line instead of cutting in at the front.

As much as his men loved their commander, the criticism of Puller's command style that had surfaced on Peleliu continued unabated after the battle. Critics cited the regiment's high rate of casualties as proof that he could not handle a unit larger than a battalion, that he underutilized artillery and other means of supporting fire, that his aggressive tactics in constantly charging well-defended Japanese positions wasted lives, and that he ordered attacks straight into enemy guns instead of turning to flanking attacks. As far as the critics were concerned, Puller had turned into a caricature of an officer who ordered ill-conceived assaults for personal gain.

Lieutenant Colonel F. P. Henderson of the operations staff said that Puller often declined fire support. "He insisted that he was going to do it with Marine infantry, ram it in there." Captain Pope, the Medal of Honor recipient for his leadership at Hill 100, wondered why Puller had to make repeated assaults against Bloody Nose Ridge when, in Pope's opinion, they accomplished little. "I had no use for Puller. He didn't know what was going on, and why he wanted me and my men dead on top of that hill, I don't know."

The facts do not fully support the criticism, which paints Puller in broad strokes while overlooking details. Puller's casualty rate of 54 percent was certainly high, but the other two regiments that fought in the ridges of Peleliu were not far behind, with the 5th Marines suffering 43 percent casualties and the 7th Regiment 46 percent. Descriptions of bloody assaults and dead marines fill the pages of Eugene Sledge's powerful memoir of the 5th Marines fighting on Peleliu, as well as numerous accounts written by marines who had labored in those ridges. Puller's 1st Marine Regiment absorbed ghastly casualties on Peleliu, but so did any unit that entered the Umurbrogol bloodbath.

Far from ignoring supporting fire and utilizing flanking attacks, more than half of the marine calls for naval gunfire in the first two days of combat came from Puller, and he had utilized flanking attacks as far back as Nicaragua. The hills and ridges of Peleliu, combined with the mutually supporting Japanese defenses, constricted freedom of movement and all but negated flanking attacks. Consequently, Puller and the other marine commanders on the island relied on the common marine tactic of frontal assaults.

Rupertus owns a large share of blame for any mishap that occurred on Peleliu, as he had made it clear to Puller and other regimental commanders that they were to take the island fast. Puller claimed that, in light of those orders, he had no alternative but to gain ground each day no matter what it might cost.

Chesty's marines believed in the colonel who commanded from the front, shared their risks, and preached that everyone in his unit, including himself, was expendable. Because of that fondness, they outperformed expectations against the stiffest opposition. A common statement made by veterans of Puller's units, before Peleliu and afterward, was that each marine would have followed Chesty to hell. They backed up those words with their actions in the hell that was Peleliu.

Brigadier General O. P. Smith toured Puller's sector in the aftermath of the battle in the Umurbrogols. After surveying the harsh terrain and examining the destruction left by the violent fighting, he concluded that Puller deserved praise for what he accomplished. "I went over the ground he captured, and I didn't see how a human being had captured it, but he did. He believed in momentum; he believed in coming ashore and hitting and just keep on hitting and trying to keep up the momentum until he'd overrun the whole thing." He added, "No, there was no finesse about it, but there was gallantry and there was determination."

Puller did not yet realize it, but his World War II career was over. He would soon leave Pavuvu for the journey home and for the next chapter in his military profession.

CHAPTER NINE

"GOD BLESS MARINES EVERYWHERE"

Home, November 1944–October 11, 1971

Puller rejoined his wife in November 1944. In addition to welcoming twins Lewis Burwell, Jr., and Martha Leigh the next year, Puller picked up a number of awards for his service, including a recommendation from the editors of the *Charlotte Observer* to be named Southerner of the Year for exemplifying the "traits of courage against great odds, stout heartedness and love of country."

Puller turned to his new posts. He helped train advanced skills in weaponry to marines at Camp Lejeune, North Carolina, commanded the 8th Marine Corps Reserve District in New Orleans, and took charge of the Marine Barracks at Pearl Harbor, which handled security for the military installations at that important base. His peacetime duty ended when war erupted in the Far East and brought Puller into his second conflict in six years.

"Let the Navy Paint the Damned Ship. You're Going to Fight This War."

On June 25, 1950, eight divisions of the North Korean People's Army (NKPA) advanced across the 38th Parallel separating their country from South Korea in an attempt to unify both nations under Communism. The Republic of Korea (ROK), a democracy with a military of only 95,000 men, was unable to slow the North Koreans, who rushed toward Seoul, the South Korean capital. Two days later the United Nations Security Council authorized member nations to band together to stop the invasion.

The offensive caught President Harry Truman and his military flat-footed. Douglas MacArthur, his commander in the Far East, had only four undermanned army infantry divisions in Japan to send to the Korean peninsula. They joined the South Korean military, but even that combined force, called the Eighth Army, fell back in front of the powerful North Korean military until they had retreated to Pusan in the southeast corner of Korea, the last major port under MacArthur's control. Reinforced by the 1st Marine Brigade under General Edward A. Craig, MacArthur was able to stabilize his lines around Pusan.

Now that marines were involved in the fighting, Puller was notified that, starting August 4, he would take command of his old regiment, the 1st Marines. The news sparked dozens of veteran marines who had fought under Chesty in the Pacific to write letters begging to be transferred to his command. "He's the roughest marine I ever saw," one of his former platoon officers explained, "but every man who ever served with him wants to get back with him again."

One marine at first hesitated to join Puller. When Sergeant Orville Jones was asked if he wanted to be Puller's driver, he had initial doubts. Jones had heard that most of Chesty's previous drivers had been injured or killed because of Puller's desire to operate at the front. "The word was that Puller wanted a driver who had been in combat, and preferably shot," said Jones.

That evening Jones entered an improvised beer hall at Camp Pendleton to grab a beer. As he waited in line, Puller walked in and asked who was in charge. When an officer stepped forward, Puller asked if it was true that the previous night he had run out of beer and that what he had served was warm. When the officer answered in the affirmative, Puller chose his words carefully. "It won't happen again, Lieutenant. You understand me?" He explained, "These boys are going to war, and some of them won't be coming back. They're working like hell all day and half the night to get ready, most of 'em at least sixteen hours straight. What they do with their off hours is their own business, and if they want a couple of beers, Lieutenant, they're going to get 'em."

The incident convinced Jones to accept the offer to become Puller's driver. "Well, after I heard the way the old man read off that lieutenant for serving warm beer, and not having enough of it at that, I decided anyone who cared that much about his men had to be a good man to work for."

Marines who knew Puller only by reputation were soon won over by their distinctive commander. Lieutenant George

Chambers, a platoon leader in the regiment, said that in training Chesty wore old utilities that made him appear more like a gunnery sergeant than a colonel. Marines shouted, "Hi, Gunny!" as he walked by flashing a smile and waving to the men. "His greatest touch was his earthiness, his ability to make the men feel he was one of them," said Lieutenant Lew Devine, rifle platoon commander. "They'd literally have gone to Moscow with him."

On August 22, Puller and his regiment left California aboard the transport USS *Noble* (APA-218), for deployment to the Far East. During the voyage, Puller noticed some of his marines, under the guidance of a naval officer, chipping paint off the deck, a chore normally given to seamen. "Throw those chippers over the side and go about your business," Chesty told his men. "Let the Navy paint the damned ship. You're going to fight this war."

While aboard the transport Puller devoured nine volumes on Korea's history and military heritage so he could make informative decisions during the fighting. That intellectual side to Puller might have surprised some, but his close marine friends had long judged him to be smarter than he appeared. "Oh, Lewie will fool you," said O. P. Smith. "He's more scholarly than you think." Smith added that Puller "gave the impression of being a little bit illiterate" and that his reputation "was as hard as nails, tough fighting man," but it "isn't the whole picture."

"A Soldier Who Appeared to Be Made Serene by Combat"

Puller was soon able to put his knowledge of Korea to good use. In early July MacArthur had planned an amphibious counterstroke on Korea's western coast to disrupt North Korean supply lines. His choice of Inchon, a port city twenty-five miles west of Seoul, surprised most military strategists, as treacherous currents and tides made navigating to Inchon through the narrow channels between islands nearly impossible, but MacArthur thought the benefits outweighed the risks and selected September 15 for the assault. While two battalions of the 5th Marines landed on what was called Red Beach by marine strategists, which faced a seawall at the foot of the city, Puller's 1st Marine Regiment would land at another sector called Blue Beach and capture the high ground southeast of Inchon to prevent enemy reinforcements from driving in to meet the assault.

Before the landings, Puller talked to his officers. He told those younger marines that they were fortunate to be in a war so soon, as most officers waited a generation or more to experience their first combat. He said that since the end of World War II in 1945, "we've sat on our fat duffs, drawing our pay. Now we're getting a chance to earn it, to show the taxpayers we're worth it. We're going to work at our trade for a little while. We live by the sword, and if necessary we'll be ready to die by the sword. Good luck. I'll see you ashore."

Chesty came in with the third wave and, as always, was the first man out of the landing craft. Puller climbed the fifteen-foot seawall and perched there, surveying the defenses to his front as his marines scaled the barrier. When Major James Treadwell, who commanded the amtracs in Puller's command, looked up to see Chesty sitting on the wall, he turned to other marines and shouted that if a man Puller's age could climb to the top under fire, so could they.

Over the next two days Puller made good progress against mild opposition. As his regiment moved closer to Seoul and Kimpo Airport, however, fighting slowed against veteran North Korean forces defending the capital city, but by September 19 Puller neared the outskirts of Seoul and prepared for what he assumed would be a tough fight for control of that key city.

Puller had a surprise visit from General MacArthur two days earlier. MacArthur's staff had noticed that the general took special interest whenever a message from Puller arrived at his headquarters, and the renowned commander was now eager to meet him and award him a Silver Star. When informed that MacArthur planned to hand him the award, Puller scoffed at leaving his men. "Signal them that we're fighting our way for every foot of ground," he groused. "I can't leave here. If he wants to decorate, he'll have to come up here."

MacArthur acceded to Chesty's wish. He located Puller at the top of a ridge, up close to observe his men as they mounted an attack. When one of MacArthur's staff told Puller they were surprised that he was not back at his command post, Chesty patted a map in his pocket and said, "This is my CP." MacArthur congratulated the marine colonel on his success in two wars and told him he would send the medal to Puller. "Thanks very much for the Star, General," said Puller. "Now if you want to know where those sons of bitches are, they're right over the next ridge."

Beyond that ridge stood Seoul and the city guarding its western approaches, Yongdungpo. In a series of attacks and counterattacks, over the next four days Puller battled North Korean infantry to carve an open path to Seoul. He called in artillery and air support to help seize Yongdungpo and to crush enemy defenses in hills northwest of the capital city, and on September 24 his regiment became the first American troops to enter the capital.

The grinding fight for Seoul contrasted with Puller's swift advance from Inchon to the city. He now measured progress in streets rather than miles, destroying homes and shops as his marines secured Seoul block by block. The North Koreans often abandoned houses to establish defensive positions at key intersections, where they set up barriers of sand-filled rice bags and engaged in furious street battles.

When he saw a group of marines huddled behind a barricade Puller, puffing on his pipe, walked over and calmly said, "Get up, boys. Get up and go. That's the quickest way to get it over. If you're going to get it, you can get it in the holes, too." Lieutenant Joseph Fisher watched Puller in the middle of one firefight walk openly in the street, cheering his marines. "He was going along where the fire was heaviest, just like he was back in Pendleton and as if he didn't know there was a fight within miles. I couldn't express how much good it did me and my troops to see him steady like that, just puffing that pipe. It made us feel like we could do no less than he did."

Reporter Jimmy Cannon, a popular columnist from the United States, joined Puller's regiment during the fighting for Seoul. When he asked a marine where Puller was, he pointed to the top of a nearby hill. "He was the only man standing up," wrote Cannon. "The others were in the holes. He is a small man and he smoked a pipe as he stood on a ration box to scan the ridge across the shallow valley with glasses. Snipers were on the ridge, but he ignored them." In a perceptive comment, Cannon added, "This was a soldier who appeared to be made serene by combat," a person who looked "as if he were killing time on a hunting trip. He sauntered toward me, exposing himself as if he had contempt for the marksmanship of the enemy." After talking to Puller, Cannon shared coffee with one of the marines. During their discussion, the man pointed to Puller and said, "That's the best Marine that ever lived."

At times Sergeant Jones noticed Puller sitting in the jeep, silent for long stretches as he planned his next moves. "He'd been putting himself in the enemy's shoes," said Jones, "figuring out what he'd do if he were a Korean commander." Puller used some of that quiet time to reflect on the plight of his men and of the Korean families displaced by combat. He told reporter H. D. Quigg of the United Press that he hated to destroy the homes of families who would be left destitute, but he was equally concerned about the deaths and suffering his marines would endure. A young officer told Quigg he expected heavy casualties and said of Puller, "I've never seen a guy like him. I'd follow him to hell—and it looks like I'm going to have to."

Lieutenant Joseph Fisher and his company fought off multiple attacks throughout one night while on a hill in Seoul. When dawn broke, Fisher wondered why a solitary marine raced to his position. "Then I saw that it was Colonel Puller's runner—and he had brought us a bottle of Black and White Scotch. My God, were we glad to see that!" Fisher added, "We knew then that the Old Man was thinking of us—and in fact never forgot us."

North Korean forces fled Seoul when Puller's battalions seized the high ground east of the capital and the Eighth Army arrived from the south. With the opposition in retreat, on September 29 General MacArthur and South Korean president Syngman Rhee arrived in the city to formally claim the capital.

Puller was proud that even though he had had little time to train his regiment, its performance matched that of his World War II commands. That pleased him more than MacArthur's ceremony with Rhee, which he viewed as nothing but senior officials patting each other on the back. When superiors ordered Puller to attend the ceremony, he tried to avoid it by arguing that his job was to defeat the enemy, not to restore governments, but they insisted. Instead of the stipulated uniform for the day, he left the line unshaven and wearing his blood-stained attire. A military police (MP) officer halted Puller's jeep at the gates to the capital building and told Chesty, "Sorry, colonel. Only staff cars and general officers are allowed in the compound."

"Son," Puller replied, "my men took this town."

The MP hesitated to move from in front of the jeep, causing Puller to tell his driver, "Run over him, Jones." Before Jones gunned the vehicle, the MP had leaped out of the way and Puller was on his way to the ceremony.

With combat easing in the Seoul area, Puller's regiment returned to Inchon to be shipped to their next location. The Chosin Reservoir would make combat in Seoul quickly fade.

"We're Entirely Surrounded"

After the marines secured Seoul, the United Nations' Eighth Army pushed through the capital to advance northward along the western coastline. At the same time, Puller's regiment boarded transports and left in mid-October for Wonsan, a port city across the peninsula northeast of Seoul, to occupy and defend the territory near Wonsan. While Puller remained near that city, the 5th and 7th Marine Regiments rushed north to the Chosin Reservoir.

In early November the Chinese launched multiple attacks against the 5th and 7th Marines near the reservoir, as well as another against marines near Sudong, a town not far north from Puller. Hoping to destroy the 1st Marine Division, of which Puller was a part, the Chinese massed their most experienced forces and relied on their seven-to-one advantage to succeed in annihilating what they deemed was MacArthur's best unit.

In mid-November Puller shifted his regiment north to support marine units fighting in the reservoir and to keep open the vital supply road winding down the mountains to their base at Wonsan to the south. Over the next five days, six Chinese divisions overwhelmed marines along the northern edges of the Chosin Reservoir before moving to Koto-ri, where they ran into one of Puller's battalions. With the Chinese in control of the countryside and flanking both sides of the supply route, Chesty was in danger of being cut off from friendly forces.

On November 29 swarms of enemy troops attacked Puller's battalion at Koto-ri, ten miles north of Chinhung-ni at the base of the mountains. Hand-to-hand combat ensued, and at one point Puller radioed a battalion commander, "We have contact on all four sides." The bleak situation supposedly led Puller to utter one of his most oft-repeated remarks. During one of Chesty's visits to a field hospital, a chaplain said to Puller, "Sir, do you know they've cut us off? We're entirely surrounded." Puller had a ready reply. "Those poor bastards. They've got us right where we want 'em. We can shoot in every direction now." Some historians claim that Puller never uttered the words and attribute their existence to a rumor that expanded into legend, but whether true or not, the utterance certainly fit Puller's warlike personality.

He continued to visit his men whenever possible. "Rarely a day passes in battle that Colonel Puller doesn't get to the front, visiting his most advanced platoons, examining the terrain, passing out advice and encouragement to his men," wrote correspondent Robert Martin. "And whenever he passes any of his men, he looks at them slyly and says, 'Hi, fellas.'" When Martin inquired about the availability of hot food to warm the men in the frigid temperatures, Chesty scoffed. "Hell, no, we like that canned cold stuff. Besides, we need the trucks to haul ammo."

On the last day of November, the 1st Marine Division units to the north received orders to destroy any equipment they could not take with them, join Puller at Koto-ri, and continue withdrawing to the sea. Puller remained in Koto-ri to act as a delaying force while the other regiments passed through and continued south, but when Major General O. P. Smith, commander of the 1st Marine Division, heard a correspondent refer to the orders as a retreat, he angrily countered, "Retreat, hell! We're not retreating, we're just advancing in a different direction."

Pulling back through intense fire from the mountaintops and slopes, in the bitter cold on December 6 the northern units battled their way south. A *Time* magazine reporter wrote that this retreat to Koto-ri was the worst military event he had experienced. Vehicles inched along the route through "murderous mortar, machine-gun and small-arms fire from Communists in log and sandbag bunkers," while Puller's marines, artillery, and air strikes "killed thousands of the enemy and held the road open. When the lead vehicles reached Koto-ri, the rearguard was still fighting near Hagaru to keep the enemy from chewing up the column from behind." He called the withdrawal "an epic of great suffering and great valor."

The last northern units entered Koto-ri the next day, where they prepared to pull out within twenty-four hours. Some of Puller's officers, realizing they were soon to fight the enemy alone, handed to officers leaving the next morning what they feared might be last letters to wives and parents.

The 1st Marine Division, with Puller standing at Koto-ri as the rearguard, filtered out of the city on the morning of December 8. Enemy fire rained down from the hills on both the retreating regiments as well as on Puller's men, who were tasked with clearing the ridges along both sides of a road that had to remain open if anyone was to survive. Accompanied by his bodyguard, Puller frequently left Koto-ri and climbed the hills, where he went "from hole to hole for half the night." Sergeant Jones added that "he would go to every man he could find in a foxhole and say, 'How you doing, old man? Where's your field of fire? Who's on your flank? Getting enough chow?'"

Puller could not begin his withdrawal until every unit from the north had exited toward the sea. Once that occurred, Puller's marine rifle companies leapfrogged down the road, with one unit providing cover for those pulling out behind them. Puller stayed back with the reconnaissance company, the last group fighting in the town, directing marines to hurry south to avoid a fast-approaching enemy. "We'll suffer heavy losses," he shouted to his men as they left. "The enemy greatly outnumbers us. They've blown the bridges and blocked the roads, but we'll make it somehow." Puller ignored the orders to destroy his equipment and told his staff that he would bring out every jeep, truck, and weapon possible.

Proof of Chesty's promise to bring out the bodies of as many slain marines as possible rested on his jeep, the final vehicle to leave Koto-ri. The body of a tank commander lay across the bumper, two other bodies were strapped onto the top, and three wounded men squeezed into the rear. Sergeant Jones had driven only a short distance before Puller leaped from the jeep to talk to his marines, inspiring them with his words and actions. He resembled a football coach delivering a pregame pep talk, telling squads or platoons that they were members of the 1st Marine Division and would survive. "We're the greatest military outfit that ever walked on this earth," he said to one platoon. "Not all the Communists in hell can stop us. We'll go down to the sea at our own pace and nothing is going to get in our way. If it does, we'll blow hell out of it." To another he boasted, "We're not retreating! We've about-faced to get at more of those bastards," and told them they would soon be aboard warm ships with hot food and showers.

Puller so frequently left the jeep to walk among his marines that Sergeant Jones worried that his boss's feet would freeze. Jones occasionally lured him back to the vehicle and its heater, but Puller would only remain a few minutes before jumping out again. "He kept getting out of the jeep, despite all I could do," said Jones. "He walked most of the way down."

The marines conducted a running fight with the enemy that reminded some correspondents of the retreats at Bataan and Dunkirk in World War II. Chinese soldiers attacked from canyons and fired from atop every ridge at the marines, who with numbed bodies turned to meet each challenge. The foe at times drew close enough to lob hand grenades into trucks, jeeps, and ambulances. "Not in the Marine Corps' long and bloody history has there been anything like it," wrote war correspondent Keyes Beech. He had covered the battle for Iwo Jima five years earlier, but said it was not on that Pacific island but in the arctic-like terrain of Korea that "I saw men suffering so much. The wonder isn't that they fought their way out against overwhelming odds, but that they were able to survive the cold and fight at all." He wrote that while the marines enjoyed occasional breaks in the fighting, "there was none from the cold. It numbed fingers, froze feet, sifted through layers of clothing and crept into the marrow of your bones. Feet sweated by day and froze in their socks by night. Men peeled off their socks—and the soles of their feet with them."

More accustomed to jungle fighting in equatorial climates, Puller shivered in wintry temperatures that plunged below zero and froze the water in his men's canteens. Marines compared the grueling conditions to what they imagined George Washington's Revolutionary War soldiers had encountered during their winter at Valley Forge, but despite the hardships, Puller seemed to be everywhere, casting aside the cold, the artillery, and the machine-gun and mortar fire to make certain his marines were properly deployed and to shift platoons to threatened sectors. His unit repelled two concentrated Chinese assaults, numerous smaller-scale attacks, and constant barrages from the ridge tops above.

On December 11, Puller and the last marine elements reached friendly lines at Hungnam, where they finally slept in tents and enjoyed rest and hot food. Puller, weary and numb from the cold, asked Keyes Beech to convey an important point to his readers. "Remember, whatever you write, this was no retreat. All that happened was we found more Chinese behind us than in front of us. So we about-faced and attacked."

Puller's pride in his marines' drive to Hungnam was still evident eleven years later. In a joint interview with his Nicaragua days buddy, William Lee, the pair of famous marines discussed numerous actions and events, but Puller made certain to accord praise to his 1st Marines in Korea. "We not only brought our wounded out, we brought our dead out. I can see our trucks returning from the reservoir now, Chosin Reservoir, piled high with dead and wounded men who were roped to the running boards of all of our trucks and other vehicles. And the examples set by the individual Marines, bringing out their dead and wounded from the Chosin Reservoir is outstanding."

Three days after their arrival, Puller and his regiment left Hungnam aboard the transport *General Collins*, for the southern tip of the Korean peninsula. The withdrawal through the mountains from the Chosin Reservoir helped save United Nations forces in Korea, contributed to destroying seven enemy divisions, and earned the Marine Corps positive publicity in the United States. Once again, Puller became a hero and a household name for navigating his way to success on the battlefield.

Puller's time in Korea was not quite over. Two days before Christmas, Lieutenant General Matthew B. Ridgway assumed command of the Eighth Army when his predecessor, General Walton Walker, died in a highway accident. At almost the same time, Chinese forces opened an offensive that dashed past Seoul to the south, forcing Ridgway to call on the 1st Division to help check the new drive. Puller and his regiment moved west of Pohang on the eastern coast, where for four weeks they pushed the enemy back into the hills and secured the right flank while Ridgway counterattacked on the left and center.

On January 26, 1951, Puller learned of his promotion to brigadier general. The next day, as he returned to his command post in a helicopter piloted by Captain Harold G. McRay, one of the whirling rotors hit a nearby wire, flipped the chopper over, and sent it smashing to the ground twenty feet below. Puller was flung forward through the Plexiglas nose but emerged unhurt from the wrecked helicopter.

News of what could have been a fatal accident broke in the United States. "A colorful marine general, Louis B. (Chesty) Puller, narrowly escaped death today [January 27] in a helicopter accident near his forward command post on Korea," explained an article appearing in many newspapers. Virginia knew that her husband was safe, but she wondered how much longer he could tempt fate.

She did not have long to wait. On the first day of February, Puller said goodbye to the regiment he had helmed in two wars when he was named assistant division commander. He served in that capacity until leaving for home on May 20, 1951.

Though the fighting in Korea eventually stalled, Puller's marines amassed an admirable record. They had conducted the landings at Inchon, helped liberate Seoul, driven to the Chosin Reservoir, and in the drive to the sea assisted in destroying seven Chinese divisions. For his actions, Puller received his fifth Navy Cross, the only man in Marine Corps history to be so honored. "By his unflagging determination, he served to inspire his men to heroic efforts in defense of their positions and assured the safety of much valuable equipment which would otherwise have been lost to the enemy," read the citation.

He would soon again be back in the United States with his family, attempting to maneuver around the challenges at home as deftly as he did the dangers of combat.

"He's Not Like Other Generals"

Flying home from Korea, Puller, who had earlier expressed some harsh statements about military strategy, drew up a list titled, "Things I will not discuss with the press." Once he stood before reporters after arriving in the United States, however, caution flew out the window.

"Last week," wrote *Time* magazine, "after nine months in Korea, weather-beaten Chesty Puller, 52, assistant commander of the 1st Division, veteran of the Inchon landing and the Marines' heroic retreat from the Chosin Reservoir, was back in the U.S.

to take over a training command." In rapid-fire style, Chesty claimed that lax American military training had failed to challenge the men. "I want them to be able to march twenty miles, the last five at double time, and then be ready to fight." He said that there were too many frills in training and that "our officer corps have had far too much schooling and far too little service in the field of battle." He even drew the wrath of some priests, ministers, and members of the Woman's Christian Temperance Union by adding, "Get rid of the ice cream and candy. Give 'em beer and whisky—that'll help some. Get some pride in them." Warmed up and on a roll, Puller pointed to what he labeled an alarming trend in society. "What the American people want to do is fight a war without getting hurt. You can't do that any more than you can go into a barroom fight without getting hurt."

Puller tried to explain to the nation the essence of a marine and to condense the principles he had gathered in a lifetime with the Corps. "The Marine Corps never tried to kid anybody. We tell our Marines that they are going to get hurt. We tell them they are going to go through hell. But we tell them, too, that whatever they are called upon to do, it will be no worse than Marines have done before. We try to teach them that it is a proud thing, a glorious thing, to fight as Marines have always fought, without counting the cost. And above all, we try to teach them that there are some things worse than wounds or death. For once a man lets his comrades down in battle, even though he saves himself, the knowledge that he failed them will gnaw at his heart until he dies." He emphasized his point by saying that "a training officer who sends men out to the combat battalions soft of body and ignorant of their weapons ought to be court-martialed. He is guilty of manslaughter."

Two years after being promoted to major general, Chesty Puller retired on November 1, 1955. He had spent thirty-seven years in the Marine Corps, all but ten of those overseas, but illness forced the fifty-seven-year-old Puller to the decision. At his request, at the retirement ceremony his longtime friend, Master Sergeant Robert L. Norrish, who had known Puller thirty years earlier when Puller was a lieutenant and Norrish a private, pinned on Puller the three stars representing his new rank as lieutenant general. Puller chose Norrish rather than a higher-ranking officer because "he was showing his great appreciation to the enlisted men of the Marine Corps and the junior officers."

He retired after serving in two major wars and jungle campaigns in Haiti and Nicaragua. His fellow marines called the most decorated man in the history of the Marine Corps a living legend, and General Lemuel C. Shepherd, the then current Marine commandant, wrote, "Marines should always be inspired by that tradition which honors the name Puller as a symbol of fighting courage."

Puller settled into a life of ease in Virginia, hunting, fishing, and watching his twins grow through the teenage years. He read military histories and biographies, often, as Virginia recalled, "beside the fireplace with a nice fire burning. He'd sit there for hours, reading and smoking his pipe. Perhaps he'd have a bourbon and water, or I'd make him a mint julep."

The man who had devoted an entire career to combat now became more involved with his Episcopal church, Christ Church, where he and Virginia had wed. During Sunday services, he lustily sang in an off-key voice that other attendees pretended not to notice, and he served his religious community by becoming one of the church wardens.

Above all, he cherished the frequent visits to his Saluda home from former marine comrades and from the trainees or officers at the start of their careers. He admired those young men who opted to follow his path, and eagerly shared advice. He told them to never leave the Corps until they were physically unable, and claimed that being a marine was "the greatest life there is. I miss it terribly."

"He had respect and admiration for those young Marines," said Virginia. "I remember many times when there'd be a knock at the door and I'd answer. There would stand a young man with an obvious Marine Corps haircut and he'd introduce himself to me and ask if he might pay his respects to the general or to 'Chesty.' The general would say to me, 'Bring them in, Virginia.' And the general would receive the young man."

Though she had frequently been apart from her husband, Virginia had no regrets over the life she shared with Chesty. She had seen many fascinating parts of the world and had never led a dull existence. She told Master Sergeant Robert S. Kinsman, a member of the Marine Corps public relations section, "I haven't had a chance to become bored. Being married to General Puller has been tremendously exciting. He's not like other generals." Upon hearing this from his wife, Puller said as he walked by and winked, "I hope not."

When Kinsman asked Puller about the 1962 Burke Davis biography, *Marine!*, Chesty answered he loved everything except that the book failed to give the enlisted men enough credit.

"They were the ones that did the big job, and I felt more should have been credited to them. I wish I could see every one of them again." Puller walked Kinsman out with a few last words. "Sergeant," he said, "say hello to all the Marines for me, and tell them if they get down this way to please pay a visit. God bless Marines everywhere."

On three different occasions in the 1960s, Puller asked Marine Corps Headquarters to return him to active duty so that he could serve in the Vietnam War, but the commandant rejected each request. That Southeast Asian conflict included a Puller, however, when his son, Lewis B. Puller, Jr., joined the Marines in the autumn of 1967. Chesty had never pushed his son to follow in his footsteps, but a youthful life filled with military heroes, medals, parades, and stories of his father's achievements all but ordained his path. With his father proudly standing next to him, Lewis, Jr., took the oath of allegiance before leaving for Quantico to become a second lieutenant. Chesty kissed his son on the lips and hugged him tightly for a few seconds before saying goodbye.

The next year the twenty-three-year-old 2nd Lieutenant Puller, serving in his father's old regiment, the 1st Marines, tripped a land mine in Vietnam, triggering an explosion that ripped off six fingers and so horribly shredded his legs that doctors had to amputate both, one just above the knee and the other all the way to his right hip. Upon hearing the news, Puller cried and dropped to his knees to pray for his son but regained his composure when he noticed the depth of his wife's pain. "I fell apart when I learned that young Lewis was so badly wounded, but the general helped me to pull myself together," said Virginia of the ordeal.

Lewis, Jr. survived his wounds to become an attorney at the Pentagon and an activist promoting veterans' rights. After winning a Pulitzer Prize for his 1992 autobiography, *Fortunate Son*, his life fell apart. Alcoholism and marital issues led to repeated problems, which culminated in his death from a self-inflicted wound in May 1994, twenty-three years after his father had passed away.

"One of Puller's Guys"

Throughout the 1960s, Chesty Puller struggled with a series of health issues. Strokes slowed him down, and a massive seizure in October 1970 required a lengthy hospitalization. Virginia was always at his side, helping him enjoy his favorite hobby, reading. "When he got so bad that he couldn't read, I'd read to him. He loved *Beau Geste* and he read that over and over, too." The seventy-three-year-old Puller died from pneumonia and other complications on October 11, 1971. "I know that he went to heaven wearing his slouch hat and carrying his pipe," said Virginia.

A group of marine volunteers from the Marine Barracks in Yorktown, Virginia, formed an honor guard to watch over his body until the funeral service. "Lewis would have been very pleased and proud to know that those young Marines came up on their own time to pay their honor and respect to the general," Virginia said.

Puller was buried in a cemetery alongside Christ Church, the place of worship he and Virginia had enjoyed their entire life together. "He didn't want to be buried in Washington," she explained. "He wanted it simple, and he loved this place. This is where he belongs. This is where our roots are."

"And so it was that they came by the hundreds," wrote a local newspaper reporter of the funeral service, "those who knew him well, others only by reputation—to historic Christ Episcopal Church here in Middlesex County Thursday—in respect, admiration, and sadness—to pay homage to the legendary marine who died of pneumonia Monday at the age of 73." Among the mourners were two former commandants, General Wallace M. Greene, Jr., and General David M. Shoup.

Three rifle volleys preceded a bugler's notes as "Taps" echoed above the silent mourners. Moments after, Chesty Puller's body was laid to rest, his plot later marked with a simple, flat stone. "It was just as he requested. Unpretentious and simple," said Virginia. "He didn't want a monument or a big stone or a carving of a figure mounted on a horse or anything. When you met Lewis and got to know him, you learned that he was as plain as an old shoe. He would be pleased with this place." She added, "I find comfort in the realization that there was only one Lewis Burwell Puller, and for thirty-four grand and wonderful years, he was mine!"

A person's significance can be measured by the various ways he is honored and remembered, not merely in the days after his death but especially in the decades that follow. Even a partial list illustrates the effect Chesty had on others and the monumental legacy he created with his words and actions. In boot camp, marine trainees learn of him and see his photograph hanging in multiple buildings. Drill instructors pound into the young men, most in their teens, to say "Good night, Chesty Puller, wherever you are." A bulldog mascot at the Marine Barracks in Washington, DC, has long been named Chesty, and men sewed sergeant's stripes on the dog's sweater because of the general's fondness for his sergeants. In 1982 the navy commissioned the guided missile frigate USS *Lewis B. Puller* (FFG-23) and thirty-five years later commissioned a second ship bearing his name, the mobile landing platform USS *Lewis B. Puller* (ESB-3). The Virginia Military Institute has twice honored its famous alumnus, first with a display in the VMI Museum's Hall of Valor, and then with the Chesty Puller Award, where an engraved officer's sword is presented each year to the graduating senior accepting a Marine commission who best exhibits the leadership traits of Chesty Puller.

The civilian world has promoted Puller's achievements as well. In 1976, famed director John Ford filmed a documentary titled *Chesty: A Tribute*, narrated by actor John Wayne. In 2005 the U.S. Postal Service issued four stamps honoring legendary marines, including one recognizing Puller, and an eight-foot-tall bronze statue of Puller rests at Semper Fidelis Memorial Park, adjacent to the National Museum of the Marine Corps in Quantico, Virginia. The state of Virginia placed a historical marker indicating Puller's burial site and renamed the road from West Point to Saluda the Lewis Burwell Puller Highway.

In 2009 *Leatherneck* magazine, whose target audience is

current and retired marines, compiled a list of what it called the "Top-10 Badass Marines," with a brief paragraph explaining each choice. Among them were William Lee, Chesty's friend from Nicaragua days, and Puller. While four or five explanatory sentences accompanied the other nine men, Chesty Puller, the Marine's marine, only needed six simple words. "Five Navy Crosses speak for themselves."

For almost thirty years, marines have returned to Chesty's hometown for the Chesty Puller Memorial Run. The route winds by Puller's birthplace and grave site, where at each spot the runners stop and pay silent homage to the officer before continuing. "This is our way of honoring Lieutenant General Chesty Puller and his service," explained Chief Warrant Officer Zerrick Wilson in 2017 of the run. "We wanted to give these young Marines an understanding of what he meant and how we as leaders try to live up to his leadership, twenty-four years strong." Most runners add an eleventh kilometer under the encouragement, "Run ONE MORE K for Chesty Puller!"

Perhaps the praise that Chesty would have found most rewarding came from the enlisted marines he so cherished. In the October 1998 issue of *The Old Breed News*, a newsletter published by the 1st Marine Division Association, a retired marine wrote of his gratefulness that he served under Chesty Puller. He wrote that while many veterans in all branches of the military reply to the question of which unit they served by giving a number, "When one of his men was asked his outfit, he never answered with a number. 'One of Puller's guys,' was the proud reply." The writer stated that Puller stepped on too many toes to become the Marine commandant, but the omission seemed appropriate to him, as Chesty Puller "didn't know how to lead except from the front."

In a November 12, 1971, letter written to Virginia Puller after her husband's burial service, the senior enlisted adviser to the commandant, Sergeant Major Clinton A. Puckett, expressed the thoughts and emotions he, as the most revered current enlisted marine, held about the most respected senior officer. "Mrs. Puller, there were so many things I should like to have said to you [at the funeral service]. My own emotions prevented me from expressing myself as I would like to have. We enlisted Marines admired the General as one of the greatest combat soldiers of all time. Yet it is not for his fearlessness in combat, nor his numerous decorations for which he is held in so high esteem. Rather, it was his total devotion to our beloved Corps; his true understanding of his enlisted Marines; and his sincere appreciation of all Marines regardless of rank, for which he is immortalized. The General's love for his Marines is fully recognized. Very respectfully, Clinton A. Puckett Sergeant Major, U.S. Marine Corps."

All in all, not a bad way to be remembered.